Through the Looking Glass

He leaves the new Sendak lying around,
but he's never actually read it.

THROUGH THE LOOKING GLASS

*Further Adventures & Misadventures
in the Realm of Children's Literature
by*

SELMA G. LANES

DAVID R. GODINE · *Publisher*
BOSTON

For Martha Farrar

without whose unflagging support

and sound editorial judgment

this book might never have been

First published in 2004 by
David R. Godine, Publisher
Post Office Box 450
Jaffrey, New Hampshire 03452
www.godine.com

LIBRARY OF CONGRESS CATALOGING-IN-PUBLICATION DATA
Lanes, Selma G.
Through the looking glass : further adventures & misadventures in the
realm of children's literature / by Selma G. Lanes.– 1st ed.
p.   cm.
ISBN 1-56792-262-7 (alk. paper)
1. Children's literature–History and criticism.
2. Children–Books and reading. I. Title.
PN1009.A1L33   2004
809'.89282–dc22
2004016527

First Edition

PRINTED IN THE UNITED STATES OF AMERICA

Contents

Introductory Note

ALL TOO OFTEN adults forget how seriously children take words. I can vividly recall being in first grade and beginning every school day with the singing of "My Country 'Tis of Thee." When we came to the lines "Land where our fathers died/ Land of the Pilgrims' pride," I was always uneasy. My grandfathers, both immigrants from Eastern Europe, were very much alive – as was my father. Was I then something of a fraud – an impostor – each time I sang with my classmates?

I outgrew this malaise and probably hadn't given the matter any conscious thought since childhood. Yet, when my father died seven years ago at the age of ninety, I remember grief giving way to a fleeting moment of inappropriate relief, even elation. In dying, my father had made an honest woman of me. I could now sing "Land where our fathers died" with whole-hearted pride and patriotic fervor.

A friend recently told a similar story about words and the power they can exert over children. For years she had been puzzled by the Thanksgiving hymn "We Gather Together." One of its verses ends "Sing praises to his name/ He forgets not his own." But why, she wondered, would anyone ever think that God might forget his own name?

When *Down the Rabbit Hole*, my first collection of essays about children's books, was published in 1971, it was a euphoric time in children's book publishing. The post–World War II era had brought an infusion of young talent and innovative work; public and school libraries received government grants to help upgrade their collections after years of Depression austerity followed by war-time paper shortages; and technological advances were making full-color printing more affordable. Most important perhaps, it was a time when children's book departments were still small, almost autonomous divisions of individual, privately owned publishing houses. (The era of mergers and huge conglomerates came more than a decade later.) The children's book editor was ruler of her realm, and manuscripts accepted for publication were edited with care. It was a given that words were important and to be respected. From 1974 to 1978 I was editor–in–chief of children's books at Parents' Magazine Press, the most rewarding job I ever had.

Through the Looking Glass appears at a time when few independent publishers are left in the United States. The merger fever of the last two decades has claimed the great majority: Random House has been melded into the international publishing colossus, Bertelsmann; Simon & Schuster is part of the Viacom conglomerate; G. P. Putnam's Sons, Penguin, Dial, Viking, Frederick Warne and others have been acquired by the British media behemoth, Pearson.

These gigantic, publicly owned mega–corporations must answer to their stockholders who are more interested in seeing their shares increase in value than they are in literature. There is considerable pressure to produce blockbuster books in both adult and juvenile departments. Children's books have become big business. Where once the Editor – guardian of words – ruled the roost, today a new player, the Marketing Director wields considerable power. "Can it be marketed?" takes precedence over another consideration about a prospective book: "Is it worth marketing?" One children's book writer was recently asked by her editor: "Our marketing department has come up with the title *Stinky Socks*; can you write a book for it?"

Through the Looking Glass is, in part, a nostalgic trip back to the last half of the last century, a salute to many of the writers and illustrators whose words and pictures are important enough to be remembered.

S. G. L.

Through the Looking Glass

ONE

Books for the Very Young:
Pre-Literature or Pretend Literature?

IT WAS THE CRITIC Wilfrid Sheed who said "No occupation designed for dim younger sons was ever easier to enter than book–reviewing; or, once entered, easier to rise in. You go immediately to the top. It is the least you can ask." Were it possible, the reviewer of children's books would doubtless rank still lower in Mr. Sheed's esteem.

Certainly few self-appointed guardians of the bailiwick of High Literature would be willing to consider *The Tale of Peter Rabbit* or *Babar the King* fit company for *Crime and Punishment* or even *Pride and Prejudice*, though the number of individuals touched by the Potter and De Brunhoff works is far greater than that of any book – classic or potboiler – intended for an adult audience. And there is no question that children are more impressionable, open–minded listeners and readers than adults, and that they constitute the most promising segment of the human race.

Books encountered in childhood are often remembered with affection throughout life, and some of them color the child's response to many subsequent experiences. Yet, the prevailing assumption is that books for young children are, as the British reviewer and critic Brian Alderson once summed it up glumly, "beneath serious critical attention," a category, at best, of sub–literature.

In his essay on the subject of Children's Literature for *The Encyclopedia Britannica* some years ago, Clifton Fadiman wrote: "Children's literature

3

comprises that vast expanding territory recognizably staked out for a junior audience, which does not mean that it is not also intended for senior. . . ." Some fifty years earlier, Mark Twain subscribed to much the same view in his introduction to *Tom Sawyer*, where he wrote: "Although my book is intended mainly for the entertainment of boys and girls, I hope it will not be shunned by men and women on that account."

And, addressing the same subject, the nineteenth-century American editor Horace Scudder, founder of the short-lived *Riverside Magazine* for children, observed: "The distinction between books for the young and books for the old is a somewhat arbitrary one, and many have discovered for themselves and their children that instead of one poor corner of literature being fenced off for the lamb, planted with tender grass which is quickly devoured, and with many medicinal but disagreeable herbs which are nibbled at when the grass is gone, the whole wide pasture land is their native home, and the grass more tender where fresh streams flow than it possibly can be in the paddock, however carefully planted and patched."

In his *Britannica* essay, Mr. Fadiman went on to point out: "Nevertheless, there is a sovereign republic of children's literature which includes not only those books appropriated by children from the realm of adult literature – like *Robinson Crusoe, Gulliver's Travels* and the collected tales of the Brothers Grimm, but also those books whose authors seem never to have clearly envisioned their audience – like *Huckleberry Finn*, the cycle of *The Lord of the Rings* and, more recently, Richard Adams's *Watership Down*." It includes, of course, picture books and easy-to-read stories as well, which Mr. Fadiman notes dismissively "are commonly subsumed under the label of literature but qualify as such only by relaxed standards." He softens this condescension by granting that "Beatrix Potter and several other writers for the lap-sized audience do qualify." Unfortunately we never learn on what grounds their special dispensation has been granted. Fadiman did, however, point out that "text and picture books for the very young pose an obdurate challenge to create literature out of absolutely simple materials."

With the age range for children's books presently extending downward into the crib and playpen and upward into the relatively new Young Adult (YA) category, the genre grows more crowded each publishing season. At the youngest level, there are catalogues of familiar objects; basic alphabet and counting books, pop–up and board books, and myriad straightforward works documenting various aspects of the young child's daily life: primers on getting dressed, making a trip to the supermarket, being potty–trained or paying a visit to the doctor. There are also fanciful tales, either original ones or adaptations from traditional folk and fairy tale sources. It is this last group – original tales and some of the more inspired recastings of traditional material – that provides young children's books with their strongest claim for entry into the wider realm of literature. At best, their texts and illustrations comprise a special amalgam found nowhere else in the world of books, a symbiotic relationship between words and pictures. Should we consider one without the other, we find ourselves contemplating a greatly diminished, almost meaningless offering.

From the earliest days of children's book publishing, there has existed a schism between those adults favoring works of the imagination for young children and those who feel that the child is, as one nineteenth–century educator put it, "an empty vessel" in dire need of being filled with useful, factual knowledge. The two camps have flourished side by side ever since Bishop Comenius fathered the first recognized children's book, *Orbis Sensualium Pictus* (Pictures of the World Around Us) in 1657, a precursor of such contemporary works as Richard Scarry's compendiums of simple words and pictures, all offshoots of his first such volume, *Best Word Book Ever*.

In the late eighteenth century, Charles Lamb, an exponent of the imaginative tale, wrote disgustedly to his friend Samuel Coleridge: "Knowledge insignificant and vapid as Mrs. B's books convey, it seems, must come to a child in the shape of knowledge, and his empty noodle must be turned with conceit of his own powers when he has learned that a horse is an animal ... instead of that beautiful interest

TRAINS

Which train do you think would be the most fun to run? Would it be a freight train or a passenger train?

bell

whistle

steam locomotive and tender

boxcar

signal tower

lantern

handcar

caboose

flatcar

dining car

railroad station

platform

56

baggage wagon

conductor

Richard Scarry, *Richard Scarry's Best Word Book Ever*

in wild tales which once made the child a man.... Think of what you would have been now if instead of being fed with tales and old wives' fables in childhood, you had been crammed with geography and natural history. Hang them: the cursed reasoning crew."

Closer to our own day, Dylan Thomas complained of yet another variety of useful, didactic fare for the young in his catalogue of practical gifts in *A Child's Christmas in Wales*: "And pictureless books in which small boys, though warned with quotations not to, would skate on Farmer Giles' pond and did and drowned; and books that told me everything about the wasp, except why."

Most of us could probably make a tolerably convincing case for accepting *Alice in Wonderland* or *The Wind in the Willows* into the wider world of Literature. But when it comes to books like Ludwig Bemelman's *Madeline* or Gene Zion's *Harry the Dirty Dog* or Arnold Lobel's *Frog and Toad* stories, we are likely to feel a bit sheepish and uncertain. Can we seriously entertain the possibility that at least some authors and author/illustrators of books for the very young really are addressing themselves to subject matter of more than evanescent interest? Is there, in all candor, anything more to be said for most good picture books than that most small children find them diverting from beginning to end?

The best of young children's books, factual or fanciful, are those that give the child listener some window on the wider world outside his or her own limited domestic experience. As adults, we tend to overlook the fact that no matter how enlightened our individual views of the world, no matter how many new experiences we may expose a child to daily, all children, for a long while, lead necessarily restricted lives. They are largely at their parents' or their teachers' mercies, often tender, but occasionally otherwise. There is so much that each child cannot know from home or school experience alone, and may vaguely ache to know. And despite the ubiquitous seductions of television and ever more sophisticated electronic wonders, surely books still provide the most intimate and memorable answers to a small child's thirst for crucial bits and pieces of knowledge.

What sort of books? Well, *Peter Rabbit*, for one. It has always been a source of wonderment to me that a book like Potter's *The Tale of Peter Rabbit* can be looked upon as lightweight or inconsequential by any thoughtful adult. The story it unfolds is one of narrowly averted tragedy. Its subject matter is what happens when a child does exactly what his mommy tells him not to do. Old Mrs. Rabbit is quite explicit at the tale's outset: "Now, my dears, you may go into the fields, or down the lane, but don't go into Mr. McGregor's garden. Your father had an accident there. He was put in a pie by Mrs. McGregor."

Peter, not surprisingly, disobeys; and no doubt the reason why most grownups like the book so well is that it confirms for them the wisdom of parental strictures. Had Peter only listened to his mother he would have had no difficulties, and we would have had no tale. But the reason why children like the story is entirely different. They long to know what happens should one break the rules, if one dares to leave the safety, confinement and occasional boredom of adult authority and protection. This Peter Rabbit's adventure tells them, blow by harrowing blow. That Peter manages to return home at the end – even if only to bed and a dose of camomile tea – is a major triumph. The subliminal and highly important message conveyed to the child listener is that one can, and generally does, survive disobedience. And surely Peter's misfortune of missing "bread and milk and blackberries for supper" – the reward of those good little bunnies Flopsy, Mopsy and Cottontail – is a price any red–blooded child would gladly pay for such heady, subversive, but ultimately liberating knowledge.

Subject matter of this sort is at odds with the views of those who agree with the French critic Paul Hazard who, in the 1930s, wrote that children's books "provide insurance against the time, all too soon, when there will be nothing but realities," that childhood itself is, or should be, "a fortunate island where happiness must be protected." Children, however, deal every day with realities every bit as disconcerting as those an adult faces, and on a much more basic level. They lack our knowledge and protective devices. As a friend of mine put it,

"Their armor is still in the foundry." Often a book that, at first glance, strikes a grownup as possibly disturbing – even frightening – provides just the answer a child may need to face or resolve some vague worry or troubling emotion he has been trying to hide from everyone around him.

Consider the charming, existential picture books of William Steig, whose gifts lie not so much in the drama of his plots as in the cadence of language, the idiosyncratic crotchets and heartfelt convictions he manages to express through his stories for small children. Among this author/illustrator's most endearing talents is an uncanny sense of how children view the world. When Amos, the mouse hero of *Amos and Boris*, is loading a boat with various "necessities" for a long ocean voyage, Steig includes not only the expected barrels of fresh water, compass, sextant and telescope, but also "a yo-yo and playing cards." Later, when Amos falls overboard on a starry, Van Gogh–like night and is in terror and despair, as small children often are, the author notes: "Morning came, as it always does," knowing instinctively what a comfort this simple fact can be to a frightened mouse – or a frightened child. In *Abel's Island*, Steig's 119-page novella with black-and-white pictures, a dandyish mouse hero named Abelard Hassam di Chirico Flint – Abel, for short – is caught in an unexpected hurricane and windblown out of his sheltered, well-upholstered life of Edwardian privilege and luxury into untamed, raw nature at its most alarmingly indifferent. Hear how author Steig addresses his young readers:

> Was it just an accident that he was here on this uninhabited island? Abel began to wonder. Was he being singled out for some reason, was he being tested? If so, why? Didn't it prove his worth that such a one as Amanda loved him?
>
> Did it? Why did Amanda love him? He wasn't all that handsome, was he? And he had no particular accomplishments. What sort of mouse was he? Wasn't he really a snob, and a fop, and frivolous on serious occasions, as she had once told him during

a quarrel? He had acted silly even at his own wedding, grinning during the solemnities, clowning when cutting the cake. What made him act that way when he did? Full of such questions, he went to wash his face in the river that kept him captive, and drank some of its water. It was foolish, he realized to harbor a grudge toward the river. It had no grudge against him. It happened to be where it was; it had probably been there for eons.

Clearly, this is a text in which the author holds nothing back. He is not writing for children, or adults, for that matter; he is pursuing the necessities of his unfolding tale with high seriousness and the full attention of a clearly grown-up mind and sensibility.

When my two sons were small, we read and looked at Dr. Seuss's frenetic picture-book tale, *The Grinch Who Stole Christmas*. And we were sufficiently taken with the good word doctor's description of the villainous Grinch's chief shortcoming – that "his heart was two sizes too small" – to apply it judiciously over the years to a select number of people who seemed to suffer from the same malady. Nor do we fail, to this day, to find solace in Steig's gentle handling of the death of the benevolent old pig who befriended the dog hero of his novel *Dominic*. As the grief-numbed hound tearfully buries his benefactor, he comes up with as poignantly simple and comprehensive a definition of death, for child or adult, as is ever likely to be found. "His turn was over." Something in that image suggests to the child listener both the necessity of making the most out of one's own turn while here on earth and of accepting the fact that, like all turns, this longest and most serious one must inevitably come to an end.

As adults selecting books for young children, we should always be on the lookout for those that reveal something beyond an obvious truth, that give us, as well as any child listening to them, some deeper understanding of, or new insight into the realities – or the make-believe – of childhood. We should value those books that surprise us by the freshness of their statement or graphic depiction of a truth, however small. It is a mistake ever to suppose that it makes little or no difference what version of a story is read, or whose illustrations accompany it. It is true that children can be as circumspect as professional diplomats. They may listen politely to a third-rate telling of a traditional tale that is almost putting its adult reader to sleep, but this doesn't mean they like it. Children have a high appreciation of originality and are themselves often startlingly original. This truth was impressed upon me several years ago when I went to an outdoor exhibition in Central Park. It was composed of drawings and compositions submitted by schoolchildren aged four to eight for a contest entitled IF I RAN THE PLAYGROUND.

The event had been sponsored by a neighborhood group trying to improve the local play facilities. And the children's suggestions, both in words and pictures, often combined a marvelous, hard-headed realism with a forthright earthiness and candor. One four-year-old boy had dictated a brief list to his nursery-school teacher. It was headed by the item: "No red ants in the sandbox." A seven-year-old girl drew a conventional enough playground but posted over its entrance a sign reading "No grownups or children over 100 pounds allowed." A practical six-year-old boy suggested hiring Macy's to lay a wall-to-wall carpet within the playground's iron fence to prevent children from skinning their knees on the existing pebbly tar surface. But my favorite entry was compiled by another six-year-old, a girl, who printed her own no-nonsense list. The playground of her dreams would contain: "1 little zoo, 1 wooden-toy shop, 100 balloons, 1 popcorn man, a golf course (small), 1 playful Mickey Mouse family walking around, and last: 1 teacup ride." Surely Kate Greenaway would have approved of this final item.

Adults should never discount their own reactions to books written for children, for no young child's picture book has any claim to being a work of literature if it appeals only to children. If the work has no resonance for an interested and intelligent older reader, the chances are it has little growing room or lasting appeal for a child either. Any young children's book worth its publication, or its full-color art work, is one from which both children young and old can derive pleasure and sustenance, pleasure at different levels and for different reasons, to be sure, but genuine pleasure nonetheless.

The quality of truth, or perhaps it would be more accurate to call it conviction, should be the same in a work of art directed at children or adults. This became clear to me many summers ago when, for the first time, my children and I vacationed on the Maine coast. Though none of us had been there before, we felt immediately at home. There were at least two good reasons for this: we had a meadow straight out of an Andrew Wyeth painting and a hill covered with blueberries right out of Robert McCloskey's *Blueberries for Sal*.

Adults who select picture books for children should be on the alert for stories, or slice-of-life vignettes, that end positively, that resolve any and all disturbing questions they may raise, and that expand the child's sense of the wonder and possibilities life affords. Beyond their need and craving for reality made comprehensible, young children are romantics who instinctively hold high hopes for the world and for themselves. When a child comes to the end of a picture book, the world's prospects and his own should seem somehow brighter than when the book was first opened.

There is little doubt that many of the most enduring of good children's books are written by those who best remember their own childhoods. Some years ago, *Time* magazine's then book and movie reviewer, Stefan Kanfer, mused about children's books and those who write and illustrate the best of them: "A sound PhD. dissertation could be written on the curious phenomenon of children's literature written by childless authors. From Edward Lear and Lewis Carroll to Dr. Seuss and Maurice Sendak, the phenomenon persists. The incidence is too high to be coincidental. Perhaps the writers substitute audience for family. Perhaps, like Beatrix Potter, they seem more comfortable in the domain of childhood, where fantasy is the norm and reality the intruder."

Possibly the answer is less complicated. Childless authors have what

most parents lack: the luxury of being able to look at childhood dis-
passionately, and thus perhaps with deeper honesty. Unquestionably
they are freer to give more concentrated attention to – and to be in
closer touch with – their own childhoods. They are not constrained by
the constant presence and needs of children to think always of themselves as cloaked in the sensible garb of responsible adulthood. As
Henry James once wrote of Robert Louis Stevenson, just such a childless author of remarkable stories for children: "He doesn't speak as a
parent, or an uncle, or an educator – he speaks as a contemporary
completely absorbed in his own game."

It is this quality of being completely absorbed in one's own game
that characterizes the compelling voices of childhood reading. The
memorable writers and illustrators hold nothing back. They give us
not what they think we ought to have, or what marketing directors of
publishing houses feel is likely to sell well this season, or what will keep
the child listener safely insulated from all anxiety, but rather what has
meaning for themselves. Literature, someone once said, is made by the
man who sings from the depths of his heart about something that
must be told. Certainly this quality of holding nothing back, of revealing something that has teased the author's own mind, often earns for
a work, be it directed at adult or child, the accolade of Literature.

Early in his writing career, the late E. B. White wrote to his brother
Stanley that "The rewards [of my work] are not that I have acquired an
audience, as you suggest (fame of any kind being a Pyrrhic victory),
but that sometimes in writing for myself – which is the only subject
anyone knows intimately – I have occasionally had the exquisite thrill
of putting my fingers on a little capsule of truth and heard it give the
faint squeak of mortality under my pressure – an antic sound."

Many a writer, illustrator and author/illustrator of young children's
books has experienced a similar aesthetic pleasure. The widespread
notion that a writer not quite good enough, or hard-working enough,
to produce a book for adults can certainly toss off something good
enough for children – perhaps one of those short and seemingly

effortless picture books of 32–page length, for example – couldn't be more mistaken.

It was Hilaire Belloc who based his high opinion of Hans Christian Andersen's fairy tales on three criteria: "In the first place, he always said what he thought; in the second place, he was full of all sorts of ways of saying it; in the third place, he said only what he had to say." This exactitude and economy of style, particularly in picture books, is crucial.

Belloc went on to raise a curious point: "Andersen could not have been so complete an artist," he notes, "had he not addressed himself to children." This observation brings to mind William Steig's insight on being asked what made so urbane and sophisticated a *New Yorker* cartoonist and artist turn to writing for small children. "I think," he said, "I could probably write for dumb adults, but not for smart ones. The thing I'm sure of is that I know a lot more than kids know, and this is very freeing to my particular sort of sensibility." Steig has also confessed that he is never embarrassed or afraid to reveal his deepest thoughts about the joys of being alive, about his fervent wish for immortality, in stories for children. "Yet the thought of undertaking an adult novel, something I have often considered doing, inhibits and cows me."

In her biography of E. Nesbit, the English writer Noel Streatfeild speaks admiringly of Mrs. Nesbit's "blotting–paper memory" concerning her own childhood. "She never forgot what it had felt like to be a child, the excitement and smell of a new day; the crushing fears which she herself described most vividly; the unclimbable barrier that lies between a child and a grown up, even the best of grown ups. She knew too the avalanches of grief that were so solid they could suffocate, especially when it appeared the grief was due to an injustice. She knew what it was like to be intolerably bored, and to have to accept the boredom." Mrs. Nesbit herself is worth listening to on the subject of her fears as a small girl:

> The first thing I remember that frightened me was running into my father's dressing room and finding him playing at wild beasts with my brothers. He wore his great fur traveling coat

inside out, and his roars were completely convincing. I was borne away screaming and dreamed of wild beasts for many a long night afterwards.

A child who wakes from an ugly dream does not fall asleep so quickly. For, to a child who is frightened, the darkness and the silence of its lonely room are only a shade less terrible than the wild horrors of listening, listening to the pad–pad of one's heart, straining one's ears to make sure that it was not the pad–pad of something else, something unspeakable creeping towards one out of the horrible, dense dark. One used to be quite, quite still, I remember, listening, listening.

Nesbit's biographer felt that such vivid recollections of fears indicated that Nesbit was deeply unhappy as a child, thereby lending weight to the oft-voiced opinion that an unhappy childhood is the best possible apprenticeship for those who are going to write meaningfully for children. "Carefully," Miss Streatfeild tells us, "E. Nesbit stored her impressions away in her author's lumber room of a mind, and there they remained until she was forty. She only had to open the door of her mind, and out came her childhood, fresh as the day she had put it away."

It was that gifted Victorian writer of children's tales, George Mac-Donald, who said in *The Princess and Curdie*: "There is this difference between the growth of some human beings and that of others: in the one case, it is a continuous dying; in the other a continuous resurrection ... the child is not meant to die but to be forever freshborn."

In this regard, Henry James observed that "We are never old, that is we never cease easily to be young, for all life at the same time; youth is an army, the whole battalion of our faculties and our freshness, our passions and our illusions, on a considerably reluctant march into the enemy's country, the country of the general lost freshness."

From a child's point of view, it makes little difference whether the books he or she likes are classified as literature, pre–literature or pretend literature. Yet surely, those books that linger long in memory, whether the subject matter be fanciful or realistic, the book's breadth narrow or wide, belong to literature. As Willa Cather defined it, a work of literature "must leave in the mind of the sensitive reader an intangible residue of pleasure; a cadence, a quality of voice that is exclusively the writer's own – individual, unique. A quality that one can remember without the volume at hand, can experience over and over again in the mind, but can never absolutely define, as one can experience in memory a melody, or the summer perfume of a garden. The magnitude of the subject is not of primary importance."

Or, as another turn-of-the-century American storyteller, Sarah Orne Jewett, put it: "The thing that teases the mind over and over for years, and at last gets itself put down rightly on paper – whether little or great, it belongs to Literature."

As to why certain writers and illustrators elect to devote their literary efforts to a young audience – particularly when, as one observer pointed out, the highest compliment is to have your work thumbed or chewed to death by its loving admirers – the words of the nineteenth-century English critic Gleeson White shed some light. "To delight a child, to add a new joy to the crowded miracles of childhood is no less worth doing than to leave a Sistine Chapel to astound a somewhat bored procession of tourists; or to have written a classic that sells by the thousands and is possessed unread by all save an infinitesimal percentage of its owners. It is, then, not an ignoble thing to do one's very best to give our coming rulers – children – a taste of the Kingdom of Art."

Mr. White's enthusiasm notwithstanding, there will continue to be self-appointed caretakers of the garden of High Literature who will go right on denying entry to even the best of young children's books. However, those of us who browse and delight in that secluded, still largely fenced-off pastureland can take comfort from the fact that we are likely to gain admittance to a still more exclusive paradise. It is yet another good book for children of all ages that tells us, "Except ye become as little children, ye shall not enter into the Kingdom of Heaven."

TWO

Biography: Fiction's Kissing Cousin

LIKE MANY OTHER CHILDREN, I first experienced biography at my mother's knee – or, more accurately, in her lap – when I began hearing those incredible tales that usually started, "When I was a little girl, just about the age that you are now..."

Mary Stolz, a veteran writer of fiction for children, has perfectly captured the way in which such stories are perceived. In her picture book, *Storm in the Night*, she tells about a small boy and his grandfather sitting together in the dark during a severe thunderstorm:

> Thomas sighed. "What will we do?"
>
> "No help for it," said Grandfather. "I shall have to tell you a tale of when I was a boy."
>
> Thomas smiled in the shadows. It was not easy to believe that Grandfather had once been a boy, but Thomas believed it. Because Grandfather said so, Thomas believed that long, long ago, probably at the beginning of the world, his grandfather had been a boy. As Thomas was a boy now, and always would be. A grandfather could be a boy if he went back in his memory far enough; but a boy could not be a grandfather. A cat could not grow up to be a kangaroo, and a boy could not grow up to be an old man. And that, said Thomas to himself, is that.

And so, when we as children first meet with bits of family history – usually related in the form of parental reminiscences – each of us welcomes it as the most wonderful sort of make–believe. "Long, long ago," these snippets of memory inform us, "mothers and fathers were little girls and boys." Nothing in fiction could be more incredible to children than the possibility that this revelation might be true. To be a young child is to be locked in an ever–advancing present, to find it unimaginable what the world might have been like – indeed, that it could really have existed at all – without oneself at the very center as its moment–by–moment observer and verifier.

The recollections of events from a parent's or grandparent's child-hood have, for small listeners, the character of romance. And certainly no author/illustrator for young children has better capitalized on this fact than the *New Yorker* cartoonist James Stevenson, with his wonder-ful tall tales about a grandfather, whom Stevenson always pictures in his stories as being child–size and in knee pants, but also mustachioed and with a balding pate, as a grandfather–child might reasonably be expected to look.

But let's turn our attention to the teller of such remembrances. All of us are guilty of polishing or improving upon events recalled from the past. In the first place, the memories are themselves highly selec-tive: we recall those which have had some special significance to us. And, in the telling of events from past history, there inevitably creep in touches of nostalgia for what has been and is gone – for our evanes-cent youth and innocence, if nothing else. And in this selective recall, particularly for an audience of children, there is also often injected a kind of didacticism. We strive to extract some worthwhile lesson or moral from the muddle of bygone events.

In the prologue to her work *Parallel Lives: An Examination of Five Vic-torian Marriages*, Phyllis Rose remarks on this view of life – and of biog-raphy – as being to a marked extent a creation.

> I believe, first of all, that living is an act of creativity, and that, at certain moments in our lives, our creative imaginations are more conspicuously demanded than at others. At certain

"It was a long time ago," said Grandpa. "One warm day in April I started a little vegetable garden in the backyard. I planned where I'd put all the vegetables, and I started to dig.

I was having a grand time until..."

James Stevenson, *Grandpa's Too-Good Garden*

moments, the need to decide upon the story of our own lives becomes particularly pressing – when we choose a mate, for example, or embark upon a career. Decisions like that make sense, retroactively, of the past and future together, and create, suspended between the two, the present.

Questions we have all asked of ourselves, such as, Why am I doing this? or even the more basic, What am I doing? suggest the way in which living forces us to look for, and forces us to find, a design within the primal stew of data which is our daily experience.

There is a kind of arranging and telling and choosing of detail – of narration, in short – which we must do so that one day will prepare for the next day, one week prepare for the next week. In some way, we all decide when we have grown up and what event will symbolize for us that state of maturity – leaving home, getting married, becoming a parent, losing our parents, making a million, writing a book. To the extent that we impose some narrative form onto our lives, each of us in the ordinary process of living is a fitful novelist, and the biographer is a literary critic.

This universal tendency to shape our pasts came into play in my collaboration with Lillian Gish on her autobiography for children: *An Actor's Life for Me!* Looked at from the outside, Miss Gish's early years presented a number of disquieting aspects, especially in view of what has been learned since the 1930s about early childhood trauma and child development. By the time she was six, Lillian Gish had undergone several personal upheavals: there had been three major moves by the Gish family in as many years; there was the break-up of her parents' always-fragile marriage; and, to cap it, Lillian was sent off for reasons of stark economic necessity, without her mother or much-loved younger sister, to work – for an open-ended period of time – with a road company of actors.

Certainly it was a childhood that might well have done in a less plucky or determined little girl. To Lillian Gish, however, looking back from the Olympian distance of age 89 (her age when we began working on the Viking autobiography), this unique theatrical apprenticeship, begun at so tender an age, was seen as an ideal training ground. It enabled her not only to become a family breadwinner but a world-renowned actress as well (one of the few in the pantheon that includes Eleanora Duse, Sarah Bernhardt, Ellen Terry and a handful of others).

Originally, she and I intended to pass quickly over this period. It was simply a remote biographical chapter in the actress's long résumé: "Eight years spent on the stage as a child actress in a number of traveling companies." I thought that the most interesting years would be those she spent as a major star of silent films. But, as Miss Gish began to speak of these early, difficult days, I was intrigued by this period about which I had known almost nothing before we met. Perhaps I became more and more intrigued because we were planning her recollections as an autobiography for young readers.

I remembered back to the time, at the age of eight or nine, when I had first been sent away to summer camp. I came from an unbroken home, yet how interminable that span of only eight weeks in an unfamiliar environment loomed before me. That first summer away from home was like some black tunnel I was being required to pass through before at last returning to my own comfortable room, my familiar dolls and toys and my much-missed parents. What must it have been like for Lillian Gish who, during that period of her life, really had no permanent home, and whose chief security and solace lay in the mother and small sister she was so often separated from?

This description of a traditional, middle-class child's daily regimen, as described by Annie Dillard in her autobiographical reminiscence, *An American Childhood*, makes Lillian Gish's peculiar situation still clearer:

What a marvel it was that the day so often introduced itself with my mother's firm footfall nearby. What a marvel that, so many times a day, the world, like a churchbell, reminded me to recall and contemplate the durable fact that I was here, and had awakened once more to find myself set down in a going world. In the living room the mail slot clicked open and envelopes clattered down. In the back room where our maid Margaret Butler was ironing, the steam iron thumped the muffled ironing board and hissed. The walls squeaked, the pipes knocked, the screen door trembled, the furnace banged, and the radiators clanged. . . . Mother . . . called the painters on the phone; it was time to paint the outside trim again. She ordered groceries on the phone. Larry, from Lloyd's Market, delivered. He joked with us in the kitchen while Mother unpacked the groceries' cardboard box.

Lillian Gish's childhood, from the age of six to twelve, had almost none of this structured continuity of daily experience to provide a reassuring foundation for her future. Her chief stability was her daily performance in some wildly improbable melodrama, the theatrical fare of turn-of-the-century America. For most children, then as now, moving from one place to another was a rarity, a landmark event of childhood. To Lillian Gish, staying put was the wonderment. Hers was a special childhood indeed, and both Miss Gish and I wanted to communicate that specialness without projecting adult judgment on its contents. Our hope was that children would make up their own minds about it if we could just provide enough telling details.

Well, there turned out to be so many remembered details of interest that we never got to Miss Gish's early career in silent films. We planned to devote a second book to that.

But is it really possible to uncover fresh autobiographical truths when the childhood being examined is at a distance of eighty years, and by a highly successful actress who has told bits and pieces of her life story hundreds of times over the years? Miss Gish and her sister Dorothy had been stars since 1915, and she had been interviewed by countless reporters, gossip columnists and magazine feature writers. She had also, at the peak of her career, in the 1930s, had one adult biography written and, of course, she wrote her own autobiographical memoir some years back, *Mr. Griffith, The Movies and Me*. In part, for us both, it was a trip backward psychically, to how it might have felt to be a child, helpless to alter a course already determined by others, to be required to make the best of a given situation for as long as it might go on, which from the child's vantage point, might just be forever.

In some respects, I suppose we all invent ourselves anew each time we tell the story of our lives to yet another receptive ear. First of all, our life had advanced a bit from the point at which we last thought about it. And our viewpoint has doubtless altered in some small, or large, way. The present listener may be asking a new question, or exhibiting a special sort of sympathy that was not present to the same degree ever before.

The novelist William H. Gass put it nicely in a recent *New York Times* book review of a biographical novel:

> 'Who am I?' is a question that has many answers, depending on what self is sought. Is it the legal self who hopes for an inheritance? Is it the tribal self whose finger will follow every vein that carries the family colors? Is it the psychological self, hoping for a harmony among its conflicting skills and feelings? Is it the cultural self, the native of a language, the exiled self who simply needs a passport and a port of entry? Or is it the self who is searching for a fresh essence, the ambitious self, the self of a better future, who shall eventually be described by his accomplishments the way Sir Walter Scott is now said to be the author of *Waverly?*

The quest for objective truth is never on such slippery terrain as when a biographer works with a living subject. To be sure, there are always certain ineluctable biographical facts: date and place of birth, names of parents and siblings, education, etc. And there is always the verifiable evidence of the subject's importance in the world, the reason why we are examining the life in the first place: Gish's film work, Picasso's art, James' novels, a Civil War general's battles won and lost. But let's face it, these are usually the least interesting parts of a good biography. If that's all we wanted to know, we could have learned it from a simple, straightforward chronology in *Who's Who.*

A good biographer is aided by a special sympathy for the subject at hand. It was I who had approached Lillian Gish with the proposal of a biography for children. I've been asked why Lillian Gish? Here again, biography enters the picture – my own. Among the stories my mother told me when I was quite young was how she and her older brother Sammy loved to go to the movies – silent films – on Saturday afternoons. They came from an immigrant family living in the West End of Boston, and money for such a luxury was hard to come by. My uncle had an after-school job and so was able to pay for his own ticket.

With luck, he would occasionally receive a free pass as a favor for extra work performed, so that he could take my mother along. But she, alas, could only go if she could bring her younger sister – her responsibility on Saturday afternoons. A gifted copyist, my mother took to forging passes for her charge, so that all three children could sit blissfully in the second gallery of the Bowdoin Square Theater and watch the early feature-length films. Often they brought lunch with them and sat through two full shows in a single afternoon. My mother's favorite actress was, you guessed it, Lillian Gish. I knew the plots of most of Gish's major films while still in grade school.

As a grown-up, I got the chance in the late 1950s to meet the legendary star herself. The national news service for which I was then working requested a series of Christmas features which would consist of interviewing several famous American women regarding their best-remembered childhood Christmas. I got two choices from a list of eight or ten celebrities and, of course, my first selection was Lillian Gish.

When we met, the octogenarian actress told me about sitting in the dirty, cold caboose of a freight train, traveling between theater engagements one Christmas Eve. Her sister Dorothy, then about eight, was with her. This reminiscence eventually became one of the incidents in Part One of *An Actor's Life for Me!* It was accidentally coming upon the yellowed newspaper clipping of that feature story about twenty-five years later, while clearing out an old desk, that led to the idea of a children's biography of Lillian Gish.

Working with Maurice Sendak on *The Art of Maurice Sendak* was an entirely different venture into the realm of biography. Maurice and I had met many years ago, and the two of us had become firm professional friends, in part because of our similar views on what constituted a good children's book; in part, again, because of our biographies. We both came from Jewish families who had emigrated to the United States from *shtetls* in Eastern Europe. We had both learned Yiddish as children for the same reason: we wanted to know what our parents and grandparents were saying about us when they reverted to this mysterious

LILLIAN GISH

An Actor's Life for Me !

AS TOLD TO SELMA G. LANES

ILLUSTRATIONS BY PATRICIA HENDERSON LINCOLN

Lillian Gish, *An Actor's Life for Me!*
illustration by Patricia Henderson Lincoln

language in order to keep us from understanding what was being said. We each of us had a wonderful collection of untranslatable Yiddish phrases saved for special occasions, and we could laugh and occasionally come close to tears over the same kinds of family reminiscences. In the case of *The Art of Maurice Sendak*, it was Maurice who asked if I would like to write the text for, as well as help in the selection of some 300 illustrations for, a lavish Harry Abrams coffee-table album of his art. Sendak was committed to a text of some substance, including critical as well as biographical material. I agreed to undertake the project.

Sendak felt strongly that whatever personal information and recollections his biography might contain, these should be directed toward illuminating his work and his development as an artist rather than meandering into any psychological speculations about the artist's personal life. Therefore, the book's introductory note contains this caveat, which was, in effect, a voicing of Maurice's imposed – and my accepted – limitations. It read:

> Ultimately, however, it is the artist's work that speaks most eloquently of his childhood, as it does of the illustrators he has admired and emulated, and of the places, objects and beings that have moved him deeply.

And so *The Art of Maurice Sendak* was a picture biography on more than a surface level. It contained a great many of Sendak's illustrations and drawings, both well and little known, and its deepest resonance derived from a serious and educated examination of these pictures, of the development of the artist's craft – rather than from any close look at Sendak's daily life.

Though it's cause for wonder sometimes, on reading the *New York Times Book Review* or the *New York Review of Books*, how many new biographies of the same famous men and women seem to proliferate year after year, the answer, at least in part, is that each era has its own particular interests and concerns, and one life honestly looked at, can be viewed in a great number of legitimate, enlightening ways.

From the biographer's side, it is a good rule of thumb, when researching or writing about a subject, to assume as little as possible to be irrefutable truth, to check wherever possible other sources for confirmation of the biographee's own recollections of events. Memory, as noted, plays tricks, and occasionally a story recorded as fact in the past will turn out to have been inaccurate or skewed, even when the biographee was its source.

On one such occasion, I had accepted an account of some event in Sendak's early career exactly as Maurice told it to me. Later, in researching another matter entirely, I heard a different, more plausible sequence of events from another participant. When I mentioned the discrepancy to Maurice, he paused thoughtfully and said, "Well, I don't care. My version is true to my remembrance of how it happened." We left the telling Maurice's way, because, after all, his recollection had a certain biographical interest and validity of its own.

As Sharon O'Brien writes in her fine biography *Willa Cather: The Emerging Voice*:

> Memory distorts as well as records; the images retained over the years are selective and fragmentary, fictions the adult creates as well as retains, stories he or she employs to imagine a continuous self, and to describe that self to others. Yet, precisely because they are subjective early memories, they constitute important psychological and biographical evidence. Willa Cather's stories and memories of her mother do not tell us what Virginia Cather was actually like, but they do tell us how she appeared in her daughter's imagination.

One has only to recall the Japanese film *Rashomon*. Its suspense and drama consisted of observing the same events from the viewpoints of three different participants. Each narrator began with the same reality, but, by emphasizing one aspect over another, by interpreting the same happening from a different vantage point, the participants provided the audience with three irreconcilable versions of the truth, and a far deeper comprehension of the complexity of all human interactions.

Yet, despite its shortcomings as unvarnished truth, biography does unquestionably exert a special hold on us – a hold quite separate from other stories we may read.

One of its prime fascinations arises from the fact, as Phyllis Rose again succinctly put it: "We are desperate for information about how other people live, because we want to know how to live ourselves."

Biography, then, is from both reader's and biographer's viewpoint a socially and intellectually acceptable form of voyeurism. It can be instructive, even spiritually or morally uplifting for us with regard to our own lives in flux.

Certainly in treating any biographical subject, an author is best served by humility: the character we are writing about is another being, in some areas unknowable to us. We are dealing with non-fiction, but much of the life under scrutiny will be imperfectly perceived. And so, a good or great biography is, like the superior novel or short story, a work of art and not merely a rendering of objective truth. A biographer must be grateful for whatever living, breathing nuggets of truth fall her way while she is researching a subject.

But for every nugget uncovered, hundreds of others will never be found. We must sift through facts, memories and the imperfect recollections of others, and try to piece together a portrait both faithful to evidence and true to the inner person we are daily getting to know almost as well as we know ourselves. But what we achieve will, at best, be an approximation. Leon Edel's remarkable six-volume *Life of Henry James* does not, in the end, deliver to us that complicated, involuted genius whole. Still, each biographer, no matter how grand or circumscribed his particular project, aims to add to a true, three-dimensional perception of its subject, to contribute something valid to the richness and depth of the particular biographee's overall portrait as a human being who lived and breathed, as we are living and breathing here and now.

THREE

Fantasy and Reality: Where Do They Meet?

Iɴ ᴛʜᴇ ᴡᴏʀʟᴅ of young children's picture books, where a well-told tale is a reality unto itself, the question of whether a given story is realistic or a work of fantasy seldom arises. No small child listening to *Sylvester and the Magic Pebble* is likely to raise an eyebrow at a family of donkeys living in a house, or to challenge the information that one of them has the hobby of "collecting pebbles of unusual shape and color." Just as no child listening to *The Tale of Peter Rabbit* doubts for a moment the inescapable reality of Peter's crisis, trapped as he is in the vegetable garden of the infamous Mr. McGregor. This is no animal fantasy; it is life at its most dangerous and fearsome.

Fear is an emotion familiar to childhood: fear of losing sight of one's mother, fear of the dark, fear of a particular new experience, fear of ridicule or of being inadequate to some required task. As parents and educators, we sometimes underestimate these painful realities, deluding ourselves with that comforting canard that childhood is an enviable time of freedom, of near perfect insulation from the world's cares. For even the happiest child, however, this is never so.

If, then, children are often scared and uncertain, it stands to reason that they respond strongly to those stories that offer some outside reassurance that their worries are shared and, occasionally, even overcome by other beings, real or imagined. When a young child says, "Tell me a story," he is hoping for something a bit outside his everyday experience, but something that deals nonetheless with his own real concerns.

In *The Uses of Enchantment*, the child psychologist Bruno Bettelheim makes an impassioned case for the power of the traditional folk/fairy tale to help young children deal with their most disturbing fears and anxieties. Bettelheim says:

> Contrary to what takes place in many modern children's stories, in fairy tales evil is as omnipresent as virtue.... Safe stories mention neither death nor aging, the limits to our existence, nor the wish for eternal life. The fairy tale, by contrast, confronts the child squarely with the basic human predicaments.... It is characteristic of fairy tales to state an existential dilemma briefly and pointedly. This permits the child to come to grips with the problem in its most essential form, where a more complex plot would confuse matters for him. The fairy tale simplifies situations.

Simplification, or myth-making, is one of childhood's natural gifts. It is the young child's earliest means of making sense out of the things that happen to him. Almost from the moment of birth, each child is at once realist and fantasist. The world is a totally magical and mystifying place to an infant. There is the wonder of changing light at different hours of the day, the mystery of giant figures moving around the crib, of myriad new sounds and sensations. In order to give some manageable shape to this experiential chaos, the young child begins very early to make magical connections between happenings and their seeming causes. These magical connections cannot really be called fantasizing, because they arise from the child's lack of understanding of the many explicable real links between events in his life. They are valiant attempts at giving some coherent structure to realities he does not, as yet, understand.

There is little difficulty in young children's accepting at face value the existence of a magic pebble, or of a feisty young rabbit wearing a blue jacket with brass buttons. These storybook facts make as much sense as a good deal else in the complex world all around them. Distinctions between reality and fantasy do not become meaningful to children until they have accumulated sufficient experience of living to know or care about the differences.

As children grow older and enter school, they acquire a great many explanations for questions that have long puzzled them. They gain more and more mastery over fact, until the infantile world of magical connections is gradually brought closer and closer to that familiar place of all-too-predictable, mundane happenings that we grown-ups inhabit for most of our waking hours. That earlier, private and often comforting mythic structure of the world, however, doesn't simply vanish. It continues to live somewhere in the unconscious of us all, child and grownup, the rich source of our dreams and imaginings, a place capable of being reached on occasion by those writers – often authors of fantasy – who somehow manage to strike a resonant chord.

We ourselves can also reach it under favorable circumstances. Even the most hard-headed and fact-favoring adult among us harbors, at times, the secret hope for a magical solution to some knotty real-life difficulty. And who of us, in the twilight of certain late summer afternoons, given a wide enough expanse of suggestive green lawn, cannot at least entertain the possibility of fairies dancing in the dusk, turning cartwheels in the grass?

Many serious-minded adults question whether it is sensible or advisable, once a child clearly knows the difference between fact and fiction, to continue to encourage literary side trips into the world of make-believe. Wouldn't we be better off giving our children realistic books to read and learn from? Is there anything fantasy offers that a good realistic work cannot match or even surpass?

It was the Edwardian aesthete Logan Pearsall Smith who wrote: "They say life's the thing, but I prefer reading." And, of course, reading teaches us all, children and adults, more about life than we could ever hope to learn from experience in a single lifetime of unadulterated living. Even when we read for pure enjoyment or escape, inevitably, in some way small or large, we are broadening our knowledge of the world, or of ourselves. Any author worth the reading writes because he is eager to reveal to the reader some cherished truth. To be sure, authors of fiction have a story to tell us, but they would not be telling this particular story unless it was intensely meaningful to them and, therefore, possibly to us as well.

Every one of William Steig's little books for young children – *Amos and Boris, Dominic, Abel's Island, Farmer Palmer's Wagon Ride, Roland the Minstrel Pig*, etc. – impart to the listener, above and beyond the entertainment value of the simple, good-natured tales they tell, Mr. Steig's deep conviction that life is worth living, not so much for the high adventure it occasionally affords, but for the solid ties of affection and duty that bind us to those we love, for the gratuitous beauty of the world that is always there to be discovered and enjoyed. The best of M. B. Goffstein's quirky little fables celebrate the sweet pain of solitude and the unexpected rewards of the creative life. Clyde Robert Bulla's starkly realistic novellas telegraph the author's abiding faith in the rightness of acting responsibly, out of honest feeling and humane values. And throughout each of Eleanor Cameron's novels, the sense of place looms large. In two of them – *The Court of the Stone Children*, a time fantasy, and *To the Green Mountains*, a realistic novel with a post-World War II setting – the general themes might be summed up in exactly the same way: An adolescent girl, unhappy with where she is presently living, manages to get her parents to move to a more congenial home.

In one of her early novels, *A Room Made of Windows*, Mrs. Cameron's eleven-year-old heroine, Julia, cannot imagine ever moving away from the little 7 by 9-foot bedroom where she has begun to write stories – even if it means sacrificing her widowed mother's chance for a happy second marriage. To a Cameron heroine, place is destiny.

But where, since their aims are the same – to reveal important truths to the reader through the tales they tell – do writers of fantasy part company with realistic storytellers? Jane Langton, an accomplished writer of fantasy, usually for older children, has said of the craft of fiction: "The very best that any writer can do is to give the reader a momentary illusion of life." In other words, even authors of the most realistic fiction do not serve us reality, but rather a selective representation of the real. By the very act of transposing to paper what the writer sees out there in the world, she gives us an artificial thing: not life but art. What, then, makes one artifice on paper realistic and another a fantasy?

On this point, E. M. Forster in his *Aspects of the Novel* is most explicit:

Our easiest approach to a definition of any aspect of fiction is always by considering the sort of demand it makes on the reader.... What does fantasy ask of us? It asks us to pay something extra. It compels us to an adjustment that is different from an adjustment required by a work of art, to an additional adjustment. The other novelists say, 'Here is something that might occur in your lives.'; the fantasist says, 'Here is something that could not occur.

Ultimately, Forster provides a simple description of exactly what it is that fantasy demands of us, which separates it unequivocally from a realistic work: fantasy implies the supernatural, even where it does not fully acknowledge it.

What of this element of the supernatural in books for children? Does it present an impediment to the growing child's relationship to reality? More often than not, works of fantasy are set in our own familiar world, peopled by the most mundane and believable of characters. Take the Tuck family in Natalie Babbitt's *Tuck Everlasting*. There are Ma and Pa Tuck and two grown sons, ages twenty–two and seventeen. They are as plain as bowls of porridge. Yet, by a quirk of fate, they just happened, more than two hundred years ago, to have drunk unwittingly from the stream of eternal life. As a result, they can never grow old or die. This one supernatural event is so tightly and convincingly woven into the fabric of the novel that we willingly suspend any doubts we might have and join the book's heroine in a consideration of the work's central question: What if we could choose the gift of eternal life? Would we want it? Every child who reads Mrs. Babbitt's mesmerizing fantasy joins the heroine, young Winnie Foster, in confronting this possibility. *Tuck* is a fantasy, to be sure, but its subject is life's deepest and most terrifying reality – the inevitability of death. This it faces more directly and comfortingly than any realistic novel for children that comes to mind. One of the advantages that a work of fantasy often has over a realistic work is that it takes us by surprise: it catches us off guard, and makes us look at something in a fresh, clear light – even so charged a subject as death.

There are, of course, realistic works that treat, with sensitivity, the same subject: Doris Buchanan Smith's *A Taste of Blackberries* for one. Simply, with tenderness and intelligence, the author tells how a boy of eight is affected by, and manages to reconcile himself to, the sudden death of a friend who is stung by a bee while they are out berry-picking together. Good as the work is, however, its very particularity does not grip the imagination in the way that *Tuck Everlasting* does.

But fantasy need not be so ambitious. Take that exemplar of nannies, *Mary Poppins*. Blown by a brisk east wind into the lives of two unexceptional middle-class English children, Jane and Michael Banks, she settles into the comfortable real world of a correct, somewhat stuffy post-Victorian household. It's not an exciting place, by any means, until she begins using her magical powers to broaden her charges' horizons and, along the way, to improve their manners and deportment. Could any adult wish for a more effective mentor in instructing children to mind their Ps and Qs than this irritable yet irresistible martinet?

The illusion of reality in a work of fantasy must be many times stronger than in a realistic novel, for the author must overcome the reader's natural incredulity. There is nothing more conducive to real-life yawns than a disembodied fantasy unanchored to solid chunks of recognizable reality. Creating the illusion of reality, however, is never easy, not for writers of realistic fiction, nor for fantasists. In a realistic work, the author is always up against severe and knowledgeable critics. The young reader knows how his own contemporaries sound when they talk among themselves, and what the atmosphere is like at a Friday-night school dance. He will measure the author's picture of the world against his own. In a fantasy, on the other hand, the writer must satisfy both the needs and logic of his made-up world and the reader's sense of the credible. A fantasy in particular must have well-delineated characters to whom we can relate; these characters must react in ways we can understand, with motivations we can believe.

So richly textured and cumulatively convincing are the setting and characters in the opening chapters of Richard Kennedy's swashbuckling fantasy *Amy's Eyes* that the reader willingly accepts the author's surprise revelation of a doll that comes to life under a particular set of circumstances. Yet, when this magical occurrence is burdened by over-use in too long and meandering a tale, Kennedy's ambitious fantasy founders. Literary fantasies, like successful soufflés, must be prepared unerringly. Most important of all, they must be served at exactly the right moment. Should the reader's disbelief be suspended over too many pages or plot excursions, the most promising literary soufflé suddenly falls flat.

Can a successful work of fantasy do things that a realistic novel cannot? Fantasy can, as we've seen, bring a child into meaningful contact with difficult subject matter, with the darker side of human existence – with cruelty and evil – without threatening the child's own inner security. Children often sense the conflict and muddle of adult lives around them, without necessarily being able to grasp the complex issues at stake. A fantasy like Zilpha Keaty Snyder's *Beneath the Root* manages to grapple with the problems of evil and injustice in the world in a clear-cut, direct manner that would have been impossible in a more realistic novel.

Unlike *Mary Poppins*, *Tuck Everlasting* or *Amy's Eyes*, all of them fantasies firmly planted in this world, Mrs. Snyder creates another place, Green-Sky, with its own rules of survival and its own unique environment. Within this made-up, simpler world, Mrs. Snyder offers young readers a major subject for consideration: the dangers of absolute power, the spectacle of a seemingly admirable and productive society perpetuating itself by suppressing all opposition and by closing its eyes to its own increasing deception and evil. In a realistic novel, it would have been far more difficult to handle so complex and thorny a theme as clearly and directly for a young reader.

Of course, all works for children do not fall clearly into one camp or the other. There are tales like Lawrence Yep's *Dragonwings*, realistic overall, but with subject matter so exotic to most of its readers that it might just as well be fantasy. Mr. Yep tells about a young Chinese boy, Moonshadow, who arrives in San Francisco at the turn of the century to join his father, Windrider. Because the culture from which Mr. Yep's characters spring is so alien to our own, the dream of Moonshadow's father – one that leads him to build a successful airplane and fly it – seems more fantastic than it otherwise might.

The same could be said of Frances Hodgson Burnett's perennially popular *The Secret Garden*, first published in 1911, that *Wuthering Heights* and *Jane Eyre* of children's books rolled into one. An isolated Yorkshire country house with its hundred unexplored rooms, locked garden and mysterious cries in the night, is a fantasy world complete, both for its orphaned heroine Mary Lennox and for its mostly girl readers. What the moor lad Dickin says on first seeing the secret garden that Mary has discovered could stand as a description of the novel itself: "Eh! It is a queer, pretty place. It's like as if a body was in a dream!" But what a perfect vehicle it proved to be for Mrs. Burnett's story, and for her impassioned and advanced ideas on how children and gardens can best flourish.

By comparison, the most popular of today's "young adult" novels – those dealing realistically with a variety of peer pressures, teen-age sex, the drug scene, abortion and divorce – seem decidedly tame. While they are often sought out by precocious readers aged nine and up as primers of behavior for a new phase of life, they lack the heady romanticism and liberating sense of the world's possibilities that the best works of the imagination – usually fantasies of one sort or other – encourage. That feeling of privilege, of having been to a far-off, special place, comes only rarely in a lifetime of reading. Our happiest recollections of it occur in childhood.

Thus, the borderline between a realistic work and one of fantasy is often hazy. There are works of fantasy that seem more real than many days of our lives. There have been realities in our century that defy human belief: Hitler's Germany for one. As Ursula LeGuin remarked in her speech accepting the 1973 National Book Award: "At this point, realism is perhaps the least adequate means of understanding or portraying the incredible realities of our existence ... it is by the imagination above all that we achieve perception, and compassion and hope."

FOUR

On "Judging"

IN OCTOBER OF 1973, I was invited to serve as one of three judges for the *New York Times Book Review*'s annual selection of The Ten Best Illustrated Children's Books of the year. As a critic and reviewer of children's picture books, I had always felt quite free to wince at, or to disdain outright, the predictably safe and uninspired selections often made by other judges in other children's book competitions. All too frequently, it seemed that the annual Caldecott Medal awarded by the American Library Association went to the right artist for the wrong book or – when, rarely, a selection committee screwed up its courage and opted to be adventurous – to the wrong artist for absolutely the wrong book. (For me Gail Hayley's *An African Tale*, and, years later, Eve Bunting's *Smoky Night*, illustrated by David Diaz, certainly fell into this latter category.)

It was, then, with high hopes and more than a little anxiety that I entered the New York Times Building that October 9. At last, the choice and responsibility were partly mine. (My two fellow judges were Walter Chappell, a respected artist and book designer, and Hilton Kramer, the *Times*' own art critic.) With ten selections to be made, we would be hopeless clods indeed if we couldn't come up with at least a few truly deserving choices. This particular year, the *Times*' children's book editor, George Woods, had the inspired idea of keeping the judges entirely separate from one another. He felt, with some considerable evidence to back him up, that choices by committee tend to smack of compromise,

38

to be the result of horse-trading sessions in which highly opinionated people swap their individual top preferences: You grant me my three favorites and, reluctantly, I'll agree to three of yours that, frankly, I think are pretty rotten. And, perhaps, if the contest is a charmed one, three or four judges will ultimately settle on one or two titles that all of them agree are eminently deserving. Woods felt that in giving each of three judges complete autonomy to choose four personal favorite books of 1973, the result would be a possible maximum of twelve choices for the year or a minimum of a unanimous four, which would constitute so rare an instance of unanimity among "experts" as to merit memorializing in *The Guiness Book of World Records*.

Arriving at the *Book Review*'s eighth-floor offices about 10 A.M., I was ushered into a conference room, its large table piled high with 218 picture books. These were the titles that had already been initially screened and pre-selected by the *Book Review*'s own children's book staff.

If you are a purist you may well think, "Aha! Here is the first evidence of possible unfairness. How do we know what irrational prejudices or pet likes on the part of the screeners may have already eliminated some entirely worthwhile, possibly even superior offerings?" Well, the answer is we don't. However, the original invitation encouraged all three judges to request any particular favorites they might have from the year's output. Also, in fairness, it should be said of those whose job it is to evaluate or review children's books, so much dross comes across their desks in the course of a year's parade of some two thousand picture-book titles that they are unlikely to pass over something of marked originality or distinction. Even when they don't like a particular work, they are so pleased to encounter a book out of the ordinary that they are not apt to overlook it.

Well, there I sat, alone with a table full of children's picture books. At first, the mind boggles at the size and absurdity of the task: 218 books! How could the *Book Review* staff reasonably expect this to be a labor of two or three hours' time? I had been told that if I came in by ten o'clock, I should end by about one P.M. and join George and his assistant for lunch in the *Times'* Executive Dining Room to celebrate my job's completion. I was told, too, that Walter Chappell, who had been in the day before, finished his selection in just under two hours. I also knew that Hilton Kramer was slated to follow me that very afternoon. Any undue dawdling on my part would not be appreciated. Both George and his assistant had, however, assured me that I could always return if I needed to deliberate longer, but I had the distinct feeling that everyone hoped I'd get on with it, and make up my mind by morning's end.

Bravely, I lit into the nearest stack. It was a little like taking a deep breath and jumping off a diving board into murky waters of indeterminate depth. Since I was there alone with a virgin yellow pad before me, I began purposefully to take notes – a form of whistling in the daylight. This is probably the point at which to confess that certainly I had come into the room with preconceived ideas: some favorites among the 1973 books that I had already seen. Weeks earlier, I had finished a long book roundup for a new education magazine, *LEARNING*, and many of the titles I had reviewed there struck me as eminently worth consideration here: *A Prairie Boy's Winter*, written and illustrated by the Canadian primitive painter William Kurelek was one; *Cathedral*, a first book written and illustrated with love and meticulous care by David Macaulay, a young American architect in love with French Gothic cathedrals, was another. Also on my list were Tomi Ungerer's demonic confection, *No Kiss for Mother*, with its mordant black–and–white drawings of the world's rottenest kitten; Raymond Briggs' *Father Christmas*, a kind of comic strip romp in the company of a thoroughly English Santa Claus on his night–before–Christmas rounds; William Steig's *The Real Thief*, a light–hearted novella about a misunderstood goose, full of Steig's seemingly effortless and charming line drawings; Maurice Sendak's illustrations for the Brothers Grimm's *The Juniper Tree*; and a funny, offbeat book the *Times* itself had sent me for review a few weeks earlier, the mysterious and wordless *Bus 24* by a French illustrator, Guy Billout. Also free–floating in my head were

William Kurelek, *A Prairie Boy's Winter*

familiar names like Janina Domanska, Peter Parnall, William Pène Du Bois, and Peter Spier, all of whom, I knew from my catalogue browsing, had done one or more picture books during the year.

What does a judge bring to a critical assessment of a picture book? The artist Janina Domanska put it very well when she observed, "Children are a marvelous audience because they can take every new thing. I think a book is supposed to create, to be strong and new." I agree wholeheartedly. I've also always liked something Arthur Rackham said: "The most fascinating form of illustration consists of the expression by the artist of an individual sense of delight or emotion aroused by the accompanying passage of literature." And, finally, I often recall something the author Jane Langton wrote a couple of years ago about a children's book contest that she happened then to be judging: "In trying to work out standards for myself, I find that a major one is the author's enthusiasm, a sense of love – almost of passion – between the author (or illustrator) and his material. I am also swayed by those books that make a mark on the reader – that leave him in some way different than he was before."

Thus, with rag-tag bits and pieces of verbal and emotional baggage, along with my own ingrained likes and dislikes, I began slowly to leaf through the ten or twelve stacks before me. It didn't take long to find myself naturally, almost unthinkingly, dividing my candidates into three categories. There were the outright rejects: books that were by no means badly illustrated, but books without surprises or marked individuality; then, there was a large pile of "worth considering" titles; and, finally, a smaller stack of definitely-in-the-running books. One of the first notes I wrote to myself as I sorted was, "With so many books to consider, there is a decided advantage given to those that you know already." But is this prior knowledge not two-edged? In the course of my sorting, I came across a number of other works by artists and writers I had come to respect over the years: Edward Ardizzone, Adrienne Adams, Eric Carle, Barbara Cooney, Brian Wildsmith. In some way, knowing an artist's capabilities may turn out to his or her disadvantage. Through the afficionado's mind parades all the memorable work one remembers by a given artist, and if the volume in hand seems too similar to earlier work, or perhaps just slightly under peak perform-ance, that work will be set aside – even though it may be superior to the work of an unknown author or artist that strikes the judge's fancy. I found myself dismissing anything that seemed to fall short of a known artist's best work. In some cases this troubled me. There was, for example, Margot Zemach's highly polished, witty and thoroughly pleasing rendition of a Welsh folktale, *Duffy and the Devil*. It was fault-less, yet, to me, it was no better than other of her improvisations and perhaps not quite as original as some. So I left it out in the end, with genuine regret. I found, too, that certain artists I had long admired produced wonderfully competent work this year and yet the end result never quite reached that level of consequence or visual excitement that cried out for a prize.

Another of the notes I wrote myself, and it seemed wonderfully subtle and wise at the time (but rather pompous in hindsight), was: "You are not choosing the ten best illustrators, nor necessarily the ten best books, but the ten in which illustration and text are in such per-fect synchronization that the amalgam achieves a life of its own." Thus I felt free to pass over good stories with dull illustrations, or smashing illustrations that struggled in vain against dull texts.

Within about an hour and a half, I found I had enough selections in the "definitely in the running" pile to concentrate on these alone. To be certain I wasn't being too hasty, I went through the "maybe" pile one last time. I even upgraded a couple of titles. I now faced an almost manage-able pile of twenty to twenty-four books to consider for my final selec-tion of four.

By now it was perfectly clear that even if I sat there for several hours more, the dilemma would be the same: eliminating sixteen to twenty books I liked a lot to end up with the four final selections that were my portion. It was a little past noon by this point, and I felt there was a certain virtue in being under time pressure. It encouraged ruthlessness: Okay, for better or worse, I had been granted a degree of autonomous power. The time had come to wield it autocratically. My own biases acknowledged, I chose what I liked best.

Taking a deep breath, I wrote my final four choices on a clean sheet of yellow paper. They were *A Prairie Boy's Winter* by William Kurelek; *Cathedral* by David Macaulay; *Bus 24* by Guy Billout and *The Juniper Tree*, Maurice Sendak's collection of Grimm tales. You've heard earlier about the first three. As for Sendak's work – which turned out to be the only unanimous choice of all three judges – it was a masterful performance in black and white. Not only had several years of research, thought and sketching gone into the final drawings, but certain of the illustrations are hauntingly memorable: i.e., the palpably real baby being spirited away by a half-dozen goblins. The artist's frontispiece drawing for the story "The Goblins" has a subtlety and mystery almost surpassing that of the Grimm tale itself.

I not only handed in my selections by about ten minutes to one, I also wrote for myself a note on another piece of the same yellow pad. Perhaps it was to assuage my conscience about the inherent arbitrariness of all contests. It said simply: "Profound regrets to leave off my list *The Woman Who Lived in Holland* by William Holdsworth, *The Clay Pot Boy* with illustrations by Arnold Lobel, *The Star-Spangled Banner* by Peter Spier and *The Magician* by Uri Shulevitz." I have that note to this day. It should also be said that in every contest, there is an ultimate unfairness. Good books, like special people, are unique and cannot really be compared to one another in any just way. As Jane Langton noted of that earlier contest she had judged: "These books are apples and oranges, pianos and prunes, washtubs and weasels." Still, I left the Times Building that day not unpleased with myself. For better or worse, I had done my best.

Parsons School of Design Lecture
December 14, 1973

FIVE

Pictures at Two Exhibitions

BEATRIX POTTER: A MINIATURIST OF UNCOMMON QUALITIES

ONE OF THE first things apparent to a viewer of the comprehensive 1988 Beatrix Potter exhibition at New York's Morgan Library
(*Beatrix Potter: The Artist and Her World*) was how of a piece Miss Potter's
graphic gifts were, from childhood on. It may come as a surprise to
some that she had a serious interest, in her twenties and early thirties,
in the accurate drawing of insects, fungi and fossils. She often used her
brother Bertram's microscope to undertake studies of butterflies'
wings, spiders, mites and beetles at various magnifications. These
painstaking efforts were in keeping with her lifelong fascination with
the careful observation of insects and small animals.

The earliest illustration in the exhibition, a page from a sketchbook
painted when she was eight, is a watercolor of several varieties of
caterpillar, depicting their colors and markings, as well as postures
while dining, while in motion and while at rest. Already the artist can
be characterized as patient, noticing and trustworthy. Her acute powers of observation are confirmed in the first drawings of various pets
she and her brother kept in their nursery, particularly those of her rabbit, Benjamin Bouncer. A brown watercolor study of 1880, done con-
fidently when she was fourteen, with a dry brush, gives an uncanny
sense of the fur's texture, of the latent energy and wary watchfulness
of the sitter. Six penciled heads of Benjamin, done from various angles

in the same year, capture the aliveness of the subject and subtle nuances of expression and mood.

The earliest watercolor of marked individuality and accomplishment, *The Library, Wray Castle, July 1882*, was done when Potter was sixteen, and it contains all the elements that were to distinguish her mature work. Loving attention is given to the room's Gothic woodwork; its solid furnishings; fireplace and mantle; the red fabric walls and cushions; and the individual volumes on the book shelves. Beckoning us to examine the room and its contents, the work is at once intimate and objective. Approximately 14 by 10 inches, it is one of Potter's larger watercolors.

By this time, Potter had already been studying drawing with a Miss Cameron for four years. When these lessons ended a year later, the young Beatrix coolly assessed their worth in the journal that she kept in code: "I have learned from the freehand, model, geometry, perspective and a little watercolour flower painting. Painting is an awkward thing to teach except the details of the medium." In 1883, Beatrix was given twelve "expensive lessons" with another teacher, a "Mrs. A.," who came highly recommended to her father. Anticipating this new instruction, Beatrix wrote, "Of course, I shall paint just as I like when not with her." Of painting as an art, the student already had her own ideas: "I am convinced it lies chiefly with oneself."

From 1885, there is a commanding pen–and–ink drawing, 7 ¼ by 4 ½ inches, of "A corner of the schoolroom, 2 Bolton Gardens," part of the nursery room that remained the creative center of Potter's life for her first thirty years. Unlike the intimate watercolor of Wray Castle's library, this work is almost scientific in its cool detachment. It is a matter–of–fact catalog of the space's contents: fireplace and screen, cages with birds, a finely proportioned table and high chest of drawers beautifully particularized and, just by the way, a tortoise crawling across the floor. Clearly the artist had more than a passing interest in furnishings and a good eye for proportions and oddments of detail. (A year earlier, at eighteen, she had written in her journal: "If ever I had a house

I would have old furniture, oak in the dining room and chippendale in the drawing room. It is not as expensive as modern furniture, and incomparably handsomer and better made.") Like the corner of the room itself, the drawing is all business.

In 1888, while visiting her paternal grandmother's house, Camfield, she made a mesmerizing watercolor study of a weasel, capturing its reddish brown coloration, feral face, lively tail and elongated proportions. Though she had trouble remembering people's names, she was particularly sensitive to personality differences in her pets – even among various snails. Because she studied animals so closely, she occasionally took note of human beings' similarities to them, once comparing in the journal her Aunt Harriet to a weasel, her Uncle Henry to a crow.

What the painter John Millais, a family friend, said about her work as a young woman remained true throughout her career: "Plenty of people can draw, but you and my son John have observation."

In 1890, Potter's gifts for animal drawing and painting took a commercial turn when she and Bertram decided they wanted to buy a printing machine at a cost of £16. The artist set her mind to earning money by producing a series of animal cards for the Christmas trade, using the durable Benjamin Bouncer as her model. Dressing her beautifully realized rabbits (years of practice studies held her in good stead here) in the height of Victorian fashion, she sold the first half-dozen to the firm of Hildesheimer & Faulkner for £6. Delighted by this success, she continued producing animal cards, but she clearly felt that these greeting-card bunnies were, in a sense, all dressed up with no place to go. She soon began to submit groups of drawings that comprised simple animal tales: one exquisitely-painted grouping in sepia (3½ by 5 inches each) for a verse "Three little mice sat down to spin," another more simply conceived set in pencil and pen-and-ink for "A frog he would a-wooing go;" but neither set met with commercial success. That the artist was eager to expand her horizons is clear from the brilliant set of six large – for Potter – watercolors (6 by 6 inches each) called *The Rabbits' Christmas Party*. The compositions are elegant, the figures entirely believable as they arrive at, partake in and finally depart from the holiday festivities in a comfortable middle–class rabbit household. In the artist's thrall, we feel privileged to have witnessed so wondrous a celebration. If prepared for sale, the effort was apparently unsuccessful, for four of the works were given as a gift to Potter's Aunt Lucy Roscoe; the other two were presented to an American visitor. During the '90s too, Potter attempted to illustrate several popular animal tales of the time. There are examples of mostly tentative pencil drawings for *Alice in Wonderland*, the *Uncle Remus* tales and Edward Lear's *The Owl and the Pussycat*. Potter referred to these efforts as "subject drawings," perhaps to distinguish them from the pure fancy of her little animal cards. She also wrote several illustrated story letters during this decade to the children of her former governess and German teacher, Annie Moore – the most famous of which was "the Peter–Rabbit letter" to Noel Moore in September 1893.

Miss Potter's serious drawing interest during the '90s however, was unquestionably fungi. There are superb examples in the show, notably an exquisite painting *in situ* of Fly Agaric (*Amanita muscaria*) c. 1895, an orange–red mushroom with white spots, surrounded by ferns and fallen leaves; and a lively study of a Parasol Mushroom (*Lepiota friessii*) elegantly displayed on a white page. These years also produced photographically precise drawings of fossils and ancient Roman objects recently excavated: shoe leathers, a variety of tools and knives. It is probable that Miss Potter thought to turn her hand to scientific drawings as a career, for she completed several plates for a Miss Martineau of the London Natural History Museum.

We will never know what, in 1901, caused her to ask Noel Moore if she might borrow back the Peter–Rabbit letter of 1893, but we can only be grateful that she turned her attention to transforming that letter into a simple picture–story book all her own. There is the pleasure of seeing the autograph copy of this book with her black–and–white drawings facing simple sentences of hand–written text. Potter originally prepared the book entirely in black and white – except for a single frontispiece drawing in color, the same one that appears in the book to this day. When no publisher would take on the book as it was, she had 250 copies printed privately in 1901. The firm of Frederick Warne came round to her way of thinking – they had originally objected to the book's small size – and, with her agreement to redo the illustrations in color, they published a commercial edition in time for Christmas 1902. And so began Beatrix Potter's career and fame as an illustrator of children's books.

Although it is the best known of her little books, *The Tale of Peter Rabbit* contains, in many respects, the least typical or evocative of her water–colors. Those earliest book illustrations lack the specific Lake Country locale of her later tales and, in most cases, they lack much in the way of background detail at all. This becomes apparent when we compare the many later landscape studies from her sketchbooks with the remarkable transformations they undergo for use in her little books.

Take the forthright 1903 sketchbook study of a stone wall with attendant vegetation (9 by 7 inches approximately) and its subsequent incorporation into a setting where old Mr. Benjamin Bouncer prances

Beatrix Potter,
The Tale of Peter Rabbit

upon it in the 1904 book, *The Tale of Benjamin Bunny*. Not only has the earlier sketch been condensed into an oval vignette scarcely 2 by 1½ inches in size, but the colors have been softened, the vegetation abbreviated and rearranged for maximum effect. Though all the salient elements of the larger picture have been compressed into the smaller one, the end result has a heightened, dreamlike quality. It is as if in the process of condensation, the original watercolor's contents have been effectively summarized and clarified. These near-magical transformations of her well-observed, matter-of-fact watercolor sketches are what give the books their endearing charm. In every instance where a sketchbook study is seen in conjunction with the final book illustration, the sketch has been improved – sharpened – by its reduction in size and by the artist's subtle alterations in color and composition.

It was, of course, this eventual combining of the small animals she knew so well with the background landscapes and cottage interiors of the Lake Country she loved that gave her work its unique quality and lasting appeal.

Another small marvel in her tales is how every real-life background has been scaled to accommodate the size of the story's particular protagonists. There is a wonderful watercolor of Anna Maria, the rat wife of Samuel Whiskers in the tale that bears his name, shown running across a living room on her way to steal some dough. The room is shown from her eye-view. Only the bottom third of the space and its contents are visible – just what Anna Maria would see as she ran.

It has been commented upon that Beatrix Potter drew the human figure poorly, and it is true that people are largely absent, or kept in distant perspective, in her books. In part, this was because a human being's size introduced a discordant note. Our concentration is so much on the small animal protagonists that human beings would somehow diminish the illusion of reality Potter so wonderfully creates. It is as if at a Punch and Judy show, we were suddenly to see the giant hand of the puppeteer. One of Miss Potter's rejected illustrations for *The Tale of Pigling Bland* bears this out. A shadowy portrait of the author beside one of the small pigs is altered in the final illustration so that only Miss Potter's hand (and that reduced in size) remains visible.

As Potter became more comfortable with the spinning of tales – she wrote and illustrated twenty–three in all, though the best of them had appeared by 1913 – she became adept at selecting likely backgrounds for her little dramas. She once delayed renovating the kitchen of Hilltop, her cottage in Sawrey, because the cast–iron stove would be a necessary backdrop in *The Tale of Samuel Whiskers*.

The truth is that, as competent and pleasing as her larger sketchbook watercolors are, were they all we knew of Beatrix Potter, she would have been just another competent but not especially distinguished gentlewoman watercolorist of the Victorian era. It was her remarkable gift for miniaturizing her work for its appearance in the tales that gives the paintings their evocative power and enduring worth.

MAURICE SENDAK: A BORROWER OF EPIC PROPORTIONS

IN OUR JUDGMENTS OF ARTISTS – be they painters, sculptors or chil-dren's book illustrators – the quality of originality is often strained. The sculptor Louise Nevelson has spoken of her earliest encouragement by a grade–school teacher: "She held this up [Louise's drawing of a flower] and said it was the best because it was original. That word was very big to a child. I clocked it; I knew that to be original was what it was all about."

Perhaps the most refreshing impression one took from the exhibi-tion of *The Art of Maurice Sendak* at the Philip H. & A. S. W. Rosenbach Foundation in Philadelphia is how little originality of style counts in any evaluation of this master illustrator's art. Marking the artist's gift to that institution in 1970 of the bulk of his drawings, and spanning the whole of Sendak's career to date – from his first earnest efforts for Marcel Aymé's *The Wonderful Farm* (1951) to several faultless drawings from his picture book, *In the Night Kitchen* (1970) – the work on exhibit comprised a moving record of the slow mastery of style, of several styles, of any style in fact, that happened to serve the Sendak work at hand.

Given our valuation of originality, such a prelude may seem to derogate the artist's work. On the contrary, it is high tribute to an illustrator who, from the outset of his career, has steadily rated inner content above graphic pyrotechnics. What is wholly original in Sendak has been so since his first rather pedestrian drawings (not exhibited in the Rosenbach show) for a little-known work published by the United Synagogue Commission on Jewish Education, *Good Shabbos, Everybody* (1951). He has an uncanny ability to make palpable the emotional reality of a tale, the atmosphere in which its child and adult characters exist, and the psychological bonds and tensions which unite and separate them. There are already in the gestures and expressions of the grandparents and small children in that earliest work, as well as in the claustrophobic sense of Jewish family solidarity he manages to project, a preview of the touching portrayal of childhood happiness and security Sendak began to create six years later for Else Holmelund Minarik's five Little Bear books. Looked at in one way, the Rosenbach show chronicles Sendak's rise from parochial and humble Brooklyn beginnings as a self-taught cartoonist, onward and upward into the aristocracy of children's book illustrators, a fit companion for Walter Crane, Randolph Caldecott or the gifted French illustrator Louis-Maurice Boutet de Monvel.

Though Sendak stands unchallenged as the leading children's book illustrator of our time, the artist seems oddly out of joint with the mainstream of American children's book illustration in the '50s and '60s. During an era when bold use of color, abstract design, outsize format and showy technical virtuosity abounded, his work has always remained low-key, curiously retrograde and nineteenth century in spirit. From the exhibited selections, made by both the artist and Clyde Driver, the Foundation's curator, Sendak clearly emerges as a conscientious and respectful student of the past, an innovator within a long tradition rather than a smasher of stylistic idols. As Sendak himself has put it: "I borrowed techniques and tried to forge them into a personal language."

Born in Brooklyn in 1928, Sendak and his older brother Jack drew pictures from childhood on, and even bound their own books of tales. Maurice studied art in high school – about the only subject he enjoyed – and worked after school and on weekends for All–American Comics filling in backgrounds for such strips as *Mutt and Jeff*. His first full–time job after high school was at a Manhattan window display house where he remained until 1948 when he and Jack tried to start their own business, manufacturing animated wooden toys. The carving and engineering were Jack's province, the painting and decorating Maurice's. Two of their creations were in the exhibition, one an ingenious Red Riding Hood tableau in which the wolf springs from grandma's bed when the child activates a lever. Though the brothers had no success marketing their handiwork – the toys would have been too expensive to produce in quantity – F. A. O. Schwarz did hire Maurice for its own window display department. While working there, he briefly attended night classes at the Art Students League and, through the store's book buyer, met Ursula Nordstrom, the children's book editor of Harper & Row. After seeing his sketchbook, she invited him to illustrate his first full-fledged entry into children's books, Marcel Aymé's *The Wonderful Farm*.

Sendak considers much of the published and unpublished work he did in the early '50s as a sort of working apprenticeship. One way or other, the artist had been preparing himself for his career since childhood. During his early teens, Sendak recalls, "I spent hundreds of hours sitting at my window, sketching neighborhood children at play ... there is not a book I have written or picture I have drawn that does not, in some way, owe them its existence." The black–and–white line drawings for *A Hole Is to Dig*, his first collaboration with Ruth Krauss – and the book that brought him his earliest fame – owe their existence to this early sketchbook. Then, too, between the ages of sixteen and eighteen, long before he had received a formal book commission, Sendak illustrated several books strictly for his own pleasure, among them Bret Harte's *The Luck of Roaring Camp*, Oscar Wilde's *The Happy Prince* and Hans Andersen's *The Little Match Girl*. Though none of these early efforts appeared in the Rosenbach show, they are ultimately promised to the Foundation in Sendak's will. "I couldn't bear to part with them now," the artist says. "When I look at them, they remind me of my state of mind at that time, an apartment I lived in and a street where I was very happy."

The seven books he illustrated for Meindert de Jong during the early '50s represented a gradual broadening of his graphic technique. He feels that the realistic demands made by De Jong's stories, set in a variety of locales unfamiliar to him, required that he do research outside his own immediate experience, find new modes of expression – in short, to move out of Brooklyn. In these tales he moved as well from the pen and ink line drawings of his earlier work to experiments with brush and wash.

At the same time Sendak was developing his technique along conventional lines in his published work, he was moving in quite another direction in sketchbooks filled with fantasy pages done for his own diversion during the years 1952–1957. Selections from this collection comprised the only catalog there was of the Rosenbach show, and they further confirm the constancy of the artist's inner vision. Themes – obsessions, perhaps – which are to play so central a role in all his own later work (children falling through space, being devoured, losing their clothes, cavorting in the altogether and ending up at a feast or safe in bed after an assortment of harrowing adventures) – are all touched upon in these freely–executed pen sketches, each sequence drawn within the playing–time span of a single piece of music. "Often I worked to chamber music," the artist recalls, "and best were the short piano pieces that practically guaranteed a page finished safely." Sendak remembers these drawings fondly as "the only homework to which I energetically applied myself, the only school that ever taught me anything." The pages, some perfunctory in execution and others of high polish and charm, comprised a sort of graphic free-association process through which the artist liberated both imagination and hand for the more personal works to come during the '60s and '70s.

The first book Sendak both wrote and illustrated, *Kenny's Window*, in 1956, is a dreamy and still tentative evocation of the Brooklyn boy he must have been. As the viewer threaded his way among well-lit cases and along well-filled walls in the two small rooms which comfortably contained the entire exhibition, it became apparent that Sendak's vision comes into sharp focus between the years 1957 and 1962. His surer touch begins to show in such works as *Little Bear* (1957), which marks the start of his romance with the great German and English illustrators of the nineteenth century. His painterly *The Moon Jumpers* (1959) distinctly promises the later *Where the Wild Things Are* (1963), and his own *The Sign on Rosie's Door* (1960) is far more in focus graphically and verbally than either of the prior books he both wrote and illustrated. Other works of these years, *No Fighting, No Biting* (1958) and *What Do You Say, Dear?* (1958), also move into the nineteenth century, which was to be Sendak's spiritual home for some time to come. In the late '50s and early '60s, too, Sendak grows more interested in the niceties of bookmaking. End papers begin to loom large, and ornamental page borders.

At various times, to different interviewers, Sendak has provided a varying list of those artists who have deeply marked his work. The names range from William Blake whom he calls "the chief head influence on my art" to the Frenchman Louis-Maurice Boutet de Monvel; from Thomas Rowlandson to Heinrich Hoffmann; from the English Victorian illustrators, Arthur Hughes and George Pinwell, to the turn-of-the-century American comic-strip artist Winsor McCay. In another vein, he has also mentioned the '30s movie extravaganzas of Busby Berkeley, Buster Keaton, King Kong and Mickey Mouse as markedly influencing his art. And in 1970 when he accepted the Hans Christian Andersen Awards' illustrator's medal in Bologna, Italy, he mentioned yet another influence, Attilio Mussino, illustrator of Collodi's *Pinocchio*. Of this artist Sendak told his listeners: "My eyes were opened by the offhand virtuosity of the man, the ease with which he commanded a variety of styles, controlled them all, blending them and still managing to keep them subservient to the tale. He taught me at one and the same time respect for finish and style as well as a certain disregard for these qualities. Style counts, I now saw, only insofar as it conveys the inner meaning of the text being illustrated."

Time and again one is struck by the persistence of Sendak's imagery. The earliest work in the exhibition – aside from a Mickey Mouse drawn by "Murray Sendak" at age six – is a small oil painting of a childhood friend, Rosie, lent by the artist's brother and dated 1948. Through the primitive brushwork and sentimental characterization, true Sendak lovers can quickly recognize the prototype for black-eyed Mimmy in *Good Shabbos* of 1951 and the more polished Rosie of *The Sign on Rosie's Door* nine years later. There is also a recurring, soggy-legged lion who appears in a work illustrated for his brother Jack's book, *Circus Girl* (1957), and in his own *Higglety Pigglety Pop!* (1967) a decade later. The lion is memorable because he hasn't changed at all. Early and late, his foreleg is so badly conceived as to look like nothing so much as a well-stuffed lion suit. (The lion in his Nutshell Library volume, *Pierre* (1962), suffers the same lion-suit syndrome, but being a broader rendition it is less obtrusive.) Though consistently badly drawn, the lion is curiously electric, magical in effect.

As more and more in the early '60s Sendak settled into the nineteenth century, "early and late," he acquired and discarded a variety of styles with ease. The viewer saw in a juxtaposition of a Rowlandson drawing borrowed from the Philadelphia Museum how much Sendak's work for *Lullabies and Good Night Songs* (1965) – and *The Bee Man of Orn* (1964) and *The Griffin and the Minor Canon* (1963) – owed to this early nineteenth-century caricaturist. A Blake drawing from *The Gates of Paradise* could be seen as a decided influence on, of all lighthearted works, The Nutshell Library, just as the work of a Blake protégé, Samuel Palmer, clearly had a marked effect on both the illustrations for Randall Jarrell's *The Bat-Poet* (1964) and *The Animal Family* (1965). Randolph Caldecott, too, recurs as an influence. (Sendak even dips pen to him by branding his initials on the saddle of one of his own "Caldecott" drawings.) In 1962, perhaps resisting the pull into Victoriana and an ever more fussy concern with cross–hatching and the imitation of steel engravings, Sendak came briefly under the sway of Winslow Homer's watercolors. A Homer sketch of Bermuda placed beside a Sendak illustration for Charlotte Zolotow's *Mr. Rabbit and the Lovely Present* (1962) shows how the artist not only emulated Homer's technique but also took over Homer's composition almost brazenly.

Yet, in the end, the intensity of Sendak's personal vision minimizes all questions of borrowings and influences. As authors enrich their vocabularies, so Sendak simply continues to add new techniques to his graphic repertoire.

Accompanying his increased reliance on both the German and English illustrators of the nineteenth century was Sendak's increased dependence on family photographs. As one caption written with the artist's concurrence put it, "The look of people frozen in time, the look of the photograph has been turned to personal affect." Many of the drawings for Isaac Bashevis Singer's *Zlateh the Goat and Other Stories* (1966) derive directly from old–world family photographs of his grandparents, great aunts and uncles. The baby in his *Higglety Pigglety Pop!* (1967) is drawn almost exactly from a family photograph of himself as an infant, as is another photograph of his brother Jack transposed into a drawing for a Randall Jarrell memorial volume. In *Higglety*, too, several drawings are memories of toys, street scenes and objects that Sendak remembers from his childhood as if they were photographed – or etched – in his mind.

In the two works closest to his heart, *Where the Wild Things Are* (1963) and *In the Night Kitchen* (1970), Sendak feels the dominant influences were cinematic: *King Kong* in the former and, in some wholly unconscious way, *The Gold Diggers of 1935* in the latter. (By six, Sendak frequently accompanied his mother on Friday night forays to the movies

– to get the free dish of the week – and he saw such films at an impressionable age.) Many who know the work of the American comic-strip artist, Winsor McCay, feel much more is owed to his strip *Little Nemo in Slumberland*, which has much the same format and even sequences remarkably close in spirit to Sendak's world of the Night Kitchen. But Sendak is, above all, eclectic in his borrowings. There is a page from the German artist Wilhelm Busch's classic *Max und Moritz* showing a baker popping two dough–crusted boys into an oven, a fate identical to Sendak's Mickey.

Yet, two small dummies, roughly–sketched precursors of each of these works, show how the matter of visual debts is entirely secondary. The books' cores are pure Sendak. *Where the Wild Things Are* grew directly (albeit slowly) out of a dummy dated eight years earlier (November 17, 1955), titled *Where the Wild Horses Are*. Less than an inch high and about five inches long, that dummy is a small gold mine of elements which later appear in other Sendak works, as well. A small boy sails off to an island, follows a sign to where the wild horses are, is attacked, kicked out of his clothes by the horses, but luckily finds a ship and sails back home. Though all the raw material for *Wild Things* is there, the graphic form was not evolved for some time to come.

The small dummy for *In the Night Kitchen* precedes this work by only one year. It is far closer to the final book in conception than *Wild Things* but the *mise-en-scène* is not at all developed. There is no hint of the final staging of the Night Kitchen with its skyscrapers built of kitchen utensils and supplies, no Oliver Hardys, no marvelous art déco curtains. Even the *Little Nemo* resemblance is absent.

As his career progressed – fifty–nine books up to 1970 – Sendak's inner vision had deepened and his technical virtuosity increased. In his speech at Bologna, the artist confided a new vision of what he wanted his future to be. "I no longer want simply to illustrate – or, for that matter, simply to write. I am now in search of a form more purely and essentially my own.... I must turn to music to describe something of what I am after. The concentrated face of Verdi's *Falstaff*, or a Hugo Wolf song, where music and words mix and blend and incredibly excite, defines my idea. Here words and music form a magic compound, a 'something else' – more than music, more than words." Sendak would like his picture–book art to move into the realm of the something else – having "the immediate beauty of music and all its deep, unanalyzable mystery." A visionary of childhood who has also made himself a master graphic technician, he has set the goal for his work of the '70s and beyond. As an artist he has no plans to rest on his laurels.

Frank R. Stockton, *The Griffin and the Minor Canon*
illustration by Maurice Sendak

Beatrix Potter, *The Tale of Mrs. Tiggywinkle*

SIX

The Tale of Mrs. William Heelis, The Last & Happiest of Beatrix Potter's Creations

I<small>T</small> C<small>OMES</small> A<small>S</small> something of a shock to realize that Beatrix Potter's life (1866–1943) spanned a period from the birth of the modern children's picture book – with the first antic graphic improvisations on traditional nursery rhymes by her countryman Randolph Caldecott in 1878 – to the still recent revolution in the genre heralded by the advent of author/artist Theodore S. Geisel (alias Dr. Seuss) and his irreverent, homegrown nonsense in the late 1930s. Furthermore, as Jane Crowell Morse's modest and beguiling collection, *Beatrix Potter's Americans: Selected Letters*, makes apparent, the connecting links were more than a matter of coincidental dates. The young Beatrix Potter saw and admired Caldecott's ingenious inventions as they were published, and her father, Rupert, bought several original Caldecott drawings during the illustrator's all–too–brief career. As for Seuss, Miss Potter's earliest American visitor, Anne Carroll Moore of the New York Public Library, forwarded a copy of the good doctor's first published work, *And to Think That I Saw It on Mulberry Street*, for Christmas 1937. The seventy–one–year–old creator of Peter Rabbit enthusiastically proclaimed it "the cleverest book I have met with for many years: The writing and movement of the pictures, the natural truthful simplicity of the untruthfulness." Then she added disarmingly, "I think my own success was largely due to the straightforward lying – spontaneous, natural, barefaced!"

Whatever the specific ingredients, Beatrix Potter's unprecedented success as the author/illustrator of some twenty little animal stories for children was all achieved between 1900 and 1913, the year in which Miss Potter, at age forty–seven, became Mrs. William Heelis, the wife of a country solicitor slightly her junior. Until this happy event, she had remained the dutiful, if restive, daughter of upper–middle–class, quintessentially Victorian parents – a cosseted captive to inflexible proprieties regarding the conduct of single ladies of quality. Once married, however, she won instant release from both parental and societal strictures. At last she was free to live, as she had long yearned to do, in her beloved Lake District village of Sawrey, the locale of two sizable properties she had bought with a small inheritance and her book royalties.

Mrs. Heelis enthusiastically devoted herself to breeding Herdwick sheep, maintaining her cottages, collecting old furniture and china, and working for the National Trust to preserve the natural beauties of the Westmorland countryside. Among her neighbors, Mrs. Heelis's fame was as a formidable competitor at local sheep fairs and ram shows. For a time, she was even the forceful president of the Herdwick Sheep Breeders Association, which held its meetings in a local tavern. So completely did Mrs. Heelis submerge her identity as a children's book artist and writer of international renown that Margaret Lane, her eventual English biographer, confessed, "I had long believed that Beatrix Potter was dead," when in 1941 she accidentally discovered that the author was very much alive.

Curiously, Mrs. Heelis rebuffed, often rudely, all efforts by her fellow countrymen to visit the author of *Peter Rabbit* in Sawrey. She wished neither to be known as Beatrix Potter, nor to be troubled by eager sightseers. It was almost as if she considered England too small a country in which to juggle the exigencies of two separate identities. Yet she was warmly cordial to a number of Americans who wrote and asked permission to call, beginning with Miss Moore in the summer of 1921 and continuing in a steady trickle through almost two decades. Not only librarians, editors and publishers came, but whole families who had loved her books – many of these visitors from in and around Boston. She explained her liking for Americans on several grounds, the foremost being, as she wrote to one, that "You really appreciate my little books; whereas in this country it is the popularity of a 'best seller' toy book ... a conventional present." Also, it pleased the author–in–retirement that her own favorite tale, *The Tailor of Gloucester*, "has never sold so well as in America." Then too, her friends in the United States responded with characteristic generosity to her Windemere Fund, sending money to rescue some lakefront property from the danger of development. (In return, endearingly, she provided each American contributor with a latter–day copy of one of her Peter Rabbit illustrations.) Overall, Mrs. Heelis particularly favored New Englanders, because "they seem to me to have lived and stayed behind in those old–fashioned times and places, which this 'old' world is rapidly obliterating."

Any reader who comes to Potter's American letters anticipating a literary correspondence will, in large part, be disappointed. Mrs. Heelis's leisurely communiqués are filled with reports of livestock prices, sheep sales, harvests and haying, jam–making, bad weather and other diurnal rural concerns. "We are selling 300 sheep at Ambleside on Thursday"; "You must telephone first. I may be out, if the hay is in"; "I am often out of reach, amongst the sheep"; "We had a grand hay time and harvest"; "The poor sheep are suffering, never dry." Occasionally, she offers a remedy to one of her ailing correspondents: "Anyone with muscular rheumatism should try mustard – half a teaspoon as hot as you can drink it; it is not as nasty as it sounds."

Despite her agricultural preoccupations, she is never insular and often uncannily prescient. During the worst of the worldwide Depression she writes: "Your task of regeneration is even harder, for your country has not a background of centuries of developing character." Skeptical about the ineffectual League of Nations, she has early forebodings of the coming war and offers the hope that both England and the United States may survive to see a better world with "rule, really rule by power, not by preaching." Clear–eyed and unsentimental, she laments that "Free education has not done much for this country. Clever children could always get educated in the past, and shallow education without character is proving to be a snare."

Literary concerns are not entirely absent from these letters. At the urging of several of the American admirers, she is persuaded to publish both *The Fairy Caravan* (1929) and *Sister Anne* (1932) with a U.S. publisher, David McKay. (Neither work had the spontaneity, originality or commercial success of her earlier writings.) With Bertha Mahoney Miller, founder and first editor of *The Horn Book*, she shares an enthusiasm for beautifully-crafted old furniture. Yet she is often discouraging about another mutual interest: children's books. During a long rainy spell, she writes, "Enforced leisure does not reawaken literary inspiration. I'm sorry, Miss Mahoney. The wells of fancy have run dry!"

An added charm of these selected letters is the inclusion of twenty full-color reproductions of Potter illustrations, many of them gifts to her American correspondents, here reproduced for the first time. The six scenes of "The Rabbit's Christmas Party" rank among the most accomplished – and playful – drawings of her career.

How far behind Mrs. Heelis had left Beatrix Potter by 1942 is underscored by her instructions to Mrs. Miller regarding an entry for a new edition of *Contemporary Illustrators of Children's Books*: "I think you had better put as little as need be.... Married name, married a lawyer, farms own land in Lake District."

Were it not for the enthusiastic Americans who sought her out, delighted in her acquaintance and, afterwards, kept up the genteel transatlantic correspondence that elicited these chatty, revealing responses, we would know far less than we now do about the unwritten – but richly experienced – tale of Mrs. William Heelis. More and more, as added years, pounds, and the weathering effects of a hard outdoor existence marked her, Mrs. Heelis came to bear a surprising resemblance to one of Beatrix Potter's most memorable creations: the admirably industrious hedgehog Mrs. Tiggywinkle.

SEVEN

A Curious Literary Correspondence:
Horace Elisha Scudder &
Hans Christian Andersen

*Genius is an egg in need of warmth, in need of the fertilization
of good fortune: otherwise it will only be a wind egg.*
Hans Christian Andersen

IT WAS, by all evidence, love at first reading. Or, as the fledgling
writer and editor from Boston, Massachusetts, Horace Elisha Scudder, put it in his critical appraisal "The Fairy Legends of Hans Christian
Andersen": "His treatment of legends is parallel to Shakespeare's dram-
atizing of popular stories.... Andersen exhibits the talent of a first-rate
story teller combined with the excellencies of a poet and humorist. The
ease and sympathy with which he reaches the excellency of his art
mark him as a born artist: one whose art is his nature."

In Scudder's conclusion to this rhapsodic homage, in *The National
Quarterly Review* for September 1861, he wrote: "The secret of Andersen's
genius lies in the fact that he is essentially and always a child. He is a
child in his memory, and in his fancy and feelings.... He creates for
himself a pure world in which he lives. Whatsoever he touches is
transmuted to the same simple beauty.... The children of his creation
are immortal – immortal childhood itself is the symbol of Andersen's
genius."

It is not surprising that the twenty–four–year–old author of this handsome tribute thought to dispatch a copy to the fifty–seven–year–old subject in Denmark. Scudder did so on March 8, 1862, thus launching a literary correspondence, entirely one–sided at the outset, which would eventually bring to the American publishing firm of Hurd and Houghton first–publication rights to ten out of seventeen of Andersen's later tales. This meant that American readers enjoyed Andersen in translation some weeks or months before his Danish audience could read the same tales in the writer's native tongue. This unorthodox publishing arrangement was entirely the result of Scudder's unflagging editorial energy and enthusiasm. Yet the start of their transatlantic exchange was anything but auspicious.

As was seemly in so much younger an admirer, Scudder was duly modest in the first note accompanying his critique: "So many better minds must have reviewed your stories both in Europe and America that I thought you would, only smile at my contribution.... When a child I read your stories – all of us American children do – and now when I take them up again and read them with a more critical mind they are to me more full than ever of beauty and holy truth."

Scudder's impulse in writing to Andersen was not entirely free of an ulterior motive. The young author had just completed his own first collection of tales, *Seven Little People and Their Friends*, and his note continued: "I wished no better introduction to the public as a young author than that which should come thus in the older company of yourself.... I write this to one ... who is ... simply Hans Christian Andersen, best of story tellers."

Although Andersen acknowledged neither the note nor its flattering enclosure, he did make a diary entry for April 1, 1862: "Received today from America *The National Quarterly Review* with a glowing review which left me feeling overwhelmed and small." Three weeks later, a lengthy summary of Scudder's piece, provided by Andersen's editor, appeared in the Copenhagen newspaper *Dagbladet*.

When Scudder's first note reached him, Andersen had recently received a substantial sum from his publishers for a new edition of his collected tales; and he was preoccupied with planning a trip to Spain and Morocco. His stories had been widely translated and were even known among Hindus in India. The earliest of his fairy tales were published in 1835, and his work had been read in America at least since Mary Howitt's first English translation in 1847.

A complex, self-absorbed and moody man, Andersen was hypersensitive about his height and plain appearance. He had once described himself: "His nose as mighty as a cannon, his eyes are tiny, like green peas." Though he was a friend and frequent house guest of the Danish royal family, he was insecure enough to rage at seeming slights or insults. Both proud and ambitious, he was born in 1805 in a one-room cobbler's shop. His mother had taken in washing in order to send him to grammar school and to dress him as fashionably as his middle-class peers. But since May of 1838 he had been receiving a modest annual stipend from the Danish government. He had traveled widely in Europe, but though he had been to England twice – once as the guest of Charles Dickens and his family – his comprehension of English was meager. By nature he was a curious combination of boldness and timidity, apprehensive of new experience even as he sought it out.

Although Scudder received no reply from Andersen, eight months later the younger man sent a copy of his own first book with the confession, "This little book of mine is to some degree inspired by your inimitable *Marchen*." Still Andersen was silent. Four years would pass before Scudder, ebullient as ever, addressed his silent mentor again. In the interim the young American editor had traveled to Scandinavia and elsewhere in Europe, without making any attempt to contact the uncommunicative Dane. Andersen, meanwhile, was beginning to feel his age. In the autumn of 1863 he wrote in his diary, "The youthful spirit and the freshness of youth are over. I cannot exist in my loneliness; am tired of life." A year later he wrote: "I have no future any more, nothing to look forward to, no ideas, I am washed out!" For a while, depressed by the intermittent war between Germany and Denmark; Andersen wrote nothing.

In 1865, however, he did publish a new tale, *The Will-o'-the-Wisps*, which began, "Once there was a man who was well acquainted with fairy tales. They used to come knocking at his door. But lately he had not had any such visitor, and he wondered why the fairy tales didn't come any more."

When Scudder sent off his third communiqué, on October 25, 1866, his circumstances had altered substantially. First he tried jogging his idol's memory: "I reviewed your little tales in one of our periodicals ... and then, with perhaps too much boldness, sent you a copy of the *Review.* ... I have published two volumes and my highest praise has been in being called 'The Andersen of America.'"

His credentials thus reaffirmed, Scudder proceeded to proffer a literary enticement to the recalcitrant Dane. "We in America have not such rich soil for fairy tales, but we are doing our best to make a beautiful world about the hearts of our young countrymen. I ... am now engaged in establishing a new magazine for the young, which I am to conduct, and which is to be published in New York by Messrs. Hurd and Houghton, eminent book publishers there." Scudder had been a literary scout and reader for Henry Houghton in various publishing enterprises, and the establishment of a new children's magazine was seen by that publisher as a way to lure authors to his two-year-old firm, their work in the magazine to be a precursor to eventual book publication. Scudder's proposal to Andersen followed. "Am I too bold in asking whether you will not contribute from your store? All that you have published thus far has been translated and read over and over again. I fear that while your name is a household word with us, you have not received that just return from publishers which is every writer's due."

What Scudder referred to was the lack, as yet, of any international copyright laws. Although Andersen's work had been widely translated, almost without exception the translations were pirated. Once a new

Andersen tale appeared in Denmark, it was almost immediately trans-lated and published abroad, with no remuneration of any kind to Andersen. Scudder proposed, "If you could be induced to send me short stories from time to time, written either in Danish or German, my publishers would gladly make at once a just return and I would have the stories translated and published in our magazine. If you will send me twelve new stories, each as long as *The Kaiser's New Clothes*, we will make payment to you in such a way as you shall advise the sum of $500, or half that sum for half the number of stories." Emboldened by the appeal of such an arrangement, Scudder concluded, "I trust that I may have a reply from you upon this matter. Believe me, I am earnestly desirous of giving our children something new and fresh from Hans Andersen. How they would leap for joy! Permit me also, with all respect, to send you through the mail, a copy of my last book, *Dream Children.*"

Still no response came from Copenhagen. Andersen was recently back from a seven-month trip to France and Portugal. Looking forward to little but old age, he wrote to a friend, "I wish I were only twenty, then I'd take my ink pot on my back, two shirts and a pair of socks, put a quill at my side and go into the wide world." In January of 1867, he confided in another note, "I think Death is going to snatch me away this year."

In the same month the first issue of Scudder's *Riverside Magazine for Young People* appeared. From the start, Scudder guided the magazine and its editorial policy with a firm hand and clearly stated intentions. "We shall pay no very close attention to the line which divides books written for the young from books written for the old; but making a survey of literature, single out those writings which are worth giving to a child." Each issue would carry an original frontispiece illustration by a known and respected artist. Such illustrator-luminaries as F.O.C. Darley, John LaFarge, Thomas Nast and Henry Stephens would grace *The Riverside's* pages. New authors Sara Orne Jewett and Frank Stockton would write for it.

On March 13, 1868, a year and three months after *The Riverside's* launching, Scudder yet again wrote to Andersen with an additional proposal that would prove irresistible. Enclosing a copy of the now extant *Riverside Magazine for Young People*, Scudder repeated his offer regarding new tales from Andersen, but with this added inducement: "I am instructed by my Publisher to add that they would be pleased to make some arrangement with you by which they might publish a complete edition of your *Marchen*, which should have your authorization and in which you should have a share of the profits." Then, just in case Andersen had forgotten, Scudder added yet again: "I have for a long time been a disciple of yours, if I may so say, my first venture in literature being a book of children's stories, which sprang in part from my admiration of your writings, and I gladly took an opportunity presented to me to analyze your works in the pages of one of our reviews."

On the sixteenth of May Scudder got his first reply from Andersen. "I have received with much pleasure your esteemed favour of the 13th.... It is to me new proof that I have friends all over the world. I approve the sympathy shown me by offering a kind of remuneration for my tales. However, nearly all my tales and stories have been translated into English already; and it only happens now and then that I am disposed to write new ones. In such case I should be most happy to send you some new tales; and the last three tales, which have not been published in English, will be sent." As for the copy of *The Riverside* forwarded by Scudder, Andersen noted, "On a cursory perusal of *The Riverside Magazine* I must confess that it is my impression that the greater part of it is written for very young people, and though I know that my tales are read by young and old, and that the former enjoy what I would call the exterior, the latter the inner part, I think that my stories are not entirely in their right place in the said Magazine." After telling Scudder that he would reserve to himself the right to publish in Danish any new stories he might send, while making whatever effort he could to prevent any competing English translation, he continued, "But a matter that is of much greater interest to me, and to which you open a prospect, is to get a collection of my stories and tales published in America as a Complete Edition with my authorization. I have 136 tales and stories, which of course would make a large volume.... My biography – a true story of my life – has been, as I suppose you know, published in London and afterwards in Boston, but this is only a translation of a short biography accompanying the German edition of my complete works. In a later period ... I published a much more detailed biography in Danish, of which there are several editions. This I might be inclined also to publish in America, and in order to give it the interest of novelty – I might add to the American edition the biography of the last 13 years of my life, and the work might close with an account of the festival prepared for me last year in my native town – Odense – where I was nominated as Citizen of Honour of the town. I suppose that ... [Hurd and Houghton] can get the works translated in America." A postscript provided the only clue that Scudder would ever receive as to why Andersen had never before responded to the young editor's packets and letters: "Not being able to address you in English, the above letter has been translated by a friend."

Scudder was delighted but waited almost a month to respond in hopes that the three promised stories would arrive. They hadn't when he finally wrote, in large part to allay Andersen's qualms about *The Riverside Magazine*: "I cannot help thinking that a more full examination of *The Riverside* will show you that your tales would not be out of place ... it is our effort to adapt the magazine to the wants of children in a new country, where European civilization is found, modified by the circumstances of nature and government. But there is always a place in such a magazine for your stories, because there is always room, in the varied little public which we regard, for your books and especially for anything new." Still unable to resist injecting his own burgeoning career into whatever matter was at hand, Scudder added, "Indeed, I thought there could scarcely be higher praise given to one story [it just happened to be his own] than that pronounced by one of the most eminent of our library journals, when it said, '"Good and Bad Apples" in the March number might almost be attributed to Hans Christian Andersen.'"

Scudder spelled out more clearly the arrangement he was proposing regarding Andersen's new stories for *The Riverside*: "It seems desirable in sending us occasional new tales for the magazine, and for publication in book form, that these should be sent in advance of their publication in Denmark or Germany, say three months in advance, to enable us to bring them out simultaneously ... otherwise their peculiar value to us would be destroyed."

Scudder then added that Hurd and Houghton would pay Andersen five per cent of the retail price of every copy sold in the authorized edition, an arrangement to remain in effect for five years. Scudder added that "Messrs. Hurd and Houghton propose to manufacture and keep always on hand, in the best style of art, a complete and authentic edition of your works ... to advertise and circulate them widely and to use every means in their power to make this edition the prevailing one in the United States." Scudder informed Andersen further that the publishers expected to issue the edition in two volumes of approximately six hundred pages each: one of the author's general works, including his biography; the other of his stories for children.

The first three Andersen tales for *The Riverside* –"The Greenies," "Peiter, Peter and Peer" and "The Court Cards" – arrived shortly afterward. More conversational than narrative in tone, they were decidedly minor offerings. Scudder published the first two in the November 1868 issue of *The Riverside*, extending "A hearty welcome to that friend of all children – Hans Christian Andersen ... we fancy that if every youngster were to bring his tattered Andersen's Stories and take his place in line, that an electric telegraph could be formed by joining hands that would stretch across the continent. When it was announced that the great Dane was to write for us, all the newspapers in the country took up the word, and rejoiced at the prospect." Andersen's new association with the American publication had been proclaimed in *The*

Riverside. Scudder noted with pride: "First of all, Hans Christian Andersen, the most eminent living writer for the young, has consented to be a regular contributor to *The Riverside*: Hereafter, all his new stories will be introduced to the American public through *The Riverside*, in advance of their publication in Denmark, Germany and England." This information comprised a considerable coup for the young editor.

From this time on the two-way correspondence was firmly launched. On Scudder's part it consisted of constant encouragement of his distant star, "I anticipate with pleasure the receipt of other stories"; "Let me beg of you finally that you will favor me very soon with new stories – the charming ones already received make me hunger for more." To Andersen it meant flattering attention from a new source at a time when his creative energies were flagging, as well as steady, if modest sums, "the first I ever received from America."

When Andersen expressed gratitude to Scudder for his sympathetic attention to his stories for the magazine, Scudder responded eagerly, "I have them put into an exact English version and then go over them myself with great care, endeavoring to give those touches and quaint turns of expression which a long study of your writings has made me acquainted with. I find a great difference in the translations which have been made of your stories; without reading Danish I have frequently said: this is not Andersen; it is fine sounding when he is simple and direct. In the forthcoming Edition of your stories I hope to do something toward restoring in the translation those happy forms of expression which I feel sure are in the original."

In this same letter Scudder also informed Andersen of a practical publishing decision: the authorized American edition of his work would appear in eight volumes instead of two, thus making it easier for readers to hold each book. A more likely explanation was that Scudder had had little idea of the extent or breadth of Andersen's writings when he first made the proposal for an American edition of his works. The Dane had written five adult novels, a philosophical treatise, several travel books, plays and poetry, in addition to his tales for children and their elders.

Early in their correspondence Scudder reported a rumor he had heard that Andersen would be coming to America during 1869 and wrote enthusiastically, "I must personally beg that I may entertain you in my own house as soon as you arrive. Do me the honour, dear Sir, and be assured that our little household of my mother; my sister and myself will do all that we can to make your stay agreeable." The older man responded that the ocean crossing loomed as too long and too tiring, failing to take note of Scudder's generous personal offer of hospitality. In a later letter Andersen absent-mindedly sent greetings to the bachelor Scudder's wife, no doubt vaguely recalling some mention of a female relation by his American correspondent. It is possible, of course, that Andersen had been ill-served by his translator of Scudder's letters, but other evidence throughout their correspondence indicates that the famous author paid little heed to anything his young editor wrote that was not of immediate concern to his reputation or his pocketbook.

An inveterate worrier, Andersen fretted over the legality of authorizing a new edition of his work in English when everything was already available in one translation or another. Scudder was quick to reassure him: "The matter of republishing English books in this country is a simple one. There is no law whatever existing between the two countries which forbids the republishing in America of English books, or in England of American books.... Any American publisher, moreover, could have all your works published in England, reprint them in this city and be under no legal obligation to pay you." This baldly honest explanation was no doubt intended, in part, to make Andersen aware of how handsomely the firm of Hurd and Houghton was treating him. Soon afterward, Andersen was disturbed by exactly what an "authorized version" might mean in so far as he, the author, was concerned. Scudder responded soothingly: "Publishing the series in connection with you, we have recourse to you in any question which may arise.... We desire simply to convey the impression that in the issue of his new

American edition, the author has a voice, and a directive oversight."

Often their letters crossed in the mails. But almost always, Andersen was relating some new honor that had come his way, and Scudder was striving to convey to the oblivious Dane his bona-fide credentials as the illustrious man's editor – and colleague in writing tales for young children. In August of 1869, after reporting to Andersen that he himself was revising "with great care" the translation of Andersen's latest tale for *The Riverside*, Scudder wrote: "Let me thank you warmly for the *Illustrated News*, which I received a few days since, containing complete the articles on your genius. I shall read them as well as my knowledge of Danish will permit, and with real pleasure, for I myself once had the honor of reviewing your works in *The National Quarterly Review* of New York, and saw afterward some comments upon it in *Dagbladet* of Copenhagen." Scudder was never to receive satisfaction on these points.

In September the Danish storyteller announced that he was sending "immediately three different daily papers, from which you may learn in detail the whole course of the beautiful festivities." Andersen was referring to the ceremonies marking the fiftieth anniversary "since I, as a poor boy and entirely unknown, came here to Copenhagen." The king of Denmark had honored him with the Commander's Cross of the Order of Daneborg. The proud author continued with that enthusiasm for his own successes, "All manner of people from all classes of society have shown their kind feelings toward me and give me all this joy. Yes, I am indeed a child of fortune, and my life the most beautiful adventure that God has graciously given.... All of this is indeed quite too much kindness to show to one person, though it does not make one vain, but rather tender, reflective and humble" – and oblivious to other writers, particularly a young and geographically distant one.

By the end of 1869 Andersen had provided nine tales to Scudder's *The Riverside*. Two of them, "The Dryad" and "What Happened to the Thistle?," were more substantial than the others and altogether worthy later tales. Two adult novels by Andersen, *The Improvisatore* and *The Two Baronesses*, had been followed by a volume of *Wonder Stories* for children containing eighty–four stories and one hundred seventeen illustrations. On March 11, 1870, Scudder wrote to announce that a package containing ten copies of each book was being sent to Andersen. Scudder added: "I have also begged the privilege for myself of adding to the parcel a little book, *Stories from My Attic*, which is from my pen, and was brought out at Christmas. May my little book tell you of the continued pleasure which your stories have given me." The authorized edition, meanwhile, had by now swelled to ten proposed volumes with Scudder's decision to divide Andersen's children's tales into two volumes and to publish the autobiography, *My Life's Adventure*, as a separate volume.

Enclosing a new story, "The Candles," at the end of March 1870, Andersen acknowledged noncommittally: "*Stories from My Attic*, I take it, is a book by yourself, and I am therefore looking forward with special pleasure to reading it very soon." He then returned to more interesting matters: "Saturday April 2nd is my birthday. I shall then have completed my 65th year. This is an advanced age, according to the common calculation, but I still have the full spirit of youth, feel most at home with the younger people. But time brings nearer the last journey. I am now in the front rank of those our Lord may summon, but when? And right now I have so great a love of life. May God's will be done!"

Early in the new year, Scudder had begun to study Danish, intending himself to translate the new expanded portion of Andersen's autobiography, as well as make the selections for a proposed volume of Andersen's poetry and drama. In April he reported to his aging protégé: "Spring Song" which came in your first letter I have myself translated for the June *Riverside*, and the pretty little story "The Candles" I have also translated for the July *Riverside*.... I must tell you how much I enjoy your continuation of *Mit Livs Eventyr* [My Life's Adventure], which I am daily engaged in translating while the earlier portion is rapidly going through the hands of another." Meanwhile, three more volumes of the collected works were ready for publication: one travel book and two more novels.

Anticipating that Andersen would, at last, actually read one of his own books, Scudder wrote expectantly: "When you read my *Stories from My Attic*, you will see me in a little vignette on the title page, for the attic was a real one.... Some of the little stories, such as "Good and Bad Apples" and "Tim and Tom," I have no doubt I should never have written had not your writings taught me many things." Scudder's letters from this point on, usually contained a sprinkling of phrases in Danish, to indicate to his mentor the progress in his language lessons.

In May of 1870 Andersen forwarded two more tales, "Great Grandfather" and "The Most Incredible," the latter of which he wrote Scudder "may perhaps be considered one of my best." After asking when *The Story of My Life* would be published in its complete form, he noted in passing, "Thank you once more for the sweet and lively *Stories from My Attic*. Only this brief letter today, which accompanies the fairy tale."

A month later Andersen was greatly concerned to know the exact publication date of his autobiography. On the twenty-seventh of July Scudder wrote: "Be assured good Mr. Andersen that the work goes on with the edition of your writings. It is necessarily slow, but we hope to publish *The Story of My Life* at least by October 1, if not September 15." Once again, there rose that cry for recognition: "I am myself translating the portion in manuscript, not liking to trust it in other hands." The letter had this postscript: "My teacher in Danish was very anxious to translate some of my little stories into Danish and I venture to send you a roll of them. Give yourself no trouble about them, but if any of your editorial friends care to print the stories in their journals, they are quite at liberty to do so."

Disheartened by the outbreak of the Franco-Prussian War, which had Danish reverberations, Andersen did not write again until early November, but with long-awaited news. "Thank you for the little manuscript you sent me of *Stories from My Attic*. I saw in these something kindred to my own poetic nature, and cannot but be pleased that you like my writings. I could not wish for a better translator than a man who is spiritually akin to me. I do not know whether you would like to have one or all these stories printed in one or another Danish magazine. But in such case I must say that our position is such that we can hardly pay an honorarium." The comments were not exactly the sort of praise to turn a young author's head! Nor could the caveat that followed have helped matters much: "Also you would have to allow me in such case to make certain corrections in the language. Some of the expressions are not entirely happy, and I am almost inclined to suspect that the translation has been made by a Dane who has long been absent from his homeland."

In late November of 1870 Scudder enthusiastically acknowledged receipt of ninety-six pages of the lengthy new tale, *Lucky Peer*. "I have translated about sixty pages.... I am delighted with the story. It really seems to me one of the brightest, most human and most attractive stories which I have read from your pen.... I found the greatest pleasure in translating it, especially after the very kind manner in which you were pleased to speak of my work." Before further elaborating on his reaction to this long-sought recognition, Scudder matter-of-factly reported some startling news: "The December number of *The Riverside*, which goes out to you today, contains the announcement that the magazine is to be discontinued after this year. The Publishers have decided that it will not be expedient to go on with it, and I have ventured to make provision for the publication of such of your stories as you may be pleased to send me, to be published first in magazine form. Messrs. Scribner & Co. have begun the issue of a magazine called *Scribner's Monthly*, with which *The Riverside* is incorporated.... They were very desirous to secure your contributions, and I ventured to assure them that such single stories as you might be disposed to send me I would translate for them, and transmit to you, as before, payment for the same. I hope that in this I have not over-stepped the limits of our good understanding." He added that *Scribner's Monthly* would be printing *Lucky Peer* in three monthly installments and that Hurd & Houghton would add the book to their Andersen edition in March. Though *The Story of My Life* was ready to print, Scudder reported difficulties in procuring paper, which would delay its publication until the spring of 1881. The editor then closed this important letter: "Thanks for the kind manner in which you speak of my writings. I do not expect any honorarium at all, but if one paper or another should take them up, I should be highly honored. If it were done, could not a copy of the paper be sent to me?" As with so much else in their correspondence that did not directly concern Andersen, the matter was never referred to again by the Danish storyteller.

A few days later Scudder sent off his first note completely in Danish, informing Andersen that he would translate the remainder of *Lucky Peer* himself. "But I believe that I shall write better English than the Danish I am writing now!"

On December twentieth Andersen wrote triumphantly, "5,500 copies of the Danish edition of *Lucky Peer* already sold! a remarkable edition for our little country.... I am sorry to see *The Riverside Magazine* cease publication. I have become so accustomed by now to look upon it as an old friend who took my little children in affectionate embrace.... I know that you, dear friend, are acting in the best interests of myself and my authorship. For this I cannot thank you enough." He closed the note, "Thank you for your friendship in the past. Thank you for your sympathy."

Soon afterward, he received and responded to Scudder's Danish note: "It gave me pleasure to receive from you a letter written in Danish, and well-written besides.... It was moreover an act of attention, of friendship, for which I thank you." Having received the January issue of *Scribner's Monthly*, Andersen acknowledged, "The translation [of *Lucky Peer*] seems to be particularly happy and intelligent. Most sincere and hearty thanks for your cordial reception of me and my writings." His closing was the most effusive to date: "From your greatly devoted friend."

On April 10, 1871, Scudder could, at last, write: "*The Story of My Life* was published day before yesterday. I should have liked to bring it out on your birthday but that could not be. I think there will be a good deal of interest felt in the book and I hope to send you from time to time reviews in our best journals." Andersen replied, "Yesterday evening all the books came by boat, and I leafed through them away into the night. *The Story of My Life*, seems to me, has been rendered especially well, for which I thank you with all my heart." He then drew Scudder's attention to a few errors in the text, remarking that they could be corrected in a later printing.

By September Scudder had lost interest in the task of translating Andersen's poetry. Sales of the new, authorized American edition were modest, and he wrote the author: "It is so exceedingly difficult to get any good translation of poetry that we feel your reputation would not be advanced." Also, since the novella *Lucky Peer* comprised the tenth volume in the Andersen series, Scudder announced rather abruptly, "It is a great pleasure to me to think that this enterprise has been fortunately brought to a close. Yet it would still be more pleasant to receive new and fresh volumes from your pen."

Andersen was doubtless taken aback and suggested by return mail that his philosophical novel, *To Be or Not to Be*, written years earlier, be added to the edition: "In a land where Emerson's writings are read and printed in new editions, the inner conflict which I have tried to present could hardly give offence." Then, in what was doubtless pique at being given such short shrift, Anderson added: "*The Story of My Life*, that is the continuation which is available to Americans but not to my Danish readers, is now being read here ... and the translation has been criticized in our foremost papers."

On October 28, Scudder, who could not yet have received Andersen's letter, renewed an invitation: "So many people would be made happy by a visit from Andersen to America that we most earnestly hope you may be induced to come over NOW and spend at least six or eight months. Your publishers will most gladly charge themselves with the expenses of your passage to and from America and will entertain you in their homes in Cambridge and New York just as long as you will do them the honor to visit them; nor can we doubt that wherever you travelled in America you would find doors fly open at your approach." Certainly such a visit would boost sales of the slow-moving American edition. In his diary Andersen noted the receipt of Scudder's proposal adding: "I should like to accept but have a premonition of the torments of the sea voyage and fear not having the stamina to go through all this. I should prefer to die in Denmark."

To Scudder he replied: "I have a great desire to visit America and my friends there, but have a dread of the great ocean on which my very dear friend, Miss Wulff, lost her life on a burning ship." That he was tempted, however, was clear. Andersen confided, "I have an infinite desire and longing to see the great country to the West, and the many there who are so friendly and good to me."

Three more Andersen tales were published in *Scribner's Monthly* by the end of 1873 –"The Great Sea Serpent," "The Gardener and His Master" and "The Professor and the Flea" – but they had already seen publication in Denmark. Ironically, none of the last four stories, a final blooming of creative energy, that Andersen sent to Scudder between mid-August and the end of September 1872, ever appeared in print during Andersen's lifetime. Yet "The Story Old Johanna Told," "The Front Door Key," "The Cripple" and "Auntie Toothache" were easily among the best of Andersen's late work. In part, Scudder was occupied with other editorial duties. More to the point, perhaps, Houghton had bought *The Atlantic Monthly* in 1873, a competitor to *Scribner's Monthly*, and Scudder's loyalties remained ever firm to this one publisher.

There was yet another reason. Scudder wrote Andersen on October 11, 1872: "Pray pardon my delay in writing. You will not be surprised that my mind has been pretty well occupied when I tell you what your friendly words make me think will interest you, that I have lately become betrothed. This gives me great happiness – but it also absorbs my time largely! But so it has been since the beginning of the world and so may it ever be." In the same letter, Scudder acknowledged receipt of Andersen's tale "The Cripple." Describing his own task as its translator, Scudder wrote: "I aim to say over again what you say, as I think you would have said it, had you been English or American." There could hardly be a simpler or a better definition of the art of translation.

Andersen made no reference to Scudder's news in his next letter three months later, but he had been ill. Throughout 1873 their correspondence consisted of Scudder's apologies for the small sums in royalties being forwarded. "People here have somehow the notion that you are only a writer for children and so miss the enjoyment they might have from your larger works." On another occasion, enclosing payment for the last *Scribner's Monthly* Andersen tales, Scudder said: "I ought to explain ... that the sum paid for these stories is smaller than it would have been by $17, as we were obliged to pay for translation. I have myself been unable to do but little and we have called upon others." In part the explanation was probably another Scudder cry for recognition: take note of how much free and caring service I have provided to you over the years! Andersen responded: "Make no apologies for the sum being small; I am glad to be read and loved, although I must often smile at the erroneous ideas that most of my countrymen ... entertain as to the great sums I receive from the mighty New World." To Andersen's frequent question as to when the revised printing of his autobiography might be forthcoming, Scudder provided polite evasions. The truth was, the book was selling poorly.

Early in 1874 Scudder wrote Andersen: "Let me tell you a little piece of news which concerns me very nearly, and I hope will not be without interest to my illustrious friend.... In October last, just before that beautiful autumn month died away, I married, and now my wife and I are living here in Cambridge, a happy life in a little set of rooms with our books and pictures about us."

In March Andersen responded dejectedly with news of a continuing illness; yet he took note of Scudder's marriage. "You are now in your best years of vigor and as I see from your letter ... a married man. You have got yourself a home, a loving wife, and you are happy! God bless you and her! At one time I too dreamt of such a happiness, but it was not to be granted to me. Happiness came to me in another form, came as my muse that gave me a wealth of adventure and songs. I have no right to complain." In July of 1874 Andersen wrote more hopefully that he was, at last, feeling well. "For more than a year and a half no composition of mine has found its way to paper.... It may even be granted to me to put still more fairy tales and stories on paper. If this takes place, I shall certainly send these, my first new compositions, to you."

More stories never came. On February 12, 1875, Scudder wrote: "Have you written anything of late? I have seen no new announcement. Yet I can hardly believe that you would remain so long without a word for your friends." Regarding his own news, Scudder reported: "For myself, I have lately given up my business interest in order to devote myself exclusively to literature.... On January 2nd my wife was delivered safely of two little girls." Happily Scudder was spared any knowledge of Andersen's final ingratitude. Soon after the Dane's seventy-fifth birthday, someone in Boston wrote inquiring of him which of the various English and American translations of his work was most successful. When the letter was read to him, Andersen is reported to have answered irritably "How am I to know?" Four months later, on August 4, 1875, Hans Christian Andersen died.

Scudder wrote to Edvard Collin, Andersen's lifelong friend and the executor of his estate: "I scarcely know to whom I may turn in Denmark when I express my personal grief at the death of Andersen." Scudder then outlined their association, starting with the critical piece he had written for *The National Quarterly Review*. He characterizes as "my favorite project, the reproduction here of his writings in a uniform series.... One thing more. He wrote me once that he intended to send me a little bust in biscuit of himself." Actually, Andersen had remarked in September 1872: "If you would like to have my bust in bisque, it may be ordered for you," which suggests that Scudder might have been billed for same. Scudder continued: "I have perhaps no right to trouble you ... yet if such a memorial could be sent me, I should prize it highly and would gladly meet any expense incurred. Most of all, however, if the request be not too bold, I would gladly have some slight souvenir from Andersen's own writing table.... I owe so much to this good and great man that I earnestly desire some personal object which I can show to my children when they are grown, as coming from Andersen to their father."

Eight months later, Collin sent Scudder Andersen's letter-clip and, along with it, an offer to sell Andersen's correspondence to the American publisher. Scudder turned the latter down explaining that the authorized American edition had to date lost a good deal of money, and Hurd & Houghton could not afford to purchase the correspondence.

Thus, Scudder's good will, energy and epistolary zeal resulted in Andersen's providing ten late tales for first publication in *The Riverside Magazine* during 1869 and 1870. More lasting, perhaps, was the editor's effort to oversee the American "author's edition" of Andersen's collected writings, published in 1870 and 1871. Scudder was also responsible for forwarding to the Danish storyteller the largest sum of money he had ever received from a foreign country.

So far as any rewarding human relationship was concerned, Andersen's self-centeredness imposed severe limitations. As the Danish critic Georg Brandes put it, after reading Andersen's published letters, his was "a mind completely and entirely filled by himself and without a single spiritual interest." If there is any lesson to be learned from the Scudder-Andersen correspondence, it is perhaps this: more often than not, genius is generous with little but its talent. But that, of course, is a great deal.

EIGHT

Sendak at Fifty

MAURICE SENDAK and Mickey Mouse celebrated their 50th birthdays within a few months of each other in 1978. Probably no two figures have had a greater influence on American children during that time span than Maurice Sendak and Mickey Mouse's creator, Walt Disney. Sendak's first color drawing, at the age of 6, signed "Murray Sendak," was of Mickey Mouse, and in his high-school magazine in 1945, the earnest young artist wrote admiringly, "Walt Disney is the greatest exponent of a new art form which will leave its imprint on civilization."

Surprisingly youthful for his five decades, Sendak still has the trim salt-and-pepper beard he grew during the summer of 1971, when he began the drawings for his commanding two volumes of Grimm Household Tales, *The Juniper Tree*. Right now, the artist is at home in Ridgefield, Connecticut, putting the finishing touches on what he considers the final part of the major picture-book trilogy of his lifetime: *Where the Wild Things Are* (1963), *In the Night Kitchen* (1970) and now, *Outside Over There* (1981). Sendak has spent more than three years on this latest project. He views the books as a trilogy because "they are all variations on a particular theme." In 1956, when he published *Kenny's Window*, the first book for which he did both text and pictures, Sendak revealed that henceforth his theme would be "children who are emotionally held back by life and who manage somehow to master their troubles or fears."

85

Sendak's Ridgefield studio looks out on leafy greenery from three sides. There is no exit to the seductive countryside from this room. Among the studio's contents are a shelf full of early Mickey Mouse dolls. (Sendak owns one of the better collections of Mickey Mousiana in the United States): two shelves of 1930s Big Little Books; a number of stuffed Wild Things made for him by various admirers over the years and a 1768 print of Mozart at the piano. To one side of the artist's drawing table hangs a snapshot of his parents as newlyweds and an Old World photograph of his maternal grandparents. (Sendak was born in Brooklyn in 1928, the youngest of three children of Philip and Sadie Sendak, who had arrived in America from different Jewish *shtetls* outside Warsaw just before World War I.) These days Sendak works to the music of Mozart exclusively. As he explains it: "For *Outside Over There*, I want only the sound of Mozart. And I make my own make-believe connections. This is Grimm country; this is the eighteenth century; Mozart died in 1796; it's proper it should be Mozart. Since I'm doing the show, I can run it anyway I like."

Almost since his start as a professional illustrator in 1951, Sendak has warmed up for serious illustration by free-association sketching to classical music. "I will start at the beginning of a page, put on any music – perhaps a Beethoven quartet – and just start drawing. It's a muscular exercise of the imagination. Whatever comes, you mustn't think."

Wild Things, still the most popular Sendak work, explored a child's blatant rage at his mother for sending him to bed without supper. *Night Kitchen*, with its mesmerizing three bakers who all look exactly like Oliver Hardy, and its haunting backdrop of kitchen utensils and pantry trappings magically transformed into the skyline of Manhattan, is the artist's tribute to his own 1930s childhood. *Outside Over There* (1973), the eleventh book Sendak has both written and illustrated – and the darkest of the picture-book trio – explores the murkier impulses of sibling rivalry. It concerns goblins who steal a baby and a brave nine-year-old heroine who manages to foil their plans.

The genesis of *Outside Over There* sheds light on the way in which Sendak has always worked, each book developing organically out of one or more that preceded it. The frontispiece to Volume I of the artist's *The Juniper Tree* was a drawing of a seated baby with a compelling, other-worldly presence, for a little-known Grimm tale called "The Goblins." Its air of mystery so captured the artist's imagination that it becomes the jumping-off place for his new tale about "a little girl with a raincoat who gets caught in a storm," an image he has retained from an otherwise-unremembered book he read as a child. "It is now 40 years," Sendak marvels, "that I've been trying to push that child into a book." Ida, the heroine of *Outside Over There*, is pluckier than any other Sendak hero or heroine.

Sendak's own career is not lacking in elements of pluck. To view it from its beginnings is to be moved by the artist's mastery of any style suited to the work at hand. He has always rated interpretive illustration – pictures that expand the text – above mere graphic decoration. "My school," he says frankly, "has been imitating other artists' work."

"I have stolen rampageously," Sendak confesses, "from Monet, Manet and Winslow Homer in *Mr. Rabbit and the Lovely Present*, for example; and from Randolph Caldecott in *Hector Protector*, and a number of other works."

His confession notwithstanding, few would argue the point that Sendak has elevated the American children's picture book to a high art form. The depth of his psychological insight combined with the clarity and beauty of his personal pictorial vision have never been equaled this side of the Atlantic. He can be compared only to such a master of the form as the Victorian English artist Randolph Caldecott.

"The several themes that repeat themselves through my work," Sendak points out, "I developed when I was very young." And certainly if one examines the small dummy of *Where the Wild Horses Are*, dated November 15, 1955, one clearly sees in it the inspiration for *Where the Wild Things Are*, some eight years afterward. The work, in fact, is a lexicon of by now familiar Sendakian concerns. A small hero is divested of his clothes (like Mickey, hero of *In the Night Kitchen*); he sails off to an island (like the heroes of both *As I Went Over the Water* and *Where the Wild Things Are*); and finally, at the adventure's end, discovers a satisfying reward (like Max in *Wild Things*).

When Sendak first began serious work on the final dummy of *Outside Over There*, he had professional photographs taken of two little girls approximately the ages of Ida and her baby sister. He posed the children as he planned to use them in the book. "It's really the only way to get a proper feel for the heft of a 14-month-old baby as she is picked up by a 9-year-old child," he explains.

Not many of Sendak's admirers are aware of how seriously he takes the texts of his own tales. *Outside Over There*, for example, a story of only 185 words, took almost a year and half to write. "I have a kind of hostility toward books which are not well-written," the author-artist says. "Because the picture book is such a beautiful, poetic form, I feel it should be treated with the utmost respect." Though Sendak invariably draws to music, he writes in a perfectly silent room, red ear plugs stuffed into his ears. "Writing is the most private business," he says, "and much more difficult than illustrating.

"When I begin writing a story," Sendak explains, "I never permit myself to envision any pictures, because then you just seduce yourself. When I came to *Night Kitchen*, for instance, I was stuck with having to draw an airplane, which I do very badly. But I wanted an airplane, and so it had to become a dough airplane, because a lousy airplane that looks like a dough airplane you can get away with."

In 1967, Sendak's longest prose work to date, *Higglety Pigglety Pop! Or, There Must Be More to Life*, was published. It is a story based on the life history of his Sealyham terrier, Jennie, who appeared regularly in his work between 1954 and 1967. Of the book, the artist says, "I wrote it when Jennie was getting old and I was afraid she was going to die." Sendak wanted Jennie's last book appearance to be a no-holds-barred Jennie Spectacular, something that would immortalize her in the very

World Mother Goose Theatre in which her master had labored so long. Her *tour de force* appearance as the heroine of an old American nonsense rhyme at the tale's close does just that. Curiously, the rhyme's author, one Samuel Taylor Goodrich, was born in the very town in which Sendak now makes his home. It's also more than likely that Jennie's master used her to express many of his own feelings about the immortality of art and its triumph over the evanescence of life.

Of course, not all of Sendak's work is serious. Most controversial of his recent books was a light-hearted dog training manual done in jaunty cartoon style, *Some Swell Pup* (1976). Countless librarians, parents and teachers objected to its repeated scenes of a puppy urinating and defecating. But Sendak was delighted that most child readers were clever enough to understand the book's point. It was as much a commentary on how parents bring up children as on how children should handle a new puppy.

"Most adults," Sendak notes with regret, "are out to protect children from what they think is dangerous." Many grown-up readers, for example, were shocked and angered by Sendak's display of frontal nudity in his hero Mickey of *In the Night Kitchen*. It both puzzles and amuses the artist that no one objected to his earlier display of frontal nudity in a girl child, on the frontispiece of *The Light Princess*. "The artist," Sendak explains, "is going to put elements into his work that come from his deepest self.... That is his particular gift. The artist understands that children know a lot more than people give them credit for. Children are willing to deal with many dubious subjects that grownups think they shouldn't know about. But children are small courageous people who have to deal every day with a multitude of problems, just as we adults do. They are unprepared for most things and what they most yearn for is a bit of truth somewhere."

Though the bulk of Sendak's more than eighty illustrated books have been remarkably successful collaborations with other authors – Ruth Krauss on *A Hole Is to Dig* (1953) and many other works; Else Holmelund Minarik on the *Little Bear* series; Randall Jarrell on two tales and a long poem – the artist has in recent years more and more limited himself to books of his own choosing. These have ranged broadly from such English Victorian classics as George MacDonald's *The Light Princess* (1969) to such little-known American delights as Frank Stockton's *The Griffin and the Minor Canon* and *The Bee-Man of Orn*. One of Sendak's last collaborations – the drawings for Isaac Bashevis Singer's *Zlateh the Goat*, in 1967 – inspired the artist to provide remarkably evocative drawings for a group of Yiddish tales. For the first time, Sendak used his own family photographs from the Old Country, making a memorable pastiche of super-realistic and virtuoso imaginative elements. It was a technique the artist would further refine in his Grimm drawings, which combined elements from paintings by Dürer and other German artists, period costumes taken from a series of postcards and realistic German scenery.

Sendak looks on *The Juniper Tree* as a "kind of watershed book. It gave me a lot of new confidence about putting my own experience into books. I felt I could now put together elements from my fantasy life and objective illustration – and bizarre as they all are, make them work. I'm old enough and experienced enough to do it now. It was only after *The Juniper Tree* that I felt I could tackle Randall Jarrell's *Fly by Night* without him, and put my own experience into it. I had let it lie for ten years after his death because frankly I just didn't know what to do with it."

Sendak firmly believes that "illustrations have as much to say as the text. The trick is to say the same thing but in a different way. Its no good being an illustrator who is saying a lot that is on his or her mind if it has nothing to do with the text. But to say the same thing that the story is saying in your own personal way, contributes dimension to the story. The artist must override the story, but he must also override his own ego for the sake of the story."

Winner of the Caldecott Medal in 1964 for *Where the Wild Things Are*, and a recipient in 1970 of the international Hans Christian Andersen Award for the body of his illustration, Sendak feels deepest affinity for the picture book. "The picture book is where I put down those fantasies that have been with me all my life and where I give them a form that means something. It's where I fight all my battles and where, hopefully, I win my wars."

If there's one thing that infuriates him about his chosen battleground, it's having his books looked upon as mere nursery trifles. "When you've worked a year and more on a book, when you've put your life into it, you expect the point of view of the professionals – editors, teachers, librarians – to be somewhat larger. You certainly expect your book to be read by people of all ages."

As he looks back on his career to date, Sendak is by no means pleased with all his work. He feels that his drawings for Tolstoy's *Nikolenka's Childhood*, in 1963, were totally misguided: "You can't illustrate Tolstoy. You're competing with the greatest illustrator in the world. Pictures bring him down and just limp along." He also dislikes the illustrations he did for Hans Christian Andersen's *Seven Tales*, in 1959. He feels he tried too self-consciously to use his limited experience of Europe in the art.

But, all things considered, Sendak at fifty is more relaxed than ever before. There is little he is unwilling to try. He has recently completed the libretto to a Broadway musical version of his animated cartoon *Really Rosie*. He's also beginning work on the sets for an English-language production of Mozart's *The Magic Flute* to be performed in Houston in 1980, and on yet another libretto for an operatic version of *Where the Wild Things Are*, to be staged in Brussels and sung in Flemish and French. Sendak will do both sets and costumes. His next book project will be illustrations for a fairy tale his father told him just before he died. As for any plans to try another animated cartoon after his television special *Really Rosie*, Sendak says: "There isn't any virile children's programming at all. It's paradoxical that I look back now on what I used to condemn in Disney as vulgarity and grossness. In retrospect, he looks like a Michelangelo of animation, because there was a vigor and honesty and intensity in Disney movies that no longer exist in children's animation. It's now so tasteful, so artful, so beautiful – and so boring. Since children aren't tasteful, aren't artful, and like real things, what's happening on TV is disheartening."

Lore Segal and Maurice Sendak,
The Juniper Tree & Other Tales from Grimm
illustration by Maurice Sendak

NINE

Sendak's Graphic Grand Operas

*I no longer want simply to illustrate – or, for that
matter, simply to write. I am now in search of a
form more purely and essentially my own.*
Maurice Sendak, 1970

I T COULD BE ARGUED that Maurice Sendak's career as a children's book illustrator ended in 1970 with the publication of *In the Night Kitchen*. The three major works that followed – *Outside Over There* (1981), *Dear Mili* (1988) and *We Are All in the Dumps with Jack and Guy* (1993) – were the artist's responses to his search for "a form more purely and essentially my own."

Like William Blake's *Songs of Innocence*, they are visionary works with no pretense of a conventional narrative or any aim to reach an audience of a particular age. For want of a better description, they are graphic grand operas. Puzzling and filled with mysteriously compelling images, they linger in the memory.

Few parents, however, would choose them for bedtime reading, and even longtime Sendak afficionados were confounded by their high seriousness and intensity. Critics and reviewers were respectful but uncertain of what audience was being addressed. My own reviews published at the time of each book's publication strike me as examples of that perplexity and puzzlement.

Outside Over There

In the world of children's books, Maurice Sendak's position is unique. One would have to go back to eighteenth- and nineteenth-century England, fusing the talents of the visionary poet and artist William Blake with those of the fantasy writer George MacDonald, to approximate the inventiveness of Sendak's pictorial vocabulary and the psychological density of his vision of childhood. This vision has never been the rosy, Wordsworthian "Heaven lies about us in our infancy"; for Sendak, rather, "it is a constant miracle that children get through childhood from one day to the next, that they manage to grow up."

His earliest success as an illustrator, the tender portrayal of Brooklyn children at play for Ruth Krauss's *A Hole is to Dig* (1952), featured those quintessentially Sendakian prototypes: pint-sized protagonists who seem knowing beyond their years, somehow bearing a disproportionate share of the world's burdens on their small shoulders. Some eighty books and thirty years later, Ida, the nine-year-old, eighteenth-century heroine of *Outside Over There*, continues the type. Ida is, without doubt, Sendak's most heavily put-upon child to date. Her mother sits out the action of the tale in a near-catatonic stupor, mourning the absence of Ida's father who is "away at sea," and the small heroine is left with full responsibility for a robust armful of a baby sister, not much more than a year old. In the course of trying to lull this fractious sibling to sleep by playing on her "wonder horn" – a magical instrument that serves as metaphor for Ida's imaginative powers and resourcefulness – she fails to notice the hooded goblins who climb into the nursery and kidnap the wide-eyed (and clearly alarmed) infant. In the baby's place, the goblins leave an expressionless changeling "all made of ice."

When Ida turns to hug the changeling, she murmurs, "How I love you," a sentiment the reader-viewer instinctively senses is false – or at least misdirected. Ida's love is for her absent father. Her subsequent fury, when she discovers that the dripping, staring imposter is not her baby sister, is aimed more at the circumstances of life (over which she, like all children, has so little control).

Ida flies out the nursery window into "outside over there" in hot pursuit of the robber goblins. She starts off in the wrong direction but manages to right her course and interrupt a goblin wedding – only to discover that the villains are "just babies like her sister." Ida charms them with a song from her horn until they – like *Little Black Sambo's* wicked tigers – melt "into a dancing stream." The heroine then returns triumphantly home with her infant sister.

According to Sendak, *Outside Over There* (1981) is the final volume in his picture book trilogy, which includes *Where the Wild Things Are* (1963) and *In the Night Kitchen* (1971). The new book is likely to alarm more adults than its predecessors did. Its story is not nearly as accessible as the saga of small Max, who triumphs over a fierce – but, in the cosmic order of things, trivial and passing – rage against his mother in the first volume. Nor is it as cheerfully diverting as *In the Night Kitchen. Outside Over There* is an apocalyptic vision of the aloneness of childhood, as well as a paean to that mysterious fount of inner reserves that children – and all of us – draw upon in extremities of one sort or another. At least some parents, teachers, librarians and other grown–up buyers of children's literature are likely to ask, "What will children make of a book about, of all things, a baby's kidnapping?" The answer, I suspect, is "as much and possibly more than many adult viewers will allow themselves to." This mysteriously evocative picture book deals with nothing less than the inescapable solitude of the human condition.

Where is the curious locale of the title? On the face of it, "outside over there" is at some remove in eighteenth–century, Grimm–fairy–tale country. It should not touch us very closely. Yet, this graphic drama is compelling. Why? Certainly a good part of the book's power is due to Sendak's uncanny ability to capture the mystery of babyhood. Ida's baby sister is a commanding presence, at once embodying that rosy, warm physicality in the here–and–now that all babies possess, and an ethereal elusiveness as well – that clear picture infants often project of being tuned in to a celestial sphere no longer accessible to adults.

If *Outside Over There* is flawed, it is that its story lacks any climactic moment. The shadowy, faceless goblins are pursued, yet never confronted *per se*, because they turn out to be not some external threat, but babies just like the small selves we all once were. Confirming Pogo's waggish observation, "We have met the enemy and he is us," the goblins are, in fact, phantoms of Ida's designing. The things we fear have a terrifying aspect, yet when confronted, our worst imaginings often shrink to manageable proportions.

Like all fairy tales worthy of the name, *Outside Over There* is a nourishing vision of life. It celebrates the phoenix–like force in all of us that allows us – child and adult – to overcome occasional periods of despair to reach temporary plateaus of contentment.

At the book's end, Ida carries her baby sister victoriously through a springtime landscape. A Mozart–like figure makes music by the side of a rushing stream and a shepherd leads his flock of lambs up a hillside. Even so, it is no paradise unmarred. Close by Ida and her smiling sister is a tree with low, menacing branches reminiscent of those grasping limbs in Walt Disney's *Snow White*. The heroine still has a distracted mother and a missing father. But not only is her baby sister safe (and a potential friend, rather than a resented sibling), the real–life situation has altered for the better during Ida's absence. Her mother holds a letter from Papa that promises his eventual return. Meanwhile, "brave, bright little Ida" is charged by that beloved parent to "watch the baby and her Mama for her Papa, who loves her always." Which, the last page tells us, "is just what Ida did."

Sendak's original inspiration for this kidnap saga came to him while he was working on the illustrations for *The Juniper Tree*. Its shortest story concerns six goblins, little old men in Sendak's rendition, who spirit away a child, leaving in its place "a changeling with thick head and staring eyes."

It is perhaps not without point that in the '30s, when Sendak was only slightly younger than his heroine Ida, Bruno Richard Hauptmann was arrested, tried and put to death for the kidnapping and murder of the Lindbergh baby. This sensational horror story dominated the newspaper headlines and radio broadcasts from late 1934 until the spring of 1936, and Sendak acknowledges that the Lindbergh child was somewhere in the back of his mind when he was drawn to the Grimm tale.

In fact Sendak's mysterious goblin babies might well be associated with yet another sensational real–life story of his childhood, the birth of the Dionne quintuplets. A kind of contemporary fairy tale, theirs was also an abduction of sorts. Taken from their natural parents, they were brought up in a real–world fantasy, a curious nurseryland splendor sustained by a combination of unflagging public relations and media receptivity during the Depression.

Outside Over There is a work of Wagnerian breadth and magnitude. In place of music, Sendak's concise libretto is set to full–color pictures, the likes of which have never before adorned a work for children. If all is not happily–ever–after resolved, well, neither are life's unfathomable mysteries: Where do we come from? How do we emerge from plastic babyhood to become the finite, constricted beings we are? In what ways does each of us survive the psychic pain and trauma we inevitably suffer along the bumpy road to adulthood? In *Outside Over There*, Maurice Sendak gives us wondrous insights, if not answers.

DEAR MILI

IT IS SOMEHOW FITTING that Maurice Sendak's latest illustrations should be a suite of fifteen grandly conceived and tenderly executed paintings in watercolor and pen–and–ink for the recently discovered (and heretofore unpublished) Wilhelm Grimm tale, *Dear Mili*.

For each artist, the work was one he felt compelled to undertake. In the case of Grimm, the author's introductory letter of 1816 to the Dear Mili of the title strongly suggests that the tale is one tailor–made to provide solace for Mili's particular sad plight. From Grimm's pointed references to what happens to a flower tossed into a brook, or to a little bird that disappears from sight over a mountain (in each case, they meet – beyond the viewer's sight – with another flower and bird, and provide companionship for one another), it seems certain that Mili has suffered some grave loss: perhaps her mother has died.

Whatever the child's predicament, it touched Wilhelm sufficiently to cause him to do what neither he nor his brother Jacob had ever done before – improvise upon elements from three different tales in the already-published Grimm repertoire of 210, hoping thus to provide spiritual comfort to a specific child in distress.

Mili's story borrows most heavily from *St. Joseph in the Forest*, with important grace notes from *The Rose* and *Our Lady's Slipper*. All three tales fall within a special category designated as "Children's Legends." Christian in theme, they date from the Middle Ages (much later in time than the classic repertoire of Grimm tales) and relate small miracles.

Briefly, *Dear Mili* is the story of a good and innocent young child endangered by a war that reaches her small village. In a frantic attempt to save her last living child from "the wicked men" who wage wars, her widowed mother sends the young heroine deep into the woods "putting a piece of cake left over from Sunday in the child's pocket." The distraught parent also instructs her daughter to wait three days before returning home, when presumably the worst will be over.

Instead, the child loses her way, dies, and enters a flower-filled paradise where she comes under the protection of St. Joseph "who long ago had cared for the Christ Child here on earth." At St. Joseph's direction, she works dutifully gathering roots for their meals, but she also plays joyously with another mysterious child, her mirror image except for having golden hair where the heroine's is brown. We are told this is probably the child's guardian angel.

What is experienced by the child as the passing of three days is actually a period of thirty years. When at last she returns to her mother, that parent is a frail old woman. After a brief reunion, the two die in perfect happiness. Maternal love and filial loyalty, in the end, triumph over war and death. Could any tale be more grandly operatic?

If Wilhem Grimm felt a compulsion to write this tale just for Mili, Maurice Sendak felt equally drawn to the subject matter and the elegiac beauty of Grimm's treatment. On first reading the story in a rough translation in 1983, he experienced what he calls "a frisson" – a thrill of recognition and discovery. "I feel that this is mine," he told an interviewer from *Publishers Weekly* last spring after completing the book. "I'll share it with Wilhelm, but I swear I've gotten into his skin."

Sendak has always been drawn to stories of children at various moments of crisis and angst. Now comes the heroine of *Dear Mili*, bravely confronting the terrors of the woods (and possible death) as her beloved mother directs her to seek safety there. Approaching the age of sixty and at the height of his powers as an interpretive illustrator, Sendak faced a remarkable text and challenge.

Surely, too, Sendak's special affinity for the tale has a lot to do with growing up Jewish in the United States during World War II. He has never forgotten the morning his Polish immigrant father received news of the loss of his entire family in the Holocaust. Sendak's triumph in *Dear Mili* is that he has taken a tale composed of parochial religious elements and an overlay of nineteenth–century sentimentality, and transformed it into an affecting, timeless memorial to violated innocence.

Thus, into Grimm's tale of war and a single child's death, Sendak has woven poignant reminders of a more recent and personally felt cataclysm, World War II. When the frightened young heroine becomes hopelessly lost in the menacing woods, Sendak's illustration reveals a tangle of gnarled tree limbs and human bones on the path ahead of her. And, off in the distance, he places a haunting group of six grey-faced, starving children – concentration–camp inmates – crossing a narrow wooden bridge (from life to death no doubt). In back of them looms the smokestack of Auschwitz.

Later in the tale, in a double–page picture of a gloriously flowering paradise, a second group of spectral children is seen in the background. They were drawn from a photograph of the ill–fated French/Jewish children deported to their deaths from the town of Izeu by Klaus Barbie. The photograph was one reprinted in the *New York Times Magazine* just prior to Klaus Barbie's trial as a war criminal, while Sendak was at work on the book. In the same illustration, the heroine and her mirror–image companion stroll arm in arm among ancient gravestones with Hebrew lettering and Jewish stars clearly visible, mute reminders of the annihilation of European Jewry. This contemporary imagery, for those who take note of it, enriches rather than distracts from Grimm's tale.

Throughout *Dear Mili*, Sendak treats the ill–fated heroine's sad story with the same high seriousness that painters of the Renaissance accorded to the Passion of Christ. Though the artist has acknowledged his stylistic indebtedness to painters of the nineteenth–century German Romantic Movement – notably to Philipp Otto Runge – his serene tableaux, particularly those containing the heroine and St. Joseph, exhibit a classical restraint more akin to Renaissance painting. More conventionally beautiful than any pictures the artist has done before, his carefully composed scenes have a stopped–in–time quality.

The artist was, of course, no stranger to Grimm. If there had ever been any doubt that Sendak aspired to be more than an entertainer for the nursery, his masterly black–and–white illustrations for *The Juniper Tree* – one wondrously compact and highly distilled pen-and-ink drawing per tale done in stylistic homage to Albrecht Dürer – should have laid it permanently to rest. By way of underscoring his early personal involvement in Grimm's *Dear Mili*, the artist began by considering it as an unexpected sequel to *Outside Over There*. Thus the mother is one and the same in both works, and the baby from *Outside Over There* has grown up to be the heroine of Grimm's tale. Ida, alas, has died, and the time is some seven years later.

In *Dear Mili*, all the disparate elements of Sendak's art – his eclectic borrowings from painters and illustrators of the past, his inclusion of elements from his own life (the Holocaust, Mozart, his own earlier books, his much–loved dogs) – are all fused in one beautifully orchestrated Passion Play of a picture book. These elements are never introduced frivolously. At the outset of *Dear Mili*, two Sendak dogs are added to the scenes of domestic tranquility. They contribute to the sense of security and inviolable peace.

There are, however, two fundamental weaknesses in *Dear Mili*. One is entirely owing to Grimm: the small heroine is so unremittingly obedient and good as to be almost beyond human understanding and sympathy. The second lies in Sendak's exalted interpretation. His flower-filled paradise constitutes a remarkable memorial to all child victims of war. But while we can both respect and admire a monument to the dead, we can never love it in the way that *Wild Things* or *Night Kitchen* are loved.

That said, *Dear Mili* represents a high point in twentieth-century picture-book illustration, both for the gravity and difficulty of its subject matter and for the high degree of success the artist manages to achieve for an audience of children and adults. At a time notably lacking in spirituality or religious faith, Sendak, at the age of sixty, has fought a spiritual battle akin to the Old Testament's Jacob wrestling with an angel.

There is no question that many adults will hesitate to introduce to their children the subject of a child's death as a result of war. They may question whether or not children will understand the Grimm tale. But this is disingenuous. The subject confronts us all daily: Lebanon, Ethiopa, the West Bank, Central America. As Sendak himself puts it, "I think children read the internal meanings of everything. It's only adults who read the top layer most of the time ... kids know what's in Grimm."

Boston Review
February 1989

WE ARE ALL IN THE DUMPS WITH JACK AND GUY

NO, VIRGINIA, Maurice Sendak's *We Are All in the Dumps with Jack and Guy* is *not* a children's book. It is a work of art. That it happens also to be a picture book confuses a lot of us grown-ups who find solace in being able to put things in their appointed places. Since Sendak has earned his reputation as an illustrator and author of picture books for children – and certainly this work, with its twenty-seven glorious double spreads of heartbreakingly beautiful, ineffably sad and, occasionally, downright scary ink-and-watercolor drawings, qualifies as a picture book – then it stands to reason, by grown-up logic, that this latest book must also be directed at the very young.

This constricting notion encourages us, alas, to be sidetracked by a peripheral and, possibly, even rather ridiculous consideration: Is this dark journey (first through an inner-city slum where seemingly abandoned children live in cardboard boxes, and, later through a rural landscape in which ominously smoking chimneys evoke, intentionally, the concentration camp at Auschwitz) suitable fare for an audience of children? We might, of course, pursue this line of reasoning and ask a question more to the point: Is this present-day world – in which terrorists bomb buses and embassies; where three groups of Slavs for five years engaged in the ethnic cleansing of one another in Bosnia and Kosovo; and where TV networks nightly vie to outdo one another in airing docu-dramas of unspeakable mayhem and violence – suitable for children?

It is understandable that we all want to protect our offspring from the more awful truths of our world. But not only can't we do it because of what children see, hear and experience, to some degree, every day of their lives, but because the more we succeed in shielding children from truths they already have some inkling of, the more awful the world is likely to remain into the next generation, and generation upon generation after that.

The plain truth is that some children are both fascinated by, and touchingly concerned with, *Dumps* and its mysterious contents. (I have shared the book with two grandchildren, ages 3 and 4½, probably about a dozen times at this writing.) As soon as they caught sight of the caterwauling baby in tattered diaper on the half-title page, they were hooked. Question followed upon question: Why is the baby crying? Is he hungry? Where is his mother? They accepted with wide-eyed interest the hammock, trash barrel and assorted lean-tos, cartons and wooden crates that constitute home to Sendak's interracial cast of parentless waifs and multi-colored kittens. And, when Evil reared its ugly head, they had no trouble recognizing it in the guise of the two large, predatory rats who appear out of nowhere to make off with a sackful of kittens and the "poor little kid" whom the reader-viewer has already met even before the curtain rises on Sendak's grand-operatic fusion of two traditional, if obscure, English nursery rhymes.

Much has been made of the relentlessly dark vision this Sendak work projects, but, from a young listener/viewer's vantage point, *Dumps* is a fast-paced saga of high suspense with a few worrisome, heart-in-mouth moments and a sort of happy outcome. The artist has honored that cardinal rule in a work for the young: that it close on a positive, hopeful note. Two bad guys (the rats) temporarily get the best of a cartload of innocents (ten kittens and a woebegone child). Then the good guys, personified by two familiar Sendak kids – the truculent Jack and his more sympathetic sidekick Guy – manage, with some help from a benign and all-seeing full moon, to save the intended victims. The two heroes then return to their makeshift shantytown home determined to take on the responsibility of caring for the rescued child, to "bring him up as other folk do."

For Sendak's larger audience – those adult afficionados who have grown up on his earlier books, and those who, through the years, have responded to his ever-deepening artistry and uncanny sensitivity to the angsts of childhood – *Dumps* resonates on various levels. It both rouses painful memories and rubs salt in some contemporary societal wounds. There are haunting images, like the outsized house of cards that gives rise to the uneasy thought that our glitzy post–modern world of glass skyscrapers and luxury apartment houses may be no more than just that. From the very moment an adult viewer confronts *Dumps'* titleless front jacket, with its commanding drawing of a full moon with a wide–open black maw of a mouth, we know we are being invited to embark on a heavy trip. Though the book's cover carries no title, Sendak pulls no punches as to what's in store. Two gloomy newspaper headlines proclaim "HOMELESS SHELTERS" and "LEANER TIMES, MEANER TIMES." Counterbalancing them are a pair of cheerier headlines, "KID ELECTED PRESIDENT" and "CHILDREN TRIUMPH." In this shorthand manner, the artist summarizes his unrelenting message: the adult world is a mess, but children, with their resilience, offer humanity's best hope of redemption.

Like Picasso with his *Guernica*, painted during the Civil War in Spain in the 1930s, Sendak gives us an apocalyptic vision of our times. It is neither pretty nor comforting, but it is difficult to quarrel with its veracity. The artist's eloquent pictures reveal a world beset by ills of varying kinds: a widening chasm between rich and poor, the well and the ill; and an ever–present threat of violence of one sort or other.

The English critic/reviewer Brian Alderson complained in his *New York Times* review of *Dumps* that there is no "sanction" provided by the original nursery–rhyme texts for Sendak's interpretation or, indeed, for his coupling of the two separate rhymes. But since when have artists waited upon sanctions for inspiration? Sendak's picture books have never been literal interpretations of a text. They are, rather, "illuminations," to use his own word, free–wheeling pictorial improvisations on the text at hand. That said, this work was in no way an opportunistic or lightly conceived project. The artist had first attempted to fuse the two arcane rhymes in 1965, following his popular success with an earlier Mother Goose duo, *Hector Protector* and *As I Went Over the Water*. He had, in fact, completed a light–hearted dummy that united the two verses when he decided that the results were too inconsequential to pursue.

This same reviewer raised the question of Sendak's possible "self-indulgence." But *Dumps* can only be viewed as a self-indulgence if we consider it to be somehow wrong – or in poor taste – to take painful life experiences and transform them into a work accessible to both children and adults. Indisputably, there are incorporated into this work images of sick children recalled from a visit the artist paid to the terminal ward of the Great Ormond Street Children's Hospital in London; personal graphic references to the pain he has felt upon losing close colleagues and promising students to the AIDS epidemic; chilling reminders of photographs from the concentration camps of Europe that he saw as a teenager in the closing days of World War II.

Despite its artistry and ambitious reach, *Dumps* is far from a seamless work. The breadth and unflinching truth of Sendak's dark vision is so overpowering at the outset that the words of the first nursery rhyme seem almost superfluous, lost in the graphic panorama. In fact, Sendak has added his own compelling (if oddly incomplete) subtext to the opening rhyme: "Look what they did/ Look what they did/ The rats stole the kittens/ And the poor little kid/ Rascal! Thief! Let's play bridge/ Let's play for the kittens/ And the poor little kid." Sendak's abbreviated verse makes neither a smooth nor a fully integrated connection to the parent rhyme.

One senses in this latest work by an older, wiser Maurice Sendak, a newfound freedom, something akin to what Virginia Woolf was feeling when she wrote at the age of fifty: "You will understand that all impediments suddenly dropped off. I had no restrictions whatever and was thus free to define my attitude with a vigor and certainty I have never known before."

If, then, *Dumps* is not a children's book but, rather, a work of art, what is a work of art? It is the successful encounter of a superior talent with a subject worthy of the artistic energy expended. In *Dumps*, Sendak has given, to children and adults alike, no holds barred, his very best effort. We cannot know from what obscure and inchoate depths the vision that illuminates *Dumps* ultimately arises. The artist has given shape and power to a personal vision we will not soon forget.

Sendak has done battle with some of the big bad wolves of our time – VIOLENCE, POVERTY, AIDS and HUMAN INDIFFERENCE. None of us who has shared his picture–book nightmare will ever be quite the same.

Parents' Choice
December 1993

TEN

Edward Gorey's
Tantalizing Turns of the Screw

O feelings of horror, resentment and pity
For things which so seldom turn out for the best.
Edward Gorey
THE INSECT GOD

For those who look upon creative endeavors as manifestations of narcissism successfully objectified, surely the work of Edward St. John Gorey provides a treasure trove of droll and persuasive examples. The artist is tirelessly inventive with the anagrammatic and other fanciful possibilities of his own name. He has, over the years, published his curiously compelling works of morbose graphic humor as Ogdred Weary, Mrs. Regera Dowdy, Dreary Wodge, Madame Groeda Weyrd, Eduard Blutig (the German *blutig* is equivalent to bloody, i.e., Gorey), and Raddory Gewe.

In *The Awdrey-Gore Legacy* (1972), an opaque whodunit dedicated to Agatha Christie, Gorey not only provides an introductory note in the guise of E. G. Deadworry, but he serves up a list of red–herring suspects named Roy Grewdead, Roger Addyew, Drew Dogyear, Gray Redwood, Dedge Yarro, and Orde Graydew. The tale's "most sought–after private detective" is one Waredo Dyrge, a half-Irish, half-Japanese soldier of fortune and surely one of Gorey's most inspired anagrams. If this were not enough, Dyrge has an inseparable and ferocious dog companion,

Deary, who is named for his master's favorite reading fare –"the Deary Rewdgo Series for Intrepid Young Ladies (*D.R. on the Great Divide, D.R. in the Yukon, D.R. at Baffin Bay,* etc.) by Dewda Yorger."

In illustration as well, Gorey's work has abounded in self-portraits. In his first published work, *The Unstrung Harp; or, Mr. Earbrass Writes a Novel* (1953), Mr. Gorey is pictured – and so labeled – in a threesome that includes the hero. His second book, *The Listing Attic* (1954), provides a full-length likeness – bearded, scarved and levitated – on the back cover, accompanied by the appropriately Gorey–esque legend "O rage! O desespoir!" And, generally besneakered and fur–coated, he can be recognized as the prototype for at least one character in nearly every work. Somewhat unexpected was his streaker's appearance, back view, on a balustraded terrace in *The West Wing* (1963).

There is good reason, in fact, to suspect that Gorey's perennial fixation on the costume and *mise-en-scène* of the Edwardian era –"c. 1910" as he pinpoints it in his single prose work, *The Black Doll* (1973) – is for no more arcane reason than that the period had the great good fortune to share his own given name. But enough. To continue in this vein is to trivialize the work of one of the inspired, if perverse, artists of our time.

With the appearance of his *Amphigorey Too* (1975), a vintage selection of nineteen Gorey works spanning his prolific career from 1952 on, we could, for the first time, judge just how rich and deep runs that small lugubrious lode that Gorey mined so assiduously – and inventively – for almost a quarter of a century. The collection is noteworthy on a number of counts – not least of which is that it brings together much of Gorey's rarely seen, out-of-print work, hitherto issued only in limited editions from small private presses. Unlike the first *Amphigorey* (1972), which was a broad survey of fifteen of Gorey's better known, commercially published little volumes, the second anthology, fatter and kinkier, provided a far more intimate view of the artist.

Not only did this compendium make available Gorey's first book, *The Beastly Baby*, completed in 1952 when Gorey was still living in Cambridge (he graduated from Harvard, a French major, with the class of 1950), but it contains both of Gorey's favorite works, *The Nursery Frieze* (1964) and *[The Untitled Book]* (1971). *The Beastly Baby* is described by the author as being about "a very unpleasant baby everyone is trying to get rid of, and who is finally carried off by an eagle and bursts like a balloon." Though written a decade earlier, the book did not find a publisher until 1962 – and then only in a private edition from Gorey's own newly-inaugurated Fantod Press – because no commercial house had faith in the sales appeal of so dank and offhand an apologia for infanticide. While the casually expressionistic drawings in *The Beastly Baby* hadn't yet settled into any stylistic mold, Gorey's prose, from the outset, was commandingly spare, self-assured and elliptical. The beastly baby "was capable of making only two sorts of noises, both of them nasty. The first was a choked gurgling, reminiscent of faulty drains. It made this noise when it had succeeded in doing something particularly atrocious. The second was a thin shriek suggestive of fingernails on blackboards. It made this noise when it had been prevented from doing something particularly atrocious." Unrelievedly macabre, at moments outrageously so, it offers just enough of those redeeming flashes of wit and insight to keep it from foundering on the shoals of sophomoric callowness. "Its nose was beaky," the author tells us of the infant, "and appeared to be considerably older than the rest of it." And already in *The Beastly Baby*, there is that hallmark of Gorey's mature work: the perfect marriage of words to pictures for maximum psychological impact and suggestiveness.

The Nursery Frieze, one of the artist's simplest and most mysterious works, is, as its title proclaims, a proposed wall decoration for a baby's boudoir. Four identical animals – a charmless hybrid of hippopotamus and capybara – march stolidly across thirty-two horizontal pages. Actually the reader sees on each page only the two middle beasts in their entirety, plus the hind quarters of the first and the front end of the fourth in line. The book having been conceived as a continuing frieze, each sequence is designed to append itself to the ones preceding and following in an unbroken procession which, at the end, will run smack into its own beginning. This being so, Gorey with unassailable – if quixotic – logic elects to start his work *in media res*. This the viewer discovers when, on closer scrutiny, he notices that Gorey has half-concealed the letters of the words The – Nursery – Frieze – Edward – Gorey, one letter (or single space between words) to each page. Gorey's book begins with the E of Nursery. As his creatures lope relentlessly forward, the three heads on each page utter some of the most abstruse nouns ever gathered in one thin work – badigeon, maremma, piacle. Just as the reader is about to despair of eliciting any sense at all from the frieze, there comes the revelation of a pattern. Every fourth word rhymes: bosphorous with phosphorous, cedilla with vanilla, remorse with divorce. But what does it all mean?

With *The Nursery Frieze*, Gorey succeeds admirably in reducing sophisticated adult readers to that state of helpless bafflement and incomprehension so often experienced by small children. Slowly, like a child, the reader gains whatever mastery is possible over this puzzling work, and the victory parallels a child's: one imposes what fragmentary logic and sense one can on the enigma at hand. It is an exotically cerebral entertainment, with Gorey forcing his audience to experience the world anew – on his terms.

Significantly, perhaps, Gorey's second favorite work, [*The Untitled Book*], has a similar theme: divining some rudimentary pattern from the world's unreason. Its cover pictures the sort of funerary landscape one might find chiseled on a nineteenth-century tombstone: a tree, a shrub, a stone wall and random, ominous clouds. There is also, at stage right, the corner of a dwelling with a darkened open window, its curtain drawn back titillatingly. The tale's first scene finds a small, unsmiling boy-child at the window. Lace-collared and Fauntleroy-suited, he is one of those cosseted Gorey scions of a well-feathered Edwardian nest. The jaunty words "Hippity wippity" appear below this initial illustration. Five subsequent frames introduce five fanciful, vaguely disquieting beings – an oversized humanoid spider who leaps out of the shrub ("Oxiborick"), a frog who vaults the wall ("Flappity flippity"), an eared lizard who lopes on stage from behind the house ("Saragashum"), a bat flapping out of the tree ("Thip"), and a stocking–doll emerging from under a stone ("thap"). At the word "thoo," all five creatures join hands and dance. For one wild moment, it looks as though the stolid child may be about to applaud their performance – his hands part suggestively – when, suddenly, a horrific, disembodied black head materializes from nowhere in the sky above. From his vantage point, the child cannot possibly see it, but he can readily observe the terror of the dancing creatures who do. As they all fall down, the child averts his eyes at impending doom ("Thumbleby stumbleby"). By the next frame, however, the nameless menace has vanished as mysteriously as it had arrived. Now the five creatures follow suit, in the order in which they appeared, to other jaunty words: "Ipsifendus; Rambleby rumbleby; Quoggenzocker; Hip; hop; hoo." And, neat as a pin, it's all over. A perfectly rounded little dance–drama in which nameless threats come, are seen, and neither conquer nor are conquered. It is so self–contained and tightly choreographed a work that, its alien reality notwithstanding, it is curiously satisfying.

The choreography of Gorey's books is not a metaphorical description but rather a key to appreciating his artfully wrought little divertissements. Gorey was an avid balletomane; in any season he rarely missed either a rehearsal or performance of the New York City Center Ballet. And one of Gorey's more inspired works is the fully–illustrated little novella, *The Gilded Bat* (1966), a substantial comi–tragic tribute in thirty sequences to the ballerina's demanding life. It documents the solitary, single–minded rise of Maudie Splaytoe from the tender age of five to blooming maturity as Mirella Splatova, reigning ballerina of her era. It is, at once, a work of grim satire and deep seriousness. Nowhere does Gorey's melancholy grasp of the realities of the artist's daily existence get hammered home more insistently. As Maudie advances, through the usual blend of discipline, luck and selfless dedication, Gorey informs us periodically: "Her life was rather monotonous.... Her life went on being fairly tedious.... Her life did not cease to be some-what dreary." And, when at last she's made it to the top, Gorey reminds us, "Her life was really no different from what it had ever been."

A second ballet work, *The Lavender Leotard* (1973), is memorable, a collection of mildly sardonic vignettes of ballet life, both backstage and as a spectator sport. The work's chief claim to fame may well be that Gorey, a perfectionist, hand-painted the ballerina's skirt on every cover of the first edition in order to guarantee precisely the shade of laven-der he had in mind.

Gorey's debt to the ballet, however, runs far deeper than its value as subject matter. Long years of rehearsal and performance-watching paid off in the élan with which he graphically staged his own works. His thoroughly captivating *CATEGORY* (1973) mesmerizes the viewer through fifty wordless pages of fifty numbered cats, casually disport-ing themselves in as many graceful poses on ladders, scaffoldings, mountain tops, bicycles, rowboats, tombstones – each one positioned by his creator with as much guile and precision as the best of Balan-chine. The cat-filled front and back covers of both *Amphigorey* (1972) and *Amphigorey Too*, in fact, display the same grace and charm.

Each of Gorey's works is staged to a fare-thee-well. The action, at first glance seemingly mechanical or quaintly wooden, has been art-fully worked out to insure maximum dramatic interplay among the three crucial elements of every Gorey drama: what the words say, what is actually pictured and what the reader is encouraged to imagine on his own. The two versions of his alphabet, *The Chinese Obelisks* (1970), which appear in *Amphigorey Too*, are instructive in this regard. The first, Gorey's rough draft for the work, had never before been published. But, with the exception of two minor word changes to improve the cadence, the text is altered not at all between notebook and published work. The art, however, undergoes subtle refinements and distillations. Mostly it moves from the literal to the suggestive. Originally, for "S was the Sun which went under a cloud," Gorey pictured the event. The published version, to far greater effect, shows the result of the sun's absence: an ominously darkened street. With a sure eye, the artist repositions characters within almost every frame. Gorey's alterations tell us what we suspected all along about the quality and quantity of graphic invention invested in each of his performances: it is a rare species of visual poetry Gorey dispenses – a highly concentrated distillation of all he has gleaned over the years about the human figure on stage or page, and its ability to command our full attention.

Though Gorey can provide as lavish sets as the best New York stage designers – replete with period furnishings, wall hangings and appropriate decorative furbelows – there is neither wasted motion nor over-embellishment in any book. He also knows the dramatic value of no setting at all. His *The Inanimate Tragedy* (1966) is a *tour de force* played on unfurnished pages by a cast of assorted pins and needles, a penpoint, a glass marble, one two-holed and one four-holed button, a thumb tack, and a knotted string. Yet, other works, like the evocative *The West Wing* (1963), are wordless and entirely dependent on decor for their content. Gorey's peeling wallpaper in one airless room of *The West Wing* is more suggestive of violation and evil than any explicit rape scene. And what could be more chilling than that merest hint of a human form in the giant grease spot that appears on another, elegantly papered wall? His wordless *Leaves from a Mislaid Album* (1972), in no way matches the virtuosity of this earlier work of pure illustration.

Other noteworthy Goreys include *The Pious Infant* (1966) by Mrs. Regera Dowdy and *The Deranged Cousins* (1971). The first, a mock-eighteenth-century moral fable, is about one Henry Clump, who, on a wintry afternoon at the age of four and five months "went to give his bread pudding to an unfortunate widow." Strictly in keeping with the canon of the genre, small Henry contracts "a sore throat, which by morning had turned into a fatal illness," thus assuring his fittingly premature dispatch heavenward.

The Deranged Cousins is Gorey at his most deliciously perverse. The tale focuses on an eccentric and involuted ménage, comprised of three orphaned cousins: Rose Marshmary, Mary Rosemarsh, and Marsh

Maryrose. They live, appropriately, in a house covered with roses on the edge of a marsh. In a quarrel "over a bedslat," Rose is killed. Marsh obligingly buries her "in a field known as the Rabbits' Restroom," and Mary turns into a religious nut, while Marsh takes to drink. Dreadful deaths, of course, ensue. The work abounds in vintage, Goreyesque touches. All three characters wear the same ankle–hugging pro–Ked sneakers made famous by *The Doubtful Guest* (1957), but, Marsh, over his knickerbockers, sports a turtleneck sweater from which an outsized H (for Harvard) has clearly been removed. Only the stitched outline where it must once have been is still apparent. It is one of those inimitable Gorey details that tickles the periphery of the conscious mind, encouraging wild and unverifiable surmises.

The remainder of *Amphigorey Too*'s inclusions are of lesser weight, but often considerable charm. *Story for Sara* (1971), the saga of a small, sly girl eaten by a large, sly cat, is distinguished by Gorey's marvelously wrought Chinese–Chippendale lettering for the covers. *The Abandoned Sock* (1973) is a wistful, picaresque account of a wayward sock which abandons its mate because life "was tedious and unpleasant." And *The Salt Herring* (1971) is a nonsense tale of classic simplicity and charm, which surely succeeds in its avowed aim "to make all serious men mad, mad, mad, and to amuse children little, little, little."

Grateful as we should be for this generous anthology, its large format and well–stuffed pages can in no way give the reader unfamiliar with Gorey's work any real sense of the special, hothouse atmosphere of his volumes. Opening one of Gorey's books is as restful as entering a medieval cloister. Machine typesetting finds no refuge here. Every single word, from the Library of Congress cataloguing and copyright data to the text itself, is compulsively hand–lettered by the artist. A hermetic, unified and oddly peaceful little cosmos is the result. We willingly submit to the artist's own rules and seductively persuasive nonsense. "It was the day after Tuesday and the day before Wednesday," begins his *The Epiplectic Bicycle* (1969). Gorey's prose is always refreshingly lean and full of surprises: "And before you could say knife," or "It was too dark to hear anything." Often in his chaste and economical picture–dramas, the left–hand pages will contain only a single line of text, and all that pristine, empty space functions as a sort of vest–pocket park, encouraging the reader's darker fancies to roam freely.

There is a basic and inviolable decorum in Gorey's world. His characters, whatever their extremity of pain, fear, horror or other human suffering, are virtually unflappable. They accept their fates, whether to be ridden over by horseless carriages or swallowed by a Wuggly Ump, with resigned and well–bred grace. It is a world where, for the most part, unspeakable practices, violences and depravities take place off stage or discreetly behind drawing room screens. Those characters who actually hurl themselves from towers do so with admirable, theatrical grace – boas flapping in the afternoon breeze. The elegant, inert feet of corpses protrude decorously from underneath rocks, over rowboat gunnels and from behind half–shut doors. Though, in *The Gashlycrumb Tinies* (1963), we do see "K is for Kate who was struck with an axe;" it is a tableau of the *fait accompli* and not the crime itself.

Certain disasters, however, recur obsessively. In *The Other Statue* (1968), Lord Wherewithal is found crushed "beneath a statue blown down from the parapet." Charlotte Sophia's last remaining relative in *The Hapless Child* (1961) is "brained by a piece of masonry." The hero of *The Chinese Obelisks* is flattened by an urn mysteriously "dislodged from the sky." An antisocial bug in *The Bug Book* (1959) is squashed flat by a large stone, and in *The Blue Aspic* (1968) an ornamental sculpture falls on the Duke of Whaup during the second interval of the opera *Amable Tastu*.

Objects, too, reappear from work to work with nightmarish regularity: ladders, Chinese and Grecian urns, tunnels, elaborately balustraded terraces, wooden legs, boulders, rising water. And, not surprisingly, because Gorey's world is so hermetically sealed, characters and places recur. Not only is Mrs. Regera Dowdy the author of *The Pious Infant* and the translator of Eduard Blutig's *The Evil Garden* (1966), but the peripatetic protagonists of *The Willowdale Handcar* (1962) manage to peer in the window of Mrs. Dowdy's home in Violet Springs to admire her writing desk. Place names too recur – Nether Millstone, for one – though Gorey seems endlessly inventive in conjuring up new ones: Peevish Gorge, Chutney Falls, Bogus Corners.

Since few artists ever have confined themselves to so circumscribed a terrain, Gorey's subject matter is easily summed up. He addresses himself to the miseries and helplessness of childhood, to the loneliness and agonies of the creative life, and to the cosmic chill and ever-present perils of mere day-to-day existence. His characters – child or adult, artist or Edwardian swell – are all subject to the random unpredictability of an indifferent, probably even sinister, world. Disaster may strike from any quarter, at any time. Gorey's work is permeated by what he apostrophized in *The Insect God* (1963) as "O feelings of horror, resentment, and pity/ For things which so seldom turn out for the best."

Given the artist's overwhelmingly morbid preoccupations, it is surprising how closely his name is associated with the world of children's books. But ever since the passing from the literary scene of the illustrated adult novel in the early years of this century, there has been no comfortable home for book illustrators like Gorey, or for that matter Tomi Ungerer. Although neither artist's best work has been done for children, they tend to be thought of first as juvenile illustrators. Gorey, as it happens, has always written about children with sympathy and understanding; he clearly regards them as the prime victims of the world's unreason. His early limerick collection, *The Listing Attic*, contains several vintage examples, including the chilling:

> To his clubfooted child said Lord Stipple,
> As he poured his post-prandial tipple,
> "Your mother's behavior
> Gave pain to Our Savior,
> And that's why He made you a cripple."

Determined to earn his way as an artist, Gorey took assignments pretty much as they came in the '50s and early '60s. Not only did he do cover illustrations for a number of Anchor paperbacks (including several novels of Henry James), he also did hardcover book jackets, illustrated food features for *Woman's Day* and assorted bits and pieces for other magazines, wrote and illustrated his own children's book, *The Bug Book*, for The Looking Glass Library, and accepted a number of children's book illustrating assignments from various publishers. He did the black–and–white drawings for six collections of John Ciardi's poems during the '60s, and three handsomely designed and elegantly colored Ennis Rees books for Young Scott Books, including *Br'er Rabbit and His Tricks*.

Probably Gorey's best known and most successful work as an illustrator of children's books was *The Shrinking of Treehorn* (1971) by Florence Parry Heide. Treehorn, clearly a character in search of an illustrator like Gorey, is a stoic child with a unique problem that no adult cares to notice: he is growing smaller day by day. Gorey's thoroughly deadpan treatment of the increasingly diminutive hero's troubles is irresistible – from Treehorn's valiantly rising above droopy sleeves to his carrying his head unnaturally high in order to see the adults who constantly natter at him.

His *Little Red Riding Hood* (1972) won him a first prize in graphics at the Bologna Children's Book Fair in 1974, but elegant as is his handling of two–color illustrations in red and tan, the work has little of the graphic resonance or character of his own inventions. And his *Rumpelstiltskin* (1973) is disappointingly perfunctory, the title character too fey to be taken seriously.

Even those of his own works generally considered children's stories, like *The Bug Book* and *The Wuggly Ump* (1963), might best be characterized as cheerily lugubrious. "Sing tirraloo, sing tirralay, the Wuggly Ump lives far away," begins the latter. Yet, while three children are fed "on wholesome bowls of milk and bread" and "pass our happy childhood hours/ In weaving endless chains of flowers," the Wuggly Ump is drawing nigh. In the end, not unexpectedly, he gleefully devours the trio, and Gorey's confection ends liltingly: "Sing glogalimp, sing glugalump/ From deep inside the Wuggly Ump."

117

And though, to date, he has published five alphabet books, none of them would qualify as likely children's fare. For the letter L, in *The Glorious Nosebleed*, Gorey provides: "He exposed himself Lewdly." In *The Fatal Lozenge* (1960), P is: "The Proctor buys a pupil ices,/ And hopes the boy will not resist/ When he attempts to practice vices/ Few people even know exist." *The Utter Zoo Alphabet* (1967) introduces for Q a horrific beast: "The Quingawaga squeaks and moans/ While dining off of ankle bones." And surely the best-known and blackest of his alphabets, *The Gashlycrumb Tinies* –"A is for Amy who fell down the stairs/ B is for Basil assaulted by bears" – may delight older children but would hardly win its way into a juvenile librarian's heart.

What of the man behind this impressive body of eccentric work for children fully grown? Gorey was born in Chicago in 1925, the son of a Hearst newspaperman. Of his own childhood, he told questioners over the years remarkably little, the most revealing statement being: "I agree with people who say what happens after five is irrelevant, but I don't remember what happened before then. I always did have a leaning toward the bizarre, I guess. I was the kind of kid who thought it funny to throw an epileptic fit on a bus and that sort of thing. But I haven't the slightest idea why my work has taken the tack it has. I just do what occurs to me – if it occurs to me strong enough."

To the interviewer who inquired why his work focused so unrelievedly on violence and horror, Gorey replied without hesitation, "I write about everyday life." And indeed, in some respects he does. He is obsessed by those uncomfortable realities and spectres all of us tend to sweep into the dark recesses of the mind. As Gorey alliteratively catalogued them in *The Inanimate Tragedy* (1966), they are "Death and Distraction; Destruction and Debauchery; Duplicity and Desolation; Dissolution and Despair; Discomfort and Damage; Doom and Discrepancy; Degradation and Dismay; Danger and Deceit; Defeat and Disaster; Depravity and Disappointment; Disappearance and Damnation."

Gorey was one of those rare artists smiled upon by the muses: he was able to work to please himself. He had, over the years, gained a following sufficiently large and loyal to oversubscribe the often limited editions of his work. And for a long while, there were a number of small, eminently respectable publications – *The Partisan Review, The Evergreen Review, The New York Review of Books* and *The Soho Weekly News* – willing to publish his recondite fantasies as he turned them out, often one panel per issue, for the leisurely delectation of their own special audiences.

Oddly enough, for work so studiously removed from the sphere of day–to–day life, Gorey's oblique improvisations are remarkably revealing of their creator. *The Awdrey-Gore Legacy* is strewn with disembodied, thinly–disguised, autobiographical truths. Boxed on various pages are little rhymed nuggets from a mythical Gorey epic, "The Ipsiad," which have the unmistakable flavor of self-revelation. "To catch and keep the public's gaze," runs one couplet, "One must have lots of little ways." What better description of Gorey's lifelong literary and graphic ethos?

The book's last box perhaps phrases Gorey's own ultimate concern:

> And what if then we don't find out
> What all of it has been about?

But if any character sums up the recurring messages in almost every Gorey work, it is the beleaguered heroine of *The Eleventh Episode* (1971), whose bizarre little adventure ends, "'Life is distracting and uncertain,'/ She said and went to draw the curtain."

•

ELEVEN

A Reformed Masochist: William Steig

I T IS GROWN-UPS who determine the classics of children's literature, and not simply because they write them. Over the long haul, children's books succeed to the degree that they reflect what literate adults want their offspring to know and feel about the world. Parents being what they are – a bumbling and inarticulate lot when it comes to talking with their kids about the things that really count – and children being what they are – remarkably adept at tuning out the parental voice of reason – children's books often serve as necessary and welcome intermediaries. Long before a grown-up thinks to speak of filial obedience, say, or the meaning of life, works like *Peter Rabbit* and *The Wind in the Willows* act as subtle establishment spokesmen for us all.

Dominic, cartoonist William Steig's first full-length novel for children, is a likely candidate for classic status, at least in part because, from a current (and even more likely, a future) parent's point of view, it radiates a miraculously old-fashioned faith in the overall wonder and worth of living. While most of us would surely like our children to acquire such a faith in life, we often lack the confidence to transmit it effectively on our own. Unlike the author-artist's six prior juvenile works – picture books aimed more at young listeners and viewers than readers – *Dominic* is a picaresque fairy tale and philosophic odyssey for slightly older (eight•through twelve), more patient children, who read both for entertainment and for expansion of their knowledge of what life is all about.

A piccolo-playing young hound dog of irrepressible good spirits, *Dominic* announces on page one, in a farewell note to his neighbors: "Dear Friends, I am leaving in rather a hurry to see more of the world...." When he meets an alligator-witch who gives him the choice of following a road with "not a bit of magic ... no surprise, nothing to discover or wonder at" or a route that "keeps right on going, as far as anyone cares to go ... where things will happen that you never could have guessed at – marvelous, unbelievable things," Dominic naturally chooses the latter, the high road to adventure.

From the outset, all five of his senses – particularly his nose – are keyed to an appreciation of whatever life holds in store. Inspired by wondrous woodland odors ("damp earth, mushrooms, dried leaves, violets, mint, spruce, rotting wood, animal droppings, forget-me-nots, and mold"), Dominic improvises a piccolo melody entitled "The Psalm of Sweet Smells." Falling unexpectedly into the clutches of an unregenerately wicked band of foxes, ferrets and weasels – the Doomsday Gang – the undauntedly optimistic hound is not blind to their virtues either. "Being evil was what they were best at," he observes. "Everyone enjoys being best at something." Besides, meeting challenges is Dominic's prime pleasure. By his own efforts, the hound outwits the villains and then, in rapid succession, befriends an elderly pig named Bartholomew Badger, loses him to a peaceful death from old age and falls heir to the pig's vast fortune.

Surprisingly, for a children's book, the death scene takes place on stage, as if Steig somehow wants both young hero and young reader simultaneously to realize that there can be no meaningful appreciation of life without the pain of knowing that death is the eventual fate of us all. (Steig says that he feels no compunction about death scenes in his children's books, so long as they take place early in the action. And in his four best books, his heroes all must confront the possibility of imminent death.) As Dominic tearfully buries his friend, he comes up with as poignantly simple and comprehensible a definition of death, for child or adult, as is ever likely to be found: "His turn was over."

Newfound riches, alas, get in the way of Dominic's free-wheeling enjoyment of life, and so, lightheartedly, he dispenses with his burdensome treasure in two lavish acts of philanthropy. When the second recipient has scruples about accepting such largesse, the hero explains: "I really have no use for wealth. I'm young. I'm free, and I have a God-given nose to guide me through life. Please, say no more." Regarding Dominic's unbounded generosity, Steig recalls that "as a kid, it was my ambition to live in holy poverty – to travel as light as Dominic."

A *Sleeping Beauty* ending in which Dominic releases a beautiful black hound dog named Evelyn from a witch's enchantment seems no better or worse than many another the author might have chosen. It is simply extraneous to the tale's central message: taking life cheerfully as it comes – the bad with the good. "Fighting the bad ones in the world was a necessary and gratifying experience," Dominic concludes, looking back on his adventures. "Being happy among the good ones was, of course, even more gratifying. But one could not be happy among the good ones unless one fought the bad ones." As to any ultimate reason for things: "Why are there owls?" Dominic asks himself at a reflective moment in the woods. And his only answer is, "Why anything?"

In many ways, *Dominic* is a throwback to a more innocent and trust-

William Steig
Dominic

ing time. "What a wonderful world!" the dog exclaims early in his travels. "How perfect! . . . Every leaf was in its proper place. Pebbles, stones,
flowers, all were just as they ought to be." Steig is championing an
optimism so old-fashioned as to be almost revolutionary. A hero who
can apostrophize: "Oh Life! I am yours. Whatever it is you want of me,
I am ready to give," should somehow be preserved under glass. It's just
possible that children of the TV age, whose experiences often consist
of the passive absorption of "life" secondhand, may find in Dominic's
headlong philosophy a refreshing new model for action. For adults, the
experience is akin to stumbling into an authentic nineteenth-century
general store: the contents are somehow more appetizing than anything we've come across in years.

Most parents who are won over by Steig's sunlit philosophy for
children also have memories long enough to wonder how this mordant *New Yorker* cartoonist came to turn his considerable gifts to the
entertainment of children. As creator, in 1942, of *The Lonely Ones*, a collection of psychoanalytically oriented cartoons ("Mother loved me – but
she died" is perhaps the best known), Steig earned the title of "trusted
spokesman for the masochist" and was instrumental in launching a
profitable era of sick humor in the greeting-card industry. Yet in 1968,
around the time of the artist's sixtieth birthday, his career took a new
course – with conspicuous success: of the six children's books that preceded *Dominic*, the fifth – *Sylvester and the Magic Pebble* – won him the
Caldecott Medal in 1970; and the sixth – *Amos and Boris* – was nominated for the National Book Award in 1971.

Steig is not unique, of course, in traveling a roundabout route into
the world of children's books. Kenneth Grahame was secretary of the
Bank of England at the time he began writing *The Wind in the Willows*.
Lewis Carroll was an Oxford don and mathematician of some note
before being diverted by Alice; and both A. A. Milne and James Thurber
were admired adult humorists when they discovered a new audience
in children. About his own reasons for turning to children's books,
Steig is disarmingly candid. His initial effort, *Roland the Minstrel Pig*, was

undertaken because a *New Yorker* colleague was leaving the magazine to found his own publishing house and convinced the cartoonist that there was money to be made in children's picture books. This incentive, plus the chance "to work in a different vein at that point in my life," was enough to make Steig willing to try.

Like his first hero, Roland, who was "a natural musician – from his hoofs to his snout," Steig found himself naturally adept at speaking from the heart to an audience of children. The potentiality had probably lain fallow for some years, since many of Steig's cartoons of the '30s and '40s depicted self-assured "Small Fry" carrying on the serious business of playing baseball and football, going to school, and dreaming of future power and fulfillment. To an interviewer who asked at that time about his seeming obsession with children, particularly small boys, Steig replied that little boys "are not as quickly socially conditioned as little girls and are not as artificial as adults. They provide the best clues to the intrinsic nature of man." As it turns out, the heroes of Steig's children's books are preponderantly young male animals – a pig, donkey, mouse and hound. Indeed, one is struck by the consistency of outlook that carries over from his cartoons for adults to his books for children. In *Dominic* Steig suggests that one is in "Nature's good graces" during childhood, a thought expressed in slightly different terms years before in the introduction to *Dreams of Glory* (1953), a collection of cartoons about children. "Even the worst of us," he wrote then, "tends to cherish children and recognizes in them the bearers of the makings of a beautiful human destiny – another tide of life flung against the wall of social stupidity."

A devoted disciple as well as successful analysand of the late Wilhelm Reich, Steig would be the last to deny that elements in several of his children's works derive from Reichian principles. There are those who see in the overall optimism of *Dominic* and the dog's at-homeness in the world an example of the Reichian ideal of union with the "primal cosmic energy" in the universe. Dominic himself is a fine specimen of the Reichian free man: one who is wholly himself because he is attuned to that inner voice that nudges him gently in the right direction. In one of his papers, Reich counsels that "there is only one thing that counts: to live one's life well and happily. Follow the voice of your heart, even if it leads you off the path of timid souls. Do not become hard and embittered, even if life tortures you at times." It could be a plot summary of Dominic's woodland odyssey

Because Steig works instinctively, he is often startled by what he later discovers in his books. "It was only when *Dominic* was done," he recalls, "that I realized it was really about my father. He was the same sort of cheerful, optimistic character." Steig was just as surprised to learn that readers have been investing the ending of *Dominic* with symbolic meaning. "I hadn't attached any significance at all to Evelyn's being a black hound," he says incredulously. "But I suppose my making her black had something to do with the things I've been thinking about lately, children's books aside. I do believe that everything you do in life relates to everything else. It's only when you're consciously aware of what you're doing in a book that you're in trouble. It always mars the work." Two major incidents in *Dominic* were informed by random phrases that popped unbidden into Steig's head –"the goose hangs high" and "a wild boar weeping." *Amos and Boris*, on the other hand, began with a drawing Steig had made of an elephant pushing a whale back into the sea. With *Sylvester and The Magic Pebble* Steig felt only that he must have a donkey hero, a pebble and something magical. He has set ideas on what animals should play which roles – again purely on instinct – and no one could have been more shocked than he at the furor created by his depicting the police in Sylvester as pigs. "They just seemed the right animal for the role," he shrugs. "I had no ideological ax to grind. I never even knew that cops were being called that as an insult. I happen to like pigs." As can perhaps be surmised, the abiding charm of Steig's work for children lies not so much in the originality – or even the drama – of his plots as in the curious touches, the idiosyncratic crotchets and convictions he somehow injects into each work. There is, among Steig's other gifts, his uncanny sense of how children

view the world. When Amos, the mouse hero of *Amos and Boris*, is loading a boat with various "necessities" for an ocean voyage, Steig includes
not only the expected two barrels of fresh water, compass, sextant and
telescope but also a "yo–yo and playing cards." Later in the book, when
Amos falls overboard one starry night and is in terror and despair, the
author notes, "Morning came, as it always does," knowing instinctively
what a comfort this simple fact can be to frightened mouse or child. In
Dominic, too, during one of the hound's moments of triumph, the hero
wonders: "How did the world ever manage without me before I was
born? Didn't they feel something was missing?" It is a common thought
of childhood, just as its opposite, "How will the world get along without me when I am gone?" may occasionally occur to the aging.

Though Steig will be sixty–five in November, he could easily pass for
a man fifteen years his junior. He has a full head of graying hair, a
strong, square–jawed face, trim build and steel–blue eyes that look as
though they probably miss less now than they did forty years ago. As
to his future plans for children's books, he so enjoyed working on a
novel–length text that he has already completed a second book for
older children about a goose named Gawain who is guardian of a king's
mysteriously diminishing treasury. Steig is also thinking of doing a full
collection of his own fairy tales. Though he has no intention of giving
up his career as a *New Yorker* cartoonist for adults, he is further tempted
by the possibility of working on animations of several of his stories –
particularly Dominic, since he would like to see his son Jeremy, a jazz
flutist and piccolo player of some repute, improvise the music. He
would even like to do a book for adults, but feels that this is unlikely.
"I think I could write for dumb adults, but not smart ones," he says.
"The thing I'm sure of is that I know more than a lot of kids know."
And this "more" is likely to keep him going for some time, if adults
have anything to say about children's books – and of course they do.

Harper's Magazine
October 1972

TWELVE

Tomi Ungerer's Unlikely Heroes

I do my books for myself, for the child inside me. In that respect,
they are selfish. They are also subversive, because I think that
all children are subversive. They see hypocrisy, and they know
the truth of just about everything by instinct.
Tomi Ungerer

I F YOU WOULD truly teach young children through the books they
listen to or read themselves, give them a hero who is an unregenerately bad example, a rotter through and through. Then the young
audience will instinctively sympathize with him and, eventually, swallow any lesson – however conventional or goody–goody – that issues
from his mouth or is implicit in his fate. The sad thing about being
small is that one is constantly failing to measure up to some adult's
incomprehensible mark. Teeth are improperly brushed; clothing is
mistreated; family heirlooms are irreverently handled and thereby
mysteriously damaged. Because one of the last senses to develop is
that of proportion, most children, by the ripe old age of three or four,
are thoroughly convinced that they are bad news.

What a relief, then, to stumble upon a character undeniably worse
than oneself! Piper Paw, the kitten hero of author–artist Tomi Ungerer's
picture book, *No Kiss for Mother*, is – claws sheathed – the orneriest, most
self–centered and willful hero to hit kids' picture books since the mid–
nineteenth–century heyday of Struwwelpeter. Not only does Piper sass

127

his mother, trample on his beautifully-ironed clothes, and spend the better part of each school day wreaking havoc with a handcrafted peashooter and an arsenal of stink bombs, but the merest hint of a maternal buss is enough to kill his appetite for herring scraps or fried finch gizzards. With the domestic world handed him on a silver fish platter by doting parents, he has the *chutzpah* to be in a perpetual rage. Part of Ungerer's charm in this forty-page tantrum is his instinctive grasp of the anger of impotence that grips all small children during large chunks of their early lives. It is a rage directed at the limitations of childhood itself.

In Piper's case, there are also several legitimate gripes. He is, first of all, locked in mortal combat with a mother, Velvet Paw, who persists – despite all evidence to the contrary – in labeling him "little sugar tiger," "honey pie" and "my sweet little nestling." (Some nestling! There have probably been cuddlier vipers.) No sooner does this aggressively affectionate feline bend down to "wedge" the tale's first kiss in her sleeping son's ear, than he is off and running from her relentlessly ready lips. Aside from his dreams, about the only place he can find temporary sanctuary is behind the latched bathroom door. Here "Mother Snoop" doesn't know that he rubs his toothbrush along the edge of the sink instead of his teeth, and that he even relaxes a bit (while on the pot) by leafing through the soggy comic books he has squirreled away behind the tub.

Among Ungerer's endearing qualities are a total candor and lack of condescension. The adults in his tales treat children with loving kindness and respect no oftener than they do in life. Miss Clot, the nurse at Piper's school, for example, "prefers iodine to Mercurochrome" and sews the kitten's torn ear with "the biggest needle she can find." On the other hand, Ungerer is no romantic concerning the sweet innocence of the young. "My God, children are little bastards who chew and eat you up as they grow," he has said. "They start with the kneecaps, maybe, and slowly they devour you." Unlike Maurice Sendak, who tenderly probes the innermost fantasies of childhood, or Edward Gorey, who limns, with Arctic detachment, the horrors of being small and at the mercy of the world's unreason, Ungerer sees himself chiefly as a chronicler of the absurd. "Our world, our children, our aspirations are all absurd," he says flatly. Yet, beyond its absurdly exaggerated catalogue of childhood misconduct, *No Kiss for Mother* strikes, with therapeutic clout, at the very heart of family relationships.

The world Ungerer creates for children is one furnished for his own aesthetic and intellectual comfort. It is, in fact, here furnished out of his own childhood experience. Velvet Paw, the sugar–coated villain of the work, bears an unmistakable resemblance to the typical martyred 1930s mother – not entirely surprising from an author who was himself a '30s child and remembers that, from the age of six, he could not abide any open display of maternal affection. Ungerer's twelve–year–old daughter, Phoebe, confirms that *grandmaman* Ungerer remained a veritable "kissing fiend." The author insists, however, that the model for Piper's intransigence was not so much himself as an impossibly stubborn Burmese cat he once owned named Piper.

Perhaps because English is not Ungerer's native language, he prides himself on what he calls his "weird mastery" of it. "I really work at my prose style," he confesses. Oddball words like "tilbury" and "blunderbuss" delight him as collector's items to be woven into his tales. (The two mentioned appeared in *The Hat* and *The Three Robbers*, respectively.) Ungerer feels strongly that children enjoy unfamiliar words and euphonious, mystifying phrases. He looks upon *No Kiss* as the first of his books in which "the specificity lies more in the words than the pictures. It is a kind of *Portnoy's Complaint* of children's books."

Graphically even more than verbally, Ungerer's picture books seem always to breathe beyond the strict requirements of plot. Though the black and white pencil drawings for *No Kiss* are as simple and direct as a comic strip's – considerably less burdened with private symbols than many an Ungerer work – they are nonetheless full of the sort of particulars that invest storybook events with their own internal life. The undershorts Piper wears, for example, bear a recognizable Purina Cat

Chow design. And in the book's climactic scene, where Velvet Paw finally hauls off and socks her wayward sprout, Ungerer has placed in the background a middle-aged, pipe-smoking cat passerby whose obvious pleasure in witnessing this domestic debacle invests it with near palpable credibility.

On occasion, an Ungerer detail will disturb the adult. There was, for example, the by-now notorious hobo in *The Beast of Monsieur Racine* who carried in his pack a mysterious extra foot, dripping blood. To the artist, however, the explanation is innocuously clear. "A hobo does a lot of walking. He needs a spare foot for when one of his own gets tired and bruised."

Ungerer has long been something of an *enfant terrible* among children's book authors, one curiously immune to the usual desire either to improve or instruct the young. Because his best work has been almost equally divided among political or advertising posters, cartoons of both mildly and grossly pornographic content, and children's books, the question inevitably arises: What does so sophisticated and jaded a sensibility have to say to small children? Ungerer, who enjoys shocking his friends and critics alike, shrugs, noting: "If people weren't interested in fucking, they wouldn't have children and we wouldn't need children's books." Putting it less baldly, the artist accuses his American critics of never having fully appreciated the seriousness – or unity – of his work.

In Vienna in 1973, by contrast, the Museum of Modern Art accorded him a major retrospective –"including my erotic art, my posters, and my children's books," he says with pride. Certainly, whether he illustrates for adults or children, a limited repertoire of psychic preoccupations has always determined his graphic vocabulary. Dripping spigots, noses and watering cans, as well as sharp axes, knives and assorted pointed instruments have almost become Ungerer trademarks: what he calls "my favorite cooking pots." The same meat grinder in which mice and rats are "processed" in *No Kiss* made an earlier appearance as a visual metaphor in a work for grown-ups, *The Underground Sketchbook*

(1964). There, the drawing of a man and woman embracing reveals only the couple's upper torsos. They are standing in a meat grinder which conceals the remainder of their bodies. And if Ungerer's work for children at times contains overly sophisticated embellishments – the bathroom in which Piper sits has a douche bag hanging above the tub – there are also times when his pornographic drawings partake of a childlike innocence. In *The Underground Sketchbook*, too, can be found a clear spiritual antecedent for poor Piper Paw's dilemma in *No Kiss*: a larger–than–life mother marching briskly with a recalcitrant child in tow; the hand by which she grasps him is a sizable red lobster claw.

An Alsatian, Jean Thomas Ungerer was born in Strasbourg, France, in 1931. His father, head of a family factory that made church clocks and chimes, died when the artist was three. Ungerer grew up in a household that included his mother, two much older sisters and a brother. "My sisters taught me to draw, my brother taught me to think, and my mother taught me to use my imagination," he says in retrospect. Other early influences included the German painters Matthias Grünewald, Albrecht Dürer and Martin Schongauer, as well as two turn–of–the–century Alsatian illustrators, Hansi and Schnugg. His children's books, decidedly European in ambience from the outset, have frequently exhibited a kind of schizophrenia, seesawing between lighthearted Gallic charm and lugubrious Teutonic humor. (From the time Ungerer was eight until he was fourteen, Alsace was Nazi–occupied, and the artist received a largely German education.) There is little question that the Germanic side has been gaining the upper hand lately.

Like many other young Europeans at the close of World War II, Ungerer developed an exaggerated admiration for all things American and came to the United States in 1956. His first children's book, *The Mellops Go Flying* – about a gentle, ingenious and decidedly French family of pigs – was done for Ursula Nordstrom at Harper & Row the following year. Other early books – *Crictor* (1958), about a snake sent from Africa as a herpetologist's birthday gift to his aged mother, and *Adelaide* (1959), concerning a young flying kangaroo who leaves home to seek her fortune – are equally Gallic and sanguine in outlook. But by 1967, a darker strain crept into his juvenile work. The United States was deeply involved in Vietnam, and Ungerer began turning out vehement antiwar posters that eventually found a worldwide adult audience. One of his two children's picture books of that year, *Zeralda's Ogre*, was about a lonely monster with a big nose, sharp teeth, bristling beard, and bad temper, who liked best "of all things … little children for breakfast." Parents were forced to hide their progeny in the cellar when this brute was on one of his rampages, much as the Ungerer family, in real life, had hidden in their cellar during the closing months of World War II when the Allied Front reached Colmar, where they were then living. Of this period Ungerer has said: "There was plenty to see and remember, and my taste for the macabre certainly finds its roots there." The artist is, in fact, presently working on a book about war for older children, based on his own experiences as a teenager.

The misanthropic *Moon Man*, which took first prize in *Book World's* Children's Spring Book Festival, also appeared in 1967. The man in the moon, to satisfy his curiosity (a motivating force for many an Ungerer hero – including Piper Paw), travels to earth, where he soon realizes that "he could never live peacefully." He takes a rocket ship back home "and remained ever after curled up in his shimmering seat in space." This work could be read as prophetic of Ungerer's future. Troubled by what he felt was the increasingly totalitarian bent of this country, the artist abandoned the United States in 1971, moving with his wife, Yvonne, to a farm on a remote peninsula in Nova Scotia. Gradually he gave up advertising and poster work to devote himself primarily to producing large black and white lithographs on erotic themes (which he exhibits only in Europe) and two or three children's books a year.

Ungerer considers that his first serious juvenile work was *The Beast of Monsieur Racine* (1971). It is the story of a retired tax collector, contentedly cultivating prize pears in his own backyard (Ungerer raises sheep, geese, goats and rabbits in Canada) until the day he discovers that his precious fruit is being pilfered by a unique and amorphous

Tomi Ungerer
No Kiss for Mother

beast. Eventually, he learns that the strange predator is animated by a boy and girl secreted deep inside its skin of old blankets, a denouement that leaves many a young reader mildly disappointed. Philosophically, however, *Monsieur Racine* was a turning point in the artist's career. Its clear message – possibly as much for Ungerer as his audience – is that no one escapes the child lurking beneath the surface, so it behooves us to be on friendly terms with that hidden, motivating force. Significantly, *Monsieur Racine* (1971) was the first of his children's books Ungerer felt was good enough to dedicate to Maurice Sendak.

Another work of the same period, *I Am Papa Snap and These Are My Favorite No Such Stories*, reflected his exuberance at having broken ties with New York, at bidding good–bye to "cocktail parties, awards, creepland, publicity, etc." Toward the end of this giddy collection of one- and two–page nonsense tales, the artist portrays a character who may well represent his own ideal: "Every day, rain, shine, or overcast, he walks down to the shore. He sits on a rock to read or dream. He has no friends, no enemies. He lives in peace. No one knows anything about him. Not even his name."

Atlantic Monthly
January 1974

THIRTEEN

Odes to Two Craftsmen

EZRA JACK KEATS (1916 – 1983)

> *... weave for us a garment of brightness;*
>   *May the warp be the white light of morning,*
>   *May the weft be the red light of evening,*
>   *May the fringes be the falling rain,*
>   *May the border be the standing rainbow.*
>   *Thus weave for us a garment of brightness ...*
>
> Native American invocation

H E WOVE FOR US ALL a garment of brightness: his vibrant, full-color vision of child life in the inner city at midtwentieth century. Although Jack was a romantic, his was not a prettified picture; after all, he grew up in an urban ghetto and knew what it was to be cut off from the creature comforts and amenities of mainstream middle-class American life. Yet Jack's illustrations are beautiful because his painter's eye saw in the crumbling plaster of tenement hallways, in the graffiti scars on faded brick walls, and in the vestigial wooden doors of demolished brownstones and gutted apartment houses the bits and pieces of the rich urban ferment that can nurture the young and hopeful as well as grind down the old and defeated.

The last time I saw Jack was at a special storytelling session in the Donnell Branch of The New York Public Library in April 1983. He was not hard to spot across a crowded room. On first impression, he looked like the villain in a turn–of–the–century melodrama with his full mustache and straight jet–black hair that had a way of refusing to stay where the comb had directed it. The audience was mostly adult that evening: children's librarians, book editors, writers and illustrators – all assembled to hear that quintessential spinner of tales, Augusta Baker, retired coordinator of children's services at The New York Public Library, up from Columbia, South Carolina, on one of her infrequent visits to the big city. "Gussie" was Jack's longtime friend. He dedicated *A Letter to Amy* to her, and the joyous hand–puppet that captivates the young hero of *Louie* is aptly named Gussie. Jack looked bone–tired – sick – and we spoke only briefly about the original art for all his children's books and about his continuing search for a college library or a museum where it might be housed, cared for, and made accessible to interested viewers. Two weeks later, he was dead of a heart attack at the age of sixty–seven. (The University of Southern Mississippi is now the custodian of all Keats' children's book art.)

Almost exactly twenty years earlier, *The Snowy Day*, "the first book that was really my own," had won Jack the 1963 Caldecott Medal. Although his award preceded Maurice Sendak's for *Where the Wild Things Are* by only one year, Jack was some ten years older than most of his colleagues who gained fame in children's picture books during those golden postwar decades – the '50s and '60s. Born in 1916, he grew up in a tough, working class neighborhood of Brooklyn. He drew pictures from the age of four on and had been a muralist for the WPA and a camouflage artist for the Army Air Force during World War II – experiences that left their mark on his unique children's book illustrations.

Primarily, Jack was a painter. He saw and thought like a painter – in terms of form and composition more than of specific action to be depicted or narrative flow to be helped along. Those first books that he illustrated conventionally for other authors during the mid–1950s and early 1960s contained competent, occasionally even highly accomplished work; for example, pictures for Lucretia P. Hale's *The Peterkin Papers* and for Millicent Selsam's *How to Be a Nature Detective*. But this

Ezra Jack Keats
The Snowy Day

work wasn't memorable. It was not until Jack found his own personal graphic voice – at the outset, an amalgam of painting and pasting: blocks of bold color combined with jaunty areas of collage and, later, a rich impasto of creamy acrylic paints – that his special qualities as a picture-book artist revealed themselves.

Read aloud one of Dr. Seuss's books, and you have a child listener on tenterhooks wondering what will happen next. Turn to a Keats tale, and reader and hearer alike are quickly caught up in the look and feel of a particular city locale at a particular moment in time. *The Snowy Day* was the first full-color picture book to feature a small black hero. But Peter wasn't black in order to make a plea for tolerance or social justice. He just happened to be a small black boy making the most of a familiar childhood experience – the first snowstorm of winter. So absorbed is the viewer in the typical yet magical encounters Peter has with the newly fallen snow that the protagonist's color is noted merely in passing. It is irrelevant to the life experience being recounted.

Keats recalled in his Caldecott Medal acceptance speech: "Long before I ever thought of doing children's books, while looking through a magazine, I came upon four candid photos of a little boy about three or four years old. His expressive face, his body attitudes, the very way he wore his clothes, totally captivated me." Jack cut the pictures out and saved them. After the book was finished, he discovered that the photographs had come from a 1940 issue of *Life* magazine. Knowing Keats's keen pictorial sense, one can well imagine the magnetic appeal of a small black boy's face against the stark white of fresh snow.

To make his picture-book snow, Keats – using a toothbrush – splattered white India ink on his drawings, the better to communicate the joy and excitement of the occasion. He brought to children's book illustration a new graphic exuberance and painterly élan, in large part because he came, a voluntary émigré, from the wider world of contemporary painting. Certainly Jack turned that specialized technique – collage – into a popular art form practiced knowingly even by pre-kindergartners. One senses, too, that Jack learned more from the school of Abstract Expressionism that came into its own in post–World War II America than he ever did from his fellow picture-book illustrators. More and more, as his career progressed, Jack applied paint joyfully, masterfully – for the sheer sensual pleasure of it. He was the Jackson Pollock and Willem de Kooning of American children's picture books.

"Jack cared desperately about his artwork and about his vocation as a children's book author–illustrator," says his long-time editor at Macmillan and Greenwillow, Susan Carr Hirschman. She recalls that once, when he had mislaid the address of a child who had written to ask a question about one of his books, Jack ran an advertisement in *The Horn Book*, hoping to locate his lost young correspondent. Known for his unswerving loyalty to editors and friends, he stuck by his characters as well. Many of the twenty–two books he both wrote and illustrated were about *The Snowy Day*'s Peter, his family, his friends and their friends. Peter is the central character in *Whistle for Willie*, *Peter's Chair*, *A Letter to Amy* and *Goggles!* Through them all, like any small boy, Peter grows. By the time we meet him again in *Hi, Cat!* he is, to our surprise, a teenager and no longer at center stage. His sister Susy's generation has taken over. And it says something about Jack's sensitivity to the changing realities of urban life that his most recent young hero, *Louie*, the chum of Peter's younger sister, is painfully introverted, artistic and white.

To look through any one of Keats's picture books is a gourmet feast for the receptive eye. His endpapers comprise a kind of color tone poem to life in the metropolis. They run from an awesome lightning bolt in a gray summer sky to a lovingly rendered semi–abstract composition of orphaned wooden doors lined up to shield an excavation site; from rubbish cans with their random overflow of urban jetsam to child–scrawled stick figures along makeshift city fences. Often his endpaper images – and even images within the stories – repeat themselves from book to book; but like Matisse's reclining nudes or Picasso's harlequins, they differ with each appearance – in mood, execution and even pictorial intent.

Jack's texts are always handmaidens to his pictures. In no way are the two separate but equal, although they are definitely inseparable. There are picture books that we can readily imagine being illustrated by any one of a number of gifted artists. Ezra Jack Keats's are not among them. It is impossible to visualize one of his scripts without his own pictorial accompaniment. None of his best works are stories in the conventional sense; rather, they are mood pieces – paeans to growing up in a big city. If the overall atmosphere is vaguely melancholy – elegiac – there are grace notes of joy and hope: an electric squiggle of French blue on the hero's shirt, the glowing vermilion on his oversized cap, a passage of heartbreakingly mellow magenta, a backdrop of luscious blue–green.

His brush lingered lovingly over the faded beauty of worn and discarded objects – the pattern of roses on a tattered mattress, the dents in a battered old rubbish bin. Like the steady rain that falls in *Apt. 3* "softening the sounds of the city," his pictures manage miraculously to mute the ugliness and brutality of modern urban living. They bear concrete evidence that "beauty is in the eye of the beholder." Newly washed laundry flaps as festively as regatta pennants atop his tenement houses. Keats wrung poetry from peeling paint and drab asphalt. He once explained the genesis of his stories to an interviewer: "I have an image of certain things happening – more of a visual image – and then I hear the characters talking to each other, and the story grows in counterpoint. Sometimes my emphasis is on the pictures and sometimes on the story. The pictures do pace the book, however. . . . I hang my illustrations on my studio wall in a row so that I can see them flow and move in sequence, like a ballet. I guess I'm the choreographer."

Certainly it is easy to imagine a musical accompaniment – in a minor key, like mellow jazz or certain blues themes – for Keats's books. Leonard Bernstein's *Slaughter on Tenth Avenue* would have handsomely matched several of Keats's impressionistic librettos.

During a career that spanned almost thirty years and produced illustrations for thirty-three books, Jack was no stranger to honors and accolades. His work was translated into sixteen languages. A film version of *The Snowy Day* received a Venice Film Festival Award. In 1967 the movie adaptation of *Whistle for Willie* won Keats a personal invitation from the Empress of Iran to be her guest at the second Teheran International Festival of Films for Children. A decade later, the film *Apt. 3* took a Gold Venus Medallion at the Virgin Islands International Film Festival. And Jack's illustrations were selected on five separate occasions for UNICEF greeting cards. As for the books themselves, *Goggles!* was a 1970 Caldecott Honor Book and, the same year, *Hi, Cat!* won the Boston Globe–Horn Book Award for illustration. In 1973 Keats received the Brooklyn Museum's Art Books for Children citation; and in 1980 the University of Southern Mississippi awarded him its annual silver medallion for "an outstanding contribution to the field of children's literature."

Nothing, however, ever gave Jack more pleasure than the news, in 1974, that a roller-skating rink in Tokyo was being named in his honor, loving tribute not only to his popularity in Japan but to the runaway success of the Japanese translation of *Skates!* Certainly Jack was proud and happy when the Warrensville (Ohio) Community Library renamed its children's room for him in 1973; he would have been equally proud could he have known that the library proclaimed May 24, 1984, its first annual Ezra Jack Keats Day.

There can be no more fitting epitaph for this major picture book artist than the one he wrote – unwittingly – in *Apt. 3*, the work of the '70s that was his own favorite, according to Susan Hirschman. Like the blind man he describes, whose harmonica plays the secrets of the tenement in which he lives, Keats achieved similar effects with his paintbrush:

> He played purples and grays and rain
> and smoke and the sounds of night.
> Sam sat quietly and listened.
> He felt that all the sights and sounds
> and colors from outside had come

into the room and were floating around.
He floated with them.

Jack's readers and viewers, too, floated with him through the sights and sounds of the metropolis he knew and loved. Ezra Jack Keats expanded immeasurably our vision of what a picture book for children could be.

MARGOT ZEMACH (1931–1989)

> *I love so much seeing,*
> *I live with my eyes.*
> Oskar Kokoschka

The quotation above was selected by Margot Zemach as the leit-motif of her picture autobiography, *Self-Portrait: Margot Zemach* (Addison). Surely her joyful love of seeing is proclaimed by every quirky, energetic drawing in every tale she ever illustrated.

It was a career with no obvious apprenticeship. The first folk tale she both wrote and illustrated, *The Three Sillies* (Holt), revealed an artist thoroughly at home between book covers. She used the white page comfortably: it was the air her characters breathed. The artist could show us upstairs and downstairs, indoors and out, in a single, uncluttered picture. Her protagonists were in constant, purposeful motion, and the narrative pacing of her illustration never flagged. Here was a born picture book artist. The early titles were mostly limited in color, but Zemach could do more with a palette of brown and orange (or Mercurochrome red) in combination with black line than anyone before or since. *Nail Soup* (Follett) and *The Speckled Hen* (Holt) bear testimony to this fact.

Collaborations with her husband, Harve, as storyteller dominated the first half of her career, between 1958 and 1974. Rollicking comedies, flawlessly staged, these picture book soufflés were brimful of verbal and graphic high spirits. If the books lacked the resonance we came to expect and take for granted in the artist's later work, they did leave us smiling and eager for the next performance.

Yet, as early as *Mommy, Buy Me a China Doll* (Farrar), a more substantial Margot Zemach was beginning to be in evidence. Her rich, earthy, page-sized paintings for that Ozark ditty gave promise of graphic lodes as yet untapped. Certainly her first collaborations with Isaac Bashevis Singer were crucial in the tempering of her talent by a deeper reflection on words. Her pictures for *Mazel and Shlimazel* (Farrar) were in perfect harmony with Singer's story – expanding our sympathy for the featured players and their Old World, East-European milieu, yet displaying an unfamiliar graphic reticence, a willed and willing subordination of illustrations to the force of Singer's telling. *When Shlemiel Went to Warsaw* (Farrar) presented a different challenge. In her powerful black-and-white drawings for this collection of Singer tales, Zemach so evoked the look and spirit of *shtetl* life in that vanished Jewish world that her pictures take on the dimensions of historical documentation. Her rapport with the characters is touching.

Going abroad to live with her family in the late '60s added yet another ingredient to Zemach's art, a firsthand and more-than-superficial appreciation of other cultures and customs. The Zemachs lived briefly in Italy and Denmark, but they lost their hearts to England. Their Caldecott-Medal-winning *Duffy and the Devil* (Farrar) was no happy accident. It had the color and flavor, the authentic furnishings and costumes of England. Her Rowlandsonesque Squire Lovel and the "'gashly girl'" Duffy are indubitably coins of the realm. Zemach's wondrous watercolors are as limpid and pure as those of Beatrix Potter or Randolph Caldecott. Never was the medal that carried his name more deservedly bestowed.

Beyond Zemach's prodigious gifts as draftsman and colorist, beyond an irrepressible comedic spirit that was both hearty and healthy, she developed an exquisitely empathetic intelligence. It enabled her to make the stories she illustrated uniquely hers before ever setting pencil or pen to paper.

Zemach's mother and stepfather had been in the theater – her mother was an actress, her stepfather, Benjamin Zemach, a dancer and choreographer. Surely this environmental influence was relevant. As the artist wrote in her autobiography, "I can create my own theater and be in charge of everything. When there is a story I want to tell in pictures, I find my actors, build the sets, design the costumes and light the stage.... If I can get it all together and moving, it will come to life. The actors will work with each other, and the dancers will hear the music and dance. When the book closes, the curtain comes down."

Like any director worth her salt, Zemach always brought a highly personal vision to the work at hand. The modest English folk tale *The Three Wishes* (Farrar) reveals the subtlety of her interpretive gift. A poor woodcutter and his wife are granted three wishes by a grateful imp whom the husband has liberated from a fallen tree. The couple waste this invaluable gift with heedless chatter. First, the husband, deep in thought as to what to ask for, idly wishes for a plate of sausages to assuage his growing hunger. Appalled at this needless squandering of a wish, the wife so berates him that he angrily wishes the remainder of the sausages be attached to the end of her nose. Of course, there is nothing left to do but wish the mindless mischief undone, and the tale is told. Though comedy was Zemach's forte, she did not play the tale for its obvious laughs; nor did she take the easy route of making sport of the foolish protagonists. Instead, her pictures underscore the bonds of love and caring that unite the poor, hard-working pair. The couple's hands touch; their eyes make contact as they huddle together before the warm fire in their neat, well-tended cottage. One feels the pangs of the husband's hunger and his even greater discomfort upon having his thoughtless first wish fulfilled. Rather than making light of the hapless pair, Zemach renders us so sympathetic to the couple's plight that we feel, with them, first the enormity of their loss, following two wasted wishes, and then the wonder of their triumph when, with the third wish, they are simply able to restore things to what they were. We finish the tale realizing that love is a miracle greater than the magic they have forfeited. It is a graphic *tour de force* of no mean proportions. Zemach's greatest talent lay in reading every text anew, as if her life depended on it. That rarest gift of all – freshness of vision – was the richest source of Zemach's art.

Earlier, Zemach had achieved a comparable *sotto voce* success in her rendition of *The Little Red Hen* (Farrar), that old saw about the industrious fowl who finds a few grains of wheat and – without an iota of help or encouragement from three lazy barnyard friends – plants that wheat, harvests it, threshes it, takes it to the mill to be ground into flour and, at long last, bakes it for eating. In Zemach's version the enterprising hen is transformed from an insufferably smug goody-goody into an admirable, doting mother – just by the artist's providing her heroine with a winning brood of five plump chicks. This injected detail gives Zemach's hen a nobility of purpose rather than an edge of spite. When she announces, at tale's end, the fate of her mouth-watering bread, "I'm going to eat it myself," Zemach's final picture shows the loaf being consumed by the heroine and her quintet of appreciative chicks. Instead of the harsh message, "No work, no reward," we are left with a warming admiration for maternal tenderness and care.

One cannot help but read in an autobiographical concomitant. Zemach knew better than most about the unsung virtues of maternal caring. When Harve died suddenly in London in 1974, Margot was left with four young daughters to bring up. As she wrote in her autobiography, "Besides being a mother every day, I am working on books because it is my job. It not only buys us shoes and toothpaste but is a real privilege and a pleasure."

There is no question that Zemach's talent deepened and took on a bittersweet edge following Harve's death. "Goodbye to my best friend, the end of talking and being parents together," was the way Zemach put it in the autobiography. Her late career was filled with successful interpretations of tales from Grimm and other traditional sources, with small domestic comedies like *To Hilda for Helping* (Farrar) and with one

The Three Wishes
illustration by Margot Zemach

of the most beautiful and deeply felt of her books, *Jake and Honeybunch Go to Heaven* (Farrar). Steeped in authentic Black–American folklore, the tale was lovingly told and dazzlingly painted in the richest colors of Zemach's long career. Its 1930s Depression setting – the era in which Zemach herself grew up – was tenderly and evocatively recreated. Nonetheless, the work became embroiled in racial issues and sensitivities remote from the picture book world, and its mixed reception upset Zemach far more lastingly than the book disturbed its detractors.

Sadly, the curtain has fallen with unexpected suddenness on Margot Zemach's exemplary career, one carried on gallantly and with deserved honors while she lived a life beset by more than its fair share of family and personal tragedy. She died in 1989, at fifty–seven, of Lou Gehrig's disease. Her legacy of luminous graphic interpretations of her own and others' tales is likely to last as long as picture books continue to entertain small children, and to enrich the lives of young and old alike. Those of us long familiar with her work will cherish our own favorite stories and images. Mine include the vision of the Squire in *Duffy and the Devil* caught in all his naked amplitude out on the Cornish Moors, also the great comatose lummox of a dog named Rover who just "won't bark" in *Hush, Little Baby* (Dutton), and the rascally brother in *A Penny a Look* (Farrar), a long–stemmed rose impossibly sprouting from the lapel of his cutaway coat. But most haunting of all is the lyrical double–page image from *Jake and Honeybunch*: Jake standing on "the Moon Regulator wagon" all loaded with stars, about to roll the full moon across the night sky. Pure magic.

Margot Zemach brought a vitality and glory to the contemporary picture book. Her antic spirit is sorely missed.

Ursula Nordstrom
illustration by Maurice Sendak
from *Dear Genius*

FOURTEEN

Some Editor: Ursula Nordstrom

To those working in the world of children's book publishing during the 1960s and '70s, the unquestioned star among its top editors was Ursula Nordstrom, Director of Harper's Department of Junior Books from 1940 until her retirement in 1973. *Dear Genius: The Letters of Ursula Nordstrom*, collected, edited and provided with a great number of helpful footnotes by the critic and biographer Leonard Marcus, offers compelling evidence of how and why this esteem was richly earned.

These well chosen, often moving selections from Nordstrom's professional correspondence (some 300 letters out of thousands perused by Marcus) were all typed by the great lady herself during spontaneous moments of cajolement, cheerleading, critical acuity, empathy, enthusiasm, euphoria, insight and, on rare occasions, discouragement or indignation. Their generosity of spirit (as well as of editorial tone), their humor and sound judgment can only enhance a reputation already bordering on legend.

As ducks take to water, so Nordstrom embraced the medium of the informal letter to express her uncensored responses to a manuscript, to art work, to a new idea, to an author's or librarian's complaint. Sometimes the briefest of notes, at other times three or four pages dashed off in the white heat of inspiration, her missives are not the work of a careful craftsman or epistolary stylist. There are often words repeated, misspellings and lapses into cliché (which she unfailingly notices and passes off with an embarrassed aside: e.g., "You should forgive the originality of my prose style.") The content, however is always heartfelt and makes for rapt reading. She had that rare gift of making each of her correspondents feel like the most important person in the world.

From the beginning of her career, Nordstrom understood that talent (aka genius) was a commodity like no other, one that would repay whatever tender nurturing and respect she could offer. To UN, as she was known to all at Harper, there was nothing sadder than a gift unfulfilled. She viewed family life as a decided impediment to creativity and confided to one author in 1965: "Any children or indeed any relatives – husbands, mothers, fathers, brothers, sisters, who are connected in any way with 'my' authors – are MY ENEMIES." Three years later, she exhorted Mary Rodgers: "Bless you, dear author, take care of your health, forget children and husband ... and WORK ON THIS MANUSCRIPT." To the picture–book writer Ruth Krauss, she confessed: "As I tried to say last Thursday, I honestly have such a real reverence for creative talent that I am willing to do anything for anyone who possesses it."

Among the countless beneficiaries of her editorial bounty were the author–artists Maurice Sendak and John Steptoe. Nordstrom discovered the 22–year–old Sendak working in the window–display department at F. A. O. Schwarz. After leafing through his sketchbook, she promptly offered a first assignment: the drawings for Marcel Aymé's *The Wonderful Farm* (1951). Their relationship blossomed, and she guided his career like a doting parent. In a birthday greeting of 1955, Nordstrom wrote: "As I have said to you other years, I am very glad you got born." Planning to meet her young protégé at a regional meeting of librarians in Swampscott, Massachusetts, one autumn, she cautioned: "Bring a sweater as the hotel is right on the ocean and it may be coldish to walk by the sea."

When the artist had completed *Where the Wild Things Are* (1963), the first full-color picture book that he both wrote and illustrated, Nord-strom exulted: "It is MOST MAGNIFICENT, and we're so proud to have it on our list. When you were much younger, I remember I used to write you letters when the books were finished and thank you for 'another beautiful job' – or some such dopiness. Now you're rich and famous and need no words of wonder from me. But I must send them, anyhow ... your beautiful book is exhilirating [sic] and it reminds me that I love creative people and love to publish books for creative chil-dren." Later, when she was about to retire, Nordstrom confided: "I know how privileged I am to hear about what is going on in your head. It has been and is the greatest happiness of my professional life."

With the gifted African-American artist, John Steptoe, her relation-ship was more rocky, and the letters to him are the most poignant in the collection. Steptoe was still in high school when Nordstrom first saw his paintings and urged him to paint and write about growing up in Harlem. After their first encounter, she wrote to him: "Never forget that what you told me is something ONLY YOU know about; noone else knows just what you know about anything. And that's why it will be so important for you to put down your thoughts and emotions." When, four months later, Steptoe brought her a handwritten manu-script, Nordstrom herself typed the draft and mailed a copy to the artist. Ever so gently, she suggested that he "see if there are not places where you would like to tell a little more.... Once again, John, I am not interested in any single thing but what is IN YOUR HEAD.... I have the greatest respect for you as an artist, young as you are. I know you know what you want to do and all I want to do is recognize it when you have done it...." *Stevie*, the first children's picture book writ-ten in non-standard English, was published to wide acclaim in 1969 when Steptoe was only eighteen. Two other books followed, but Step-toe, uncertain of his direction and uncomfortable in the genteel, downtown world of publishing, began pointedly to ignore Nord-strom's efforts to reach him. Finally, out of frustration, Nordstrom wrote to Steptoe's mother late in 1970: "He is a perfectly wonderful person. I think he is very cynical about me, I can't help being white, and I suppose he can't help not liking me. But I truly love him. I love his talent, but I love him as a person, too."

Not all Nordstrom's letters were to star performers on the Harper list. To the author of a first picture book who was having great difficulty with a second manuscript, Nordstrom enthused: "You are a terrific person, with vitality and creative energy and there isn't the slightest chance in the whole world that you are not going to write many many many wonderful books. So try to get through this frustrating time without becoming discouraged. I can absolutely promise you that you will do your next book sooner rather than later and that it will be good."

To a Harper salesman who was hoping for a sequel to Ruth Krauss's *A Hole Is to Dig*, because it was selling so well, she scolded: "She doesn't do the same thing over and over again and if she ever starts she won't continue to be Ruth Krauss."

She could be droll as well, as in a reply to Edward Gorey's excuse for the non-delivery of a long-overdue manuscript: "Thanks for your card telling me you are having a nervous breakdown. Welcome to the club. I think you know that I have His and Her straitjackets hanging in my office. Come down and slip into one and we can have a good talk."

Some of her best letters, however, went to parents or librarians – those who had the responsibility of choosing books for children. When an irate school librarian announced that she had burned a copy of Sendak's *In the Night Kitchen* because of a frontal-nude illustration of its young hero Mickey, she mused: "Should not those of us who stand between the creative artist and the child be very careful not to sift our reactions to such books through our own adult prejudices and neuroses? To me as an editor and publisher of books for children, that is one of my greatest and most difficult duties. . . . I think young children will always react with delight to such a book as *In the Night Kitchen*, and that they will react creatively and wholesomely. It is only adults who ever feel threatened by Sendak's work."

Among many controversial and pioneering books that Nordstrom published and staunchly defended were the first teen-age novel to deal openly with a homosexual encounter and a first picture book that championed a small hero who likes to play with dolls.

Though she occasionally referred to her division at Harper as "the Tot Dept." or "kiddie boox," she had no patience with those who condescended to children or to those who wrote and illustrated their books. To Isaac Bashevis Singer, who was collaborating with Maurice Sendak on *Zlateh the Goat and Other Stories*, she wrote: "You've wondered why Sendak didn't do adult books. And once you asked me if I wouldn't rather be an editor of adult books. But most adults are dead and beyond hope after the age of thirty, and I think with *Zlateh* you will find a new and marvelous audience." To Louise Fitzhugh, the author of *Harriet the Spy*, she once exclaimed, "Thank God for anyone under twelve years of age."

During her later years at Harper, Nordstrom worried about the future of picture books. Production costs of full-color printing had risen drastically, and juvenile publishing was becoming far more competitive. The role of the marketing director was beginning to rival that of the editorial director. That once leisurely climate in which new talent could be nurtured, even cossetted, was no longer there. Nordstrom wrote wistfully to an old friend and author, "I'm glad I had the chance to take chances when to do a picture book in color didn't cost a fortune."

On the day – February 16, 1973 – that she retired, Nordstrom found time to reply to a child upset by the sad ending of E. B. White's *Charlotte's Web* (the death of its spider heroine): "Your letter about Charlotte's death has come to me because I published the book, *Charlotte's Web*. When I read the manuscript I felt exactly the way you now feel. I didn't want Charlotte to die, and I too cried over her death. What I think you and I both should keep in mind is that Charlotte had a good and worthwhile life. ... And something to be glad about is that she had all those children. I think the author knows that in due course a spider such as Charlotte does die, but her children live, and so will her children's children."

Ursula Nordstrom died in 1988, but her children – like Charlotte's – live on: books like *A Hole Is to Dig*, *Goodnight Moon*, *Harriet the Spy*, *Harold and the Purple Crayon*, *Little Bear* and *Stuart Little*. As Charlotte herself might have put it, "SOME EDITOR!"

FIFTEEN

E. B. White and Read All Over

Like many a veteran devotee of *The New Yorker*, I had my ear for the felicities of language honed on E. B. White's beautifully wrought "Talk of the Town" items and the earthbound sagacity of his welcome "Letter from the East." I'd rather have been White than President.

Elwyn Brooks White, the writer and subject of a hefty and ingratiating volume, *Letters of E. B. White*, was born in Mt. Vernon, New York, on July 11, 1899, the sixth and youngest child of comfortably middle-class parents. Though he lacked the miserable childhood deemed a prerequisite, in some quarters, for literary success, he never lacked – even as a small boy – that awareness of shadows ("the dark of the attic ... the sadness of afternoon") that lends resonance to word pictures. He was also, by his own admission, "lucky."

Certainly his luck was running strong in February 1925 when he bought a copy of the first issue of Harold Ross's *New Yorker* in Grand Central Station and was immediately attracted to the new magazine's seeming penchant for short items. As he later wrote his elder brother Stanley: "I discovered a long time ago that writing of the small things of the day, the trivial matters of the heart, the inconsequential but near things of this living, was the only kind of creative work which I could accomplish with any sincerity or grace.... Not till *The New Yorker* came along did I ever find any means of expressing these impertinences and irrelevancies." White was offered a part-time job with the magazine in 1927 and, either officially or as a wayward contributor, has been associated with it ever since.

This volume's opening letter, written at age nine to his eldest brother Albert at Cornell (where White would eventually go), reveals a precocious respect for the written word. Apologizing for his tardy reply to a communiqué from Albert, he explains, "I have been waiting for something to say." And it has been characteristic of his long career as essayist, poet, children's book author and epistolary champion of a free press never to rush into print, never to cry wolf and never to raise his light, pure voice in any cause that he did not firmly and fervently embrace.

White's literary output has seldom been written to tight deadline – in fact, he always took pains to keep this circumstance from ruling his work. Twice during his career, he cut even his loose bonds to *The New Yorker* to avoid such pressure. For five years, beginning in the late '30s, White provided a monthly, signed column, "One Man's Meat," for *Harper's* magazine. Trying to explain this defection to Ross, he wrote him that "a monthly department gives me about three weeks of off time, which I can devote to a sustained project like shingling a barn or sandpapering an old idea."

This juxtaposition of homely task with literary effort was never idly or coquettishly made. More and more, as White's life progressed, his rustic locutions were the hard-earned verbal dividends of a man in intimate relationship with farm life. Certainly his best children's book, *Charlotte's Web*, could never have been written, as Dorothy Lobrano Guth, the collector and editor of *Letters*, points out, "by anyone lacking an emotional involvement in the lives of domestic animals." This land/literature connection operated in reverse as well. The farm that White and his wife Katharine – also a lifetime *New Yorker* editor – bought in North Brooklin, Maine, during the '30s was paid for with earnings from steady typewriter toil.

The elements of White's mature style seem to have been in him from the beginning, that racy mixture of countrified colloquy and citified perception: "Spring dallies somewhere in the offing," he reports to his parents in 1922, "like a backward child asked to perform." One of his first published efforts as an adult was a sonnet to a bantam rooster.

"I am a dull man, personally," White confided in 1938 to his good friend James Thurber. "Nobody ever seeks me out, not even people who like me or approve of me; because after you have sought me out, you haven't got anything but a prose writer." But to what admirable extent "a prose writer" is made clear in this monumental patchwork of letters dispatched by Mr. White to family, friends and assorted well- and ill-wishers over a period of sixty-eight years, all lovingly collected and decorously annotated – only where absolutely necessary to the reader's understanding – by the subject's goddaughter, Mrs. Guth.

One of the greater delights *Letters* affords is discovering how all-of-a-piece White's entire life is – professional and personal, in correspondence with adult or child. Writing tenderly to colleague Frank Sullivan on learning of his sister's death, White adds an admonitory postscript to "establish firm emotional connections with a major-league ball club.... Without these simple marriages, none of us could survive." And to some sixth graders in Los Angeles who sent him their compositions, he answered, "I was pleased that so many of you felt the beauty and goodness of the world." By way of appreciation, he sent them "one of the most beautiful and miraculous things in the world" – an egg laid by his goose Felicity.

The letters are noteworthy as well for their revelation of White's unparalleled gift for keeping his life's priorities straight. Instinctively, he seemed to recognize threats to his own special and – as he clearly felt – fragile literary powers. At times he could be almost ruthless in attempting to guarantee ideal growing conditions for these talents. In the spring of 1927, he wrote to his wife in explanation of a plan to take a year off from all avoidable commitments: "A person afflicted with poetic longings of one sort or another searches for a kind of intellectual and spiritual privacy in which to indulge his strange excesses.... I intend ... merely to inform you of a new allegiance – to a routine of my own spirit rather than to a fixed household and office routine." To his great disappointment, that year off was never to produce the magnum opus he had hoped to write.

White's most sustained and enduring pieces of fiction, curiously enough, have turned out to be two of his three children's books, *Stuart Little* and *Charlotte's Web*. The first is a fantasy quest for ideal beauty and goodness, the second a celebration of life as it is, "the seasons, the goodness of the barn, the beauty of the world, the glory of everything." As with the body of his work, the writing for children did not come easily. *Stuart* was suggested by a dream he had in 1933 and, in a letter of 1938, he refers to the book as half–done. But in 1939, he wrote to his then–editor at Harper, Eugene Saxton, "I would rather wait a year than publish a bad children's book, as I have too much respect for children." The work finally came out in 1945.

To a mother who politely suggested that White provide a sequel to *Stuart Little*, he wrote: "There is no sequel.... A lot of children seem to want one but there isn't any. I think many readers find the end inconclusive but I have always found life inconclusive, and I guess it shows up in my work."

Charlotte's Web progressed faster. In March 1951, he wrote to Harper's Ursula Nordstrom: "I've recently finished another children's book, but have put it away for a while to ripen (let the body heat go out of it). It doesn't satisfy me the way it is." Within a year, a completely revamped *Charlotte* was ready for the printer.

E. B. White's odd failure to produce other major works may, in part, be explained by a confession to one of his correspondents: "Unlike you, I have no faith, only a suitcaseful of beliefs that sustain me. Life's meaning has always eluded me, and I guess it always will. But I love it just the same."

A profoundly sane and almost arrogantly modest writer, White is painfully aware that "the man–on–paper is always a more admirable character than his creator, who is a miserable creature of nose colds, minor compromises, and sudden flights into nobility." This knowledge may well account for White's lifelong disdain for prizes. Early in his career, he wrote his brother Stanley: "The rewards of such endeavor are not that I have acquired an audience as you suggest (fame of any kind being a Pyrrhic victory), but that sometimes in writing for myself – which is the only subject anyone knows intimately – I have occasionally had the exquisite thrill of putting my finger on a little capsule of truth, and heard it give the faint squeak of mortality under my pressure, an antic sound."

The *Letters* are an inspiring testament to one man's grace and humor in the face of life's absurdities, delights and cruel blows. Every so often, their clarity and tone are off-putting – almost as if the writer were chained to a public, *New Yorker* style. But the reverse is almost certainly true: that periodical has been permanently infected with the sound of his own voice.

Writing to his wife's aunt on the occasion of her ninetieth birthday, White gallantly noted, "You have given the kind of sober happiness that comes from knowing and loving a Lady of Quality." Keeping company with Mr. White through a lifetime of letters is full of that same joy – reading and respecting a literary Gentleman of Quality. But Mr. White perhaps said it best at the close of his *chef d'oeuvre, Charlotte's Web*: "It is not often that someone comes along who is a true friend and a good writer."

SIXTEEN

A Talk with Natalie Babbitt

IT WILL COME AS no surprise to her admirers that Natalie Babbitt's tenth book (her sixth novel), *Herbert Rowbarge* (1981), is as unlike *The Eyes of the Amaryllis* (1977), the ghostly tale of lost love that preceded it, as her exhilarating first novel, *The Search for Delicious* (1969), was radically different from its picture-book antecedent, the Edwardian rhymed farce, *Phoebe's Revolt* (1968).

Perhaps more than any other contemporary writer for children, Mrs. Babbitt gives pause to those who would fence off the realm of juvenile literature from the republic of adult *belles lettres*. Her work has risen in imaginative reach – and age level – as the three Babbitt children advanced from grade school through college. Her sons were ten and eight, her daughter six, when she wrote her first picture book, the tongue-in-cheek verse saga *Dick Foote and the Shark* (1967). Each new work offers more evidence of the originality, intelligence and high purpose that make her one of our most gifted writers for children.

To date, however, neither her distinctive narrative voice – instantly recognizable despite virtuoso alterations in pitch and mood from story to story – nor her subject matter has moved beyond the understanding of an interested older child. In all her books there is a sense of the tale's having been rendered pure, clarified to the starkness of fable. Yet the author herself has referred to *Herbert Rowbarge* as "a biographical novel for adults." And her publisher's designation, "Ages 14 and up," suggests a special work suited both to venerable children and venturesome grown-ups.

On a recent morning, Mrs. Babbitt pondered the anomalies of *Herbert Rowbarge*. She sat, smack center, on a contemporary couch in the living room of the 24th-floor New York apartment where she and her husband, Samuel Babbitt, have lived since 1979. He is a vice president with the Memorial Sloan–Kettering Cancer Center. In classic sweater and skirt, the author looked more like a denizen of the groves of academe than the occupant of a Manhattan aerie. This is hardly surprising: For more than a decade, she lived and sometimes taught in Clinton, New York, at Kirkland, an innovative women's college of which her husband was president. The author's speaking voice is mellow, on the deep side and unhesitant.

"*Herbert Rowbarge* was a long time in the working," she says. "I first had the idea for it about 10 years ago – that is, I saw how it would end. Generally I think of endings first. I get my bearings that way, then flesh things out – the setting, the characters. Plot is almost a last consideration.

"Eventually, other ingredients enter in. *Knee-Knock Rise* (1970) had something to do with the overwhelming sense of loss I experienced when my sister [two years her senior] told me there was no Santa Claus," she explains. *The Devil's Storybook* (1974) grew out of her determination to salvage a scene set in hell from a failed novel. *Tuck Everlasting* (1975) was written for her daughter Lucy who at eleven had a great fear of death. "Actually," the author says, "I don't think of *Tuck* as being about death. The tale is concerned with life – its finiteness, what this means and whether or not, ultimately, it is preferable to immortality."

Similarly, though *Herbert Rowbarge* is the story of an identical twin separated from his sibling and unaware of his existence, Mrs. Babbitt's interest was not in twinship. "*Rowbarge* is about the search for a perfect mate, for the completion of self," she says. "It's something we all do in life. What we're really looking for is ourselves. So a book about an identical twin is a symbolic way to consider this quest for the ideal other person who will totally understand and accept the self."

Because *Rowbarge* breaks several cherished canons of children's books – e.g., it neither skirts the subject of sex nor projects an upbeat view of the human condition – the author felt certain it was a book for adults. "To be truthful," she confessed, "I wasn't sure it had an audience at all. I wrote 150 pages of a first draft and was only through Herbert's third year! This was pure self-indulgence, so I set the work aside."

Rowbarge might still be gathering dust, were it not for a trip to North Carolina and a conversation there with Anita Moss of the English Department at the University of North Carolina. "She's a most perceptive reader, and I mentioned the plot of this unwieldy book that I'd probably abandon because I couldn't imagine who'd read it," Mrs. Babbitt recalls. "She said 'I would – you should go ahead and do it.'" The author did.

This involved wholesale restructuring, covering only pivotal events in the hero's history within chapters that alternate between past and present. In a prologue to the novel a narrator speaks of the biographer's need to telescope life, "like a concertina, compressing its multitude of monotones into a single blat."

The book's Ohio setting, a lakeside town and its amusement park, is one familiar to the author. She was born in Ohio in 1932, and her family lived in a succession of small towns before settling down in Cleveland. The story's Red Man Lake is the counterpart of Indian Lake, where Mrs. Babbitt spent summer vacations at her maternal grandmother's cottage. "We lived right across the street from an amusement park," she says. "My mother resented it bitterly, but my sister and I loved falling asleep to the music of the merry-go-round and the screams of the roller-coaster riders." The near-Dickensian orphanage evoked by the author is one remembered from Gallipolis, Ohio. The accidental death of Herbert's wife – run over by a horse and buggy – is the end suffered by Mrs. Babbitt's paternal grandfather. Beyond this, the author thinks of herself as a product of "an Ohio lifeview," different from that of the East. "It is, first of all, uncomplicated," she explains. "There is the feeling that certain things are right – and that's that. Also, there is a sense of the land's always being there." This latter feeling permeates the author's work, from *Knee-Knock Rise* through *Rowbarge*. Place is as memorable as any of her characters.

Herbert Rowbarge's twin daughters, Louisa and Babe – the only truly sympathetic characters in the novel – were inspired by the author's relationship with her own sister. "We were close as children," says Mrs. Babbitt. "In fact my daughter has accused me of stealing my sister's life. My sister was the one who was going to be a writer and marry a college professor. I was going to be an artist, marry a rich industrialist and ride around in a convertible."

Mrs. Babbitt, in fact, majored in art at Smith College, though she never aspired to be a painter. "My sense of color is weak," she says. "I wanted to be a book illustrator, in black and white." As an undergraduate, she enrolled in one writing course, but only because her prospective husband planned to become a novelist. "If I was going to be his wife, I wanted to understand the problems a writer faces," she elaborates. "Can you imagine any woman admitting to such a thing today?"

When her children were all in grade school, the author illustrated her first book, *The Forty-ninth Magician* (1966). The text was written by her husband. It was published by Pantheon, where the Babbitts worked with a young editor, Michael di Capua. The author followed him to Farrar, Straus & Giroux, and he has been Natalie Babbitt's career-long editor, mentor and friend. Mr. Di Capua encouraged her to try a longer prose work after she had written two picture books in verse. ("I didn't think I could write, but I knew I could rhyme," she says.) The result was *The Search for Delicious*. Still, Mrs. Babbitt considered herself primarily an illustrator. She did drawings for all her early novels and usually does her own jacket illustrations. She has also provided pictures for three poetry collections and a novel by Valerie Worth, a good friend.

"It's odd, but I never think of myself as a writer," she confesses. "I like being an artist, because you can watch yourself learning. Writing is more frustrating – every time you try something new, the problems change entirely."

The author has given considerable thought to why neither her husband nor her sister pursued the career that she is still surprised to be following. "Writing takes a certain amount of skill," she says, "but it is a talent widely distributed. You have to like what goes with writing." There is an uncharacteristic pause. "If people are very important to you," she adds with finality, "you're not going to be able to do it."

As to why each book is a radical departure from its predecessor, Mrs. Babbitt says, "Either you have to stay where you are, or change. I don't want to stand still."

New York Times Book Review
1981

SEVENTEEN

The Graphic History of Piglet and Toad

Few books have been as happy in their illustrations as A. A. Milne's foursome – *When We Were Very Young* (1924), *Now We Are Six* (1927), *Winnie-the-Pooh* (1926) and *The House at Pooh Corner* (1928) – with the line drawings of Ernest H. Shepard. There were, to be sure, *Alice in Wonderland* and John Tenniel, as well as *Mary Poppins* and Shepard's own daughter, Mary. But, in the case of the elder Shepard, it is almost unthinkable to entertain seriously the idea of any other artist's appropriating Milne. So successfully did Shepard distill the essence of Milne's whimsy the first time round, with small miracles of spirited drawing, that the work of any other artist can only diminish our experience of the four books. Even the contemporary Walt Disney Studios' animations of Pooh and his friends are respectful adaptations of Shepard's drawings.

Few illustrators, of course, come to their task under such happy circumstances. Only three years apart in age, both Milne and Shepard were products of similar late Victorian upbringings, and they shared a nostalgia for like childhoods. Recalling his reaction to Shepard's first drawings for *Pooh*, Milne said: "I remembered all that *Renard the Fox* and *Uncle Remus* and the animal stories in *Aunt Judie's Magazine* had meant to us. Even if none of their magic had descended on me, at least it had inspired my collaborator; and I had the happy feeling that here was a magic which children from generation to generation have been unable to resist."

From Milne, Shepard went on to illustrate more than thirty books for adults and children. Never, however, was he to match the triumph achieved for the Milne foursome. Shepard's role as an artist for Kenneth Grahame's *The Wind in the Willows* was probably the most challenging undertaking of his career. While charming in its own right, Shepard's work for Grahame's book had little of the verve and spontaneity of his Milne drawings. Unquestionably it was a far more difficult task to enter Grahame's complex world of the imagination than it was to accompany Milne on a light-hearted ramble through the familiar byways of a shared English childhood.

"There are certain books that should never be illustrated," Shepard opined unexpectedly in the preface to his own illustrated edition of *The Wind in the Willows*. Even as he was working on the drawings, the artist felt that Grahame's book was one of these; and history has, in a sense, backed him up. Published in 1908, the book was in its eighth edition – a classic on both sides of the Atlantic – when it was first illustrated in 1913. "Perhaps if it had not already been done," Shepard said, "I should not have given way to the desire to do it myself."

So overshadowed have the earlier illustrators been by Shepard's monumental effort for the 38th edition in 1933 that we tend to think of him as Grahame's first illustrator. He did, in fact, create the Mole, Rat, Toad and Badger we know today. But the work of his three predecessors is of interest both in gauging the magnitude of the job and in assessing the contributions of all subsequent illustrators.

The 1908 first edition, published by Methuen in London and Scribner's in New York, contained 302 pages of unrelieved text, except for an expendable art-nouveau frontispiece by Graham Robertson. Robertson, however, contributed the book's present title, and it was he who first voiced the trepidation illustrators were to feel for years to come: "There was then some talk of my providing illustrations, but time was lacking and, moreover, I mistrusted my powers, for I could not number an otter or a water-rat among my acquaintances."

The Wind in the Willows was written by no less a personage than the Secretary of the Bank of England, and that probably contributed to keeping English artists at bay for more than twenty years. It was two Americans, Paul Bransom in 1913 and Nancy Barnhart in 1922, who became its first illustrators.

Bransom was a born animal illustrator and, not surprisingly, his ten illustrations depict Grahame's characters as purely creatures of the woods. They are unclothed except in two minor instances and appear in scrupulously accurate proportion to man. So insignificant, in fact, does Toad appear in relation to the jailer's daughter in one Bransom drawing that we can only wonder why we are bothering to read about such insignificant creatures. In her twelve illustrations, Nancy Barnhart gave the animals a stature appropriate to their fictional importance and, most important in establishing their visual credibility, dressed them fully and handsomely: checked suits for Toad, spats, watch chains, handkerchiefs, etc. In truth, she transformed them into personages, animal in face only. While much influenced by Beatrix Potter, she had none of Potter's gift for establishing locale, and the setting of her illustrations remained hazy, indeed unrevealed.

Grahame's first British illustrator, Wyndham Payne, came along in 1929 and certainly suffered no excess of reverence for his task. His twenty animated drawings, the most ambitious to that date, are full of lively improvisations. Unfortunately, they have almost nothing in common with the stateliness of Grahame's prose. There is humor in *The Wind in the Willows*, but it is not a light-hearted work. Payne's contribution was to place the characters in unmistakably English countryside. His inspired conception of Toad's canary-yellow caravan has remained through all ensuing illustrations. Never mind that Payne's Mole looked like a weasel; the artist's irreverent approach proved liberating.

It was Shepard who finally placed Mole, Rat, Toad, Otter, Badger, etc., in the locale Grahame had always intended. Shepard spent an autumn afternoon sketching the Thames countryside near Grahame's house and made a map of *The Wind in the Willows* country just as he had once charted the world of *Winnie-the-Pooh*. His hundred-plus small illustrations make living presences of all the animals and bring *The*

Wind in the Willows considerably closer, particularly to a young listener who may occasionally grow impatient with the longer lyrical passages. We might argue that Shepard's Mole looks too much like an earless and upright Eeyore (with a dash of Piglet thrown in); but, still, if Grahame had had no other illustrator, he would have been well served. In 1959, Shepard added eight full-page color illustrations, but large-scale work was not his forte and these water colors are simply diluted variations of the black-and-white drawings.

Almost pure accident brought *The Wind in the Willows* its most perfect illustrator, Arthur Rackham. Probably the most gifted illustrator of his time, Rackham, an Englishman, was approached in 1936 by the American editor George Macy to illustrate James Stephens's *The Crock of Gold*. Since he liked commissions in pairs, Rackham asked if Macy hadn't another book as well. After some thought, the editor came up with the Grahame work, and an inkling of its effect on Rackham comes from Macy's recollection:

"Immediately a wave of emotion crossed his face; he gulped, started to say something, turned his back on me and went to the door for a few minutes." When Rackham regained composure he explained that he had yearned to do the book for years.

Rackham's drawings for *The Wind in the Willows* are as perfect as were Shepard's for Milne. He took whatever he fancied from those who preceded him, yet made the end result entirely his own. His animals are as believable as Bransom's, but leave no doubt as to their being creatures of the imagination. He outdid Barnhart in the costuming and housing of his animals, but with a touch distinctly masculine and unsentimental. Lacking Payne's frivolity, and with a far greater talent, he used the English countryside with almost heartbreakingly lyrical effect. Finally, while his characters are related to Shepard's, he created an unforgettable Mole in "the black velvet smoking suit" that Rat admired "awfully" but to which, surprisingly, no prior illustrator had done justice.

If Rackham had any fault, it was his uncompromising seriousness.

So much do his drawings echo Grahame that, like the text, they are not quite for children. Their somber quality may owe something to Rackham's having been fatally ill when he completed the commission. Indeed, his last drawing was of Rat and Mole embarking upon that picnic of picnics at the book's start. Some children are put off by Rackham; I know one little girl who cannot look at his Mole because he is "too scary." But Rackham's morbid streak, if this it was, is not at odds with Grahame. An author who could describe Rat's falling asleep with "slumber gathered him forthwith, as a swath of barley is folded into the arms of the reaping-machine" cannot be accused of a surfeit of sweetness and light. In any case, had Rackham turned down Macy's offer, how much poorer we all would be.

One would like to think that the hallmarks of those illustrations which endure are a combination of a unique conception and a memorable execution. Shepard, in Milne, and Rackham, in Grahame, were generously endowed with both. In Rackham's case, the artist reworked well-turned soil with brilliance. As for Shepard, he cultivated new territory with as green a thumb as children's literature has ever beheld.

EIGHTEEN

Our Homegrown Fairy Tale: The Wonderful Wizard of Oz

THE WONDERFUL WIZARD OF OZ is that rarity among children's books: one that continues – into the fifth generation at this writing – to find its way into the hearts of children. First published in 1900, L. Frank Baum's novel–length fairy tale was characterized in *The New York Times* of September 8th that year as "ingenuously woven out of commonplace material." The review went on to prophesy "It will be strange indeed if there be a normal child who will not enjoy the story." From such raw stuff as a rundown farm in Kansas, an orphaned girl–child of eight or nine, a small mongrel dog and a cyclone, Baum had spun a suspense–filled, fantastic adventure. With its curious blend of idealism, optimism, ingenuity and hard–headed pragmatism, it spoke directly to American children.

Baum's stated intention at the start of the tale makes amply clear his philosophical attitude toward fairyland in general. "The oldtime fairy tale, having served for generations, may now be classed as 'historical'.... *The Wonderful Wizard of Oz* ... aspires to be a modernized fairy tale in which the wonderment and joy are retained and the heartaches and nightmares are left out." This is not unlike our forefathers' vision of life for themselves and their offspring in the new world: a real–life fairy tale in which the wonderment and joy are achievable with all the old–world heartache and nightmare left behind. Baum's Oz books take place in a child's version of the American utopia. The fields are always

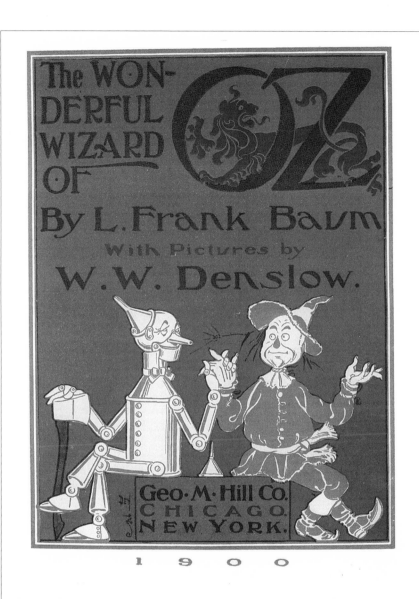

L. Frank Baum, *The Wonderful Wizard of Oz*
illustration by W. W. Denslow

green in Oz; "no disease of any sort was ever known among Ozites"; "every inhabitant of that favored country was happy and prosperous"; and the Emerald City itself shines dazzlingly green through everyone's mandatory green–tinted glasses. In Oz, as in the United States at the turn of the twentieth century, the magic does not ultimately reside in persons, not even in the Wizard, but in the material abundance of the land and the relatively smooth–running machinery of a government in which all the inhabitants fully believe. If the Ozian utopia lacked refinement, smacking more of Barnum & Bailey than of Old World elegance, it was not unlike America at that time: crude, perhaps, but filled with energy and a sense of radiant power and hope.

Where the essence of traditional fairy tales is a concern with wealth (or the lack of it) and power (marrying a handsome prince or a beautiful princess), in Baum's tale the quest of his characters is never for material possessions. (These were readily attainable in American life.) Rather they seek knowledge, courage, a heart, or – in Dorothy's case – simply the way back home.

Despite *The Wizard's* immediate success, Baum gave no thought to sequels. He was ready to move on to other tales. He had already gained some small fame as the author of *Father Goose: His Book* and *The Songs of Father Goose*, illustrated by the same Chicago newspaper cartoonist, W. W. Denslow, whose place in children's book history was assured by his bold drawings for *The Wizard*. (Though other artists, including John R. Neill, Peter Newell and Frederick Richard also illustrated *Oz*, it is Denslow's pictures that remain as intimately bound to *Oz* as John Tenniel's are to Lewis Carroll's *Wonderland*.) In 1901, Baum produced *Dot and Tot of Merryland*, an unrelated story about a doll who rules a country made of candy. This was followed by *The Magical Monarch of Mo* and *The Enchanted Island of Yew*. Though all three were about other lands of enchantment and make–believe, they failed to gain even a semblance of the popularity achieved by *Oz*.

The idea of a continuing series of Oz books, however, came not from author or illustrator, but from Baum's young readers. Smitten by

Oz–mania, they sent impassioned pleas to the author for more stories about Oz. By 1904, Baum gave in and produced *The Marvelous Land of Oz: A Sequel to The Wizard of Oz*. This only swelled the clamor from fans, and in 1907 Baum published *Ozma of Oz*, followed in the next three years by *Dorothy and The Wizard of Oz*, *The Road to Oz* and *The Emerald City of Oz*. By 1910, Baum had had enough and devised for himself a perfect escape. In *The Emerald City of Oz*, he contrived to cut off communications with his fantasy realm by means of an impenetrable Barrier of Invisibility.

For three years, Baum wrote other stories, but none assuaged the *Oz* craving. Thus, using the plot device of the wireless (a relatively new invention in 1913), Baum was able logically to reopen communication with Oz. *The Patchwork Girl of Oz* was the result. Resigned to his fate, the author also promised the children of America that he would continue to write about Oz for as long as they cared to read about it. He kept his word, producing seven more titles before his death in 1919. But not even Baum's death ended the clamor for more *Oz* books, and other sequels by a number of authors appeared until the mid 1960s. In all, the Oz series ran to forty–one books written by six different authors. Though most are out of print now, none of the fourteen *Oz* titles by Baum himself has ever been unavailable, even at the books' nadir of popularity with the adult literary establishment.

Certainly this seemingly unending march of *Oz* titles down the decades of the twentieth century had something to do with turning librarians and other critical readers against our first and most durable homegrown fairy tale. By 1930, the Children's Room of the New York Public Library had removed the entire *Oz* series from its shelves, and other library and school systems throughout the nation followed suit. Neither author Baum nor *The Wizard* was mentioned in the first editions of the two leading reference texts on children's literature: *Children and Books* (1947) by Mary Hill Arbuthnot and *A Critical History of Children's Literature* (1953) by Cornelia Meigs.

If distinction of literary style, tautness of narrative and seamlessness of plot were inflexible standards of judgment, *The Wizard* would long since have bitten the dust. Yet few works have ever spoken so directly to children, without need of adult explanation or elaboration. Thoroughly American in her gumption and skeptical good sense, the heroine Dorothy was hailed by *Collier's* magazine in 1946 as typifying "that attitude, if you'll pardon a bit of flag-waving, that did much to make this country great." There is no question that *The Wonderful Wizard of Oz* is a New World fairy tale, appealing not only to children but even to nations young in spirit. It was probably not mere happenstance that during World War II two Australian brigades in North Africa marched into battle singing, "We're off to see the Wizard/ The wonderful Wizard of Oz."

This brings us to the MGM technicolor musical extravaganza *The Wizard of Oz*, one of the best film adaptations of a children's story ever made. Starring Judy Garland, it was released in 1939 but gained its widest audiences in annual televised reruns from the mid-1950s on. After a decade of watching the film with two sons as they were growing up, I came to think of author L. Frank Baum and actor Frank Morgan as one and inseparable. During that memorable scene in the Emerald City's throne room where the Wizard (played by Morgan) is unmasked as the humbug he is, there is a touching moment illuminating the truth about both storyland wizard and real-life author.

> "Are you not a great Wizard?" Dorothy asks.
> "Hush, my dear," he said, "don't speak so loud, or you will be overheard – and I should be ruined. I'm supposed to be a great Wizard."
> "And aren't you?" she asked.
> "Not a bit of it, my dear; I'm just a common man."

And this revelation applies to Baum as well. Though he wrote some fifty books during his lifetime – most of them for children – Lyman Frank Baum was "just a common man." The author was born in 1856 in Chittenango, New York, to well-to-do parents. Though Lewis Carroll's *Alice in Wonderland* was published when Baum was nine, there is no evidence of his having read it as a child. He did know the tales of the Grimm brothers and Hans Christian Andersen and was both fascinated by their wonderment and variety and repelled by the human suffering and injustices they chronicled. He decided early that when he grew up he would write fairy tales without a "European background" and without "all the horrible and blood-curdling incidents devised by their authors to point a fearsome moral." Though he wrote plays, and even acted in them, while still in his twenties, little else he did as a young man suggested that he would become a household name in the world of American children's books. He married, fathered four sons to whom he told improvised stories at bedtime and was at various times a job printer, chicken farmer, axlegrease manufacturer, store owner, newspaper editor, salesman of chinaware, and finally, when he was just past forty, children's book author.

Baum had meanwhile spent several years living in the American heartland (from 1888 to 1891) in Aberdeen, South Dakota, a small prairie town, where he edited the local weekly; then in Chicago where he started a magazine – *The Show Window: A Monthly Journal of Practical Window Trimming* – the official publication of The National Window Trimmers of America, an association that Baum himself organized in 1898. It is a background as incongruous as that of *The Wizard of Oz* himself, whose credentials for the job as architect of the Emerald City and grand ruler of Oz were training as a ventriloquist and practical experience as a balloonist advertising the circus's arrival in town!

The curious confusion that seems so often to occur in American fairy tales and fantasies – between the world of make-believe and the wondrous realities of American daily life – is exemplified in Baum's own history. After the great success of his *Oz* books, he moved from Chicago to Hollywood for the purpose of becoming his own filmmaker of Oz. (He did, indeed, make two silent films on the realm and its inhabitants.) There he also bought an island off the California coast –

Pedloe Island – which he intended to turn into a real-life land of Oz for the children of the United States. His visionary plan never came to fruition, though a latter-day adventurer into fairyland American-style, Walt Disney, appropriated Baum's dream. In the 1950s, Disney created the first of his mundane fairylands in California, curiously combining elements of fantasy with recreated realities from an earlier America – the only fairyland that Americans old and young seem thus far to have wholeheartedly embraced.

By now, of course, *The Wonderful Wizard of Oz* has, through longevity if not literary acclaim, achieved the status of an American classic. As one of *Oz*'s earliest adult champions, Edward Wagenknecht, pointed out in 1929: "To lose your love of fairy tales is almost as terrible as to lose your sense of religion. Indeed, at bottom, it is very much the same thing, for religion and fairy lore alike spring from a sense of reverence and a sense of wonder in the face of the unexplored and unexplained mystery of life." And Martin Gardner, perhaps *Oz*'s most loyal enthusiast among contemporary adult critics, speaks for at least four generations of ex-children whose youth was enriched by the unforgettable experience of reading *The Wonderful Wizard of Oz* when he says right out, "Let me speak plainly. Baum is the Lewis Carroll and the Hans Christian Andersen of the United States. To have been so late in recognizing this now obvious fact is one of the major scandals of American letters."

NINETEEN

PC or Not to Be?

> *Perhaps we do not realize that fiction reading for*
> *children is not the same in our children's generation*
> *as it was in our own. Life cannot stand still. What*
> *was black yesterday is white today. What was white*
> *yesterday is black tomorrow.*
> Hugh Lofting

MOST OF US would like our children to grow up free of prejudice and stereotypical attitudes that constrict their thinking and freedom of action. In the past half–century, our awareness of racial and gender inequalities (along with other blatant societal injustices) has risen dramatically. Not surprisingly, children's books, too, have been drawn into the polemical fray. The pieces that follow, often prompted by what struck me as overzealous attacks on worthwhile works, may suggest that the militant pursuit of political correctness, however admirable its intent, has its own perils.

THE REHABILITATION OF LITTLE BLACK SAMBO

THERE'S STARTLING NEWS: After virtual banishment from library shelves and bookstore displays for more than a quarter of a century, *Little Black Sambo* is back in a mid–1990s politically corrected rendition. (How complete was the old Sambo's ostracism became abundantly clear in Anita Silvey's recent compendium, *Children's Books and Their Creators*. That hefty reference work makes no mention of either *Little Black Sambo* or its author Helen Bannerman.)

It is by now generally acknowledged that Mrs. Bannerman, who wrote the original little book in 1899, did so for the amusement of her two daughters who were often far from their home in India. Her intention was to spin a diverting fantasy about a brave little boy who manages to outwit a quartet of fierce and hungry tigers by his quick-witted resourcefulness. Why a Scotswoman who spent the better part of her adult life in India should have depicted clearly black protagonists with the names Black Sambo, Black Mumbo and Black Jumbo remains a mystery. (The author herself confirmed that the tale's locale was India when she explained that the Indian word "ghi" describes the pool of melted butter that the battling tigers eventually turn into). In any event, *Sambo* succeeded in pleasing generations of children around the world. I must confess that when I grew up in the 1930s, *Sambo's* great appeal to me was the crudeness and rough-hewn simplicity of Bannerman's pictures. I also loved the author's suspenseful text. And how brave and clever Sambo was.

With the passage of time, social and political sensibilities have undergone both healthy and overheated changes. As objections to *Sambo* grew louder and stronger, a genuine small black hero became a literary *persona non grata*.

Three cheers, then, for the versatile and intelligent illustrator Fred Marcellino who brings us *The Story of Babaji*. The loudest cheer is for his wise decision to retain the original Bannerman text (except for the hero's new and unmistakably Indian name). Next to be applauded are Marcellino's elegant illustrations, providing more detailed background and making it abundantly clear that Little Babaji, his Mamaji and Papaji are, indeed, Indians. But Marcellino's tigers steal the show. How ludicrous the first and second ones appear, having squeezed themselves into Babaji's small red jacket and little pair of blue pants, and how touchingly delighted is the third tiger, his ears decked out in the beautiful little Purple shoes with Crimson soles and Crimson linings. Though these tigers are not nearly as menacing as Mrs. Bannerman's originals, still their toothy grins as each basks in the certainty of being "the Grandest Tiger in the Jungle" are a delight to witness.

Curiously, the artist's accomplished illustrations transport us into a more patrician milieu. Babaji is a sophisticate compared to Sambo. Elegantly turned out, he's a Brooks Brothers hero, a decidedly less vulnerable figure than the much simpler and more endearing Bannerman Sambo. Marcellino's cover drawing depicts Little Babaji mounted on one of the tigers: our hero is fully dressed, holding his umbrella aloft and sporting a grin that indicates he's definitely in command. The scene does not appear in Bannerman's tale – it simply couldn't have – and it detracts from our sense of suspense about the story to come.

Yet Marcellino has produced a loving, intelligent and handsome rendition of a story well worth salvaging for future generations' enjoyment.

Parents' Choice
Spring 1997

The Cautious Return of **Doctor Dolittle**

HUGH JOHN LOFTING's *The Story of Doctor Dolittle*, the first of twelve adventures starring the bluff and rotund physician from Puddleby–on–the–Marsh who loved animals and learned to speak their language, was published in 1920. Like many of Beatrix Potter's tales, it had its genesis in letters written to specific children – in this case, Lofting's own. Serving as a captain with the Irish Guards during World War I, the author wrote the story–letters about the remarkable Doctor from the trenches in France. In part, they enabled him to remain close to his two children; in part, too, they transported him to a better time (c. 1830) and place (an imaginary English country town), in which a caring healer, disdainful of personal gain, attends his fellow creatures selflessly and embarks periodically on far–flung errands of mercy or scientific inquiry.

A civil engineer by profession, Lofting had undergone far–flung adventures of his own as a young man; helping to build the Lagos Railway in West Africa, working in Canada and Cuba and, eventually, marrying an American and settling permanently in the United States. Born in England in 1886, during the heyday of British Imperialism, the author doubtless imbibed his fair share of the Anglo–Saxon certitude rife in a nation of Empire builders.

Like Helen Bannerman, who wrote *Little Black Sambo* two decades earlier, Lofting was urbane – an internationalist in outlook, life experiences and sympathies – and, writing for children, he intended to provide them with a positive entertainment. Like the rest of us, he was a product of the times in which he lived and subject to the cultural blind spots and social attitudes of his day and class.

There is more than a fleeting resemblance between Lofting and his medical hero. Both were idealists, enthusiastic naturalists and formal in their attire. Dolittle is seldom pictured without his morning coat and high hat, and the author was reputed to make public appearances in a pearl–grey fedora and spats.

All this history bears some relevance to the news that this is the summer of Doctor Dolittle's return. After being in disrepute in the United States (land of their first publication) since the early 1970s, and out of print for almost a decade, both *The Story of Doctor Dolittle* and *The Voyages of Doctor Dolittle* are available again, in hard and softcover, in a new Centenary Edition punctiliously altered to offend none but the most diehard of their former critics. *Story* and *Voyages*, both out of copyright by now, are the first of eight projected Dolittle adventures to be reissued.

Among the earliest and harshest of the Doctor's detractors was the New York librarian Isabelle Suhl who, in a 1968 bulletin of *Interracial Books for Children* charged "that the 'real' Doctor Dolittle is in essence the personification of The Great White Father Nobly Bearing the White Man's Burden and that his creator was a white racist and chauvinist, guilty of almost every prejudice known to modern white Western man." In her view, "editing out a few racial epithets will not make the book less chauvinistic."

Aficionados of Doctor Dolittle and his domestic menagerie of talking animals – Dab–Dab, the duck housekeeper, and Jip, his loyal dog, among many others – will not recognize their hero in this inflamed and politicized rhetoric. We remember his enthusiasm for scientific discovery: how he stayed up all one night trying to learn the fish language of "the silver fidgit." (Not surprisingly, the ethnologist Jane Goodall credits the *Dolittle* books as being an early inspiration for her own career.) We recall, too, his generous concern for both animals and his fellow man: how he crossed the sea in a borrowed boat to save the monkeys of Africa from a dread disease; and how he convinced a judge in Her Majesty's Court of Assizes to let Bob, a dog, testify at his master's murder trial, thereby saving a life. In a tight spot, this eccentric man of science always came through. As his young assistant Matthew Stubbins put it in *Voyages*: "Just to be with him gave you a wonderful feeling of comfort and safety."

This said, his critics had grounds for dismay. The original *Dolittle* texts were marred by a sprinkling of gratuitous racial epithets. Almost all of these emanated from the Doctor's short-tempered 183–year–old parrot Polynesia, known for her command of "the most dreadful seafaring swearwords you ever heard." But such blatant blemishes were all removed by the undated, fifty–second printing of *Story*, a Lippincott "new edition from new plates," from which I read to my two sons around 1970. A reference to "darkies" had been altered to "people," "work like niggers" had become "work hard," and several other unfortunate locutions had been rendered admirably innocuous. It speaks volumes about the racial obtuseness of earlier decades that no one seemed troubled by their appearance in highly regarded works for children. Warts and all, *Voyages* won the Newbery Medal as the best children's story of 1922.

The Centenary Edition's new excisions and revisions are far more extensive. The present editors obviously hoped to obliterate for black and other minority readers every emotionally tinted word. Thus, though much of *Story* takes place in Africa, we hear no reference to skin coloration. When Doctor Dolittle's party first lands, they are no longer met by "a black man" coming out of the woods. He is simply "a man." Likewise, where once the monkeys, grateful for Doctor Dolittle's ministrations, shouted, "Let us give him the finest present a White Man ever had!", they now say somewhat flatly, "Let us give him the finest present ever given." When a comparison becomes inevitable, it is now between African and European instead of black and white. Gone too is every illustration featuring a black character: no more broad caricatures of the King of the Jolliginki or his Queen Ermintrude; no more depictions at all of Crown Prince Bumpo. Two full-page pictures retained from earlier editions have had black figures whited out – no irony intended. The engaging Prince Bumpo, heir to the throne of the Jolliginki, has even been removed from a cameo appearance on *Story's* title page. If this verbal and visual caution occasionally seems almost craven – an avoidance rather than a positive resolution of problems – Lofting is no longer alive to deal creatively with the blind spots of his own era. The most extensive text deletion is entirely commendable: the removal from *Story* of the discomforting scene in which Doctor Dolittle reluctantly agrees to transform Prince Bumpo into a white prince so that The Sleeping Beauty, his favorite fairy-tale character, will agree to marry him. Curiously, this very episode had struck me forcibly as a white child reading *Story*. It did not make Bumpo seem ridiculous, but instead poignant and vulnerable. Here was a black prince reading the same fairy tale I knew so well, and yet it had clearly not been written with him in mind. Sleeping Beauty was there to be awakened and rescued by a prince – but not a black prince. It made me realize my favored position and, perhaps for the first time, made me keenly aware of a specific and very real exclusion of blacks. Certainly its effect on black readers must have been highly distasteful. The removal of this most flagrant Dolittle liability has been so deftly managed as to leave no noticeable gap in the narrative.

Happily, none of this well–intended editorial tinkering has had the slightest effect on the tales' enduring charms. They still exude the same cheerful optimism about life's possibilities and the excitement of discovery awaiting those who will just take the time to observe carefully. More important, the *Dolittle* books are enthusiastic about the joys of using one's mind. What more can we ask of children's books?

There is, above all, the unfading magic of an adult character who has taken the time and trouble to learn the languages of various animals. Children, a species of animals themselves, are keenly sensitive to the bother and pain of being misunderstood and misinterpreted by grown–ups.

If the world were ruled by logic, then surely all this doggedly well–meaning effort would succeed, and *Doctor Dolittle* would be restored to respectability for a new generation and a new century of children. But should the whole effort come a cropper, Hugh Lofting, for one, would not be surprised. Writing with uncanny prescience in 1930 about a now forgotten book of his called *The Twilight of Magic*, he said: "Perhaps we do not realize that fiction reading for children is not the same in our children's generation as it was in our own. Life cannot stand still. What was black yesterday is white today. What was white yesterday is black tomorrow. We have no excuse for supposing that those books which were given to us as the ideal reading fare for children are the ideal reading fare for the children of today." Still, those of us who loved Doctor Dolittle as children cannot help but wish him well in this scrubbed–clean Centenary appearance.

New York Times Book Review
August 1988

FAIRY TALES RETOLD

LAY THE BLAME on centuries of prejudicial brain–washing, but it is difficult for one brought up on Andrew Lang's rainbow–hued fairy books to take seriously a sleeping prince "with skin as white as snow and lips as red as blood and hair as golden as the sun." Happily in Alison Lurie's collection of fifteen "forgotten folktales," *Clever Gretchen*, each story features a heroine who is "strong, brave, clever and resourceful" in addition to being beautiful and good. The princess/savior in "The Sleeping Prince" willingly dons a pair of iron shoes and travels "far, far, and farther still" to free the hapless hero from an enchantment. She ultimately succeeds, but in a curiously passive way: No bestower of the expected restorative kiss, she sits quietly at his side for days and weeks and months until he wakes – as he does annually – on St. John's Eve. Then, the mere sight of her breaks the evil spell.

In other tales, clever Gretchen outwits the Devil; wise Manka proves more sage than her husband the judge; Elena, a kind–hearted sister, rescues her baby brother from a terrible witch; and Mastermaid (progenitor of Superman?) saves an inexperienced princeling from a cruel and demanding employer. So it goes in each story – a heroine carries the day. Yet, despite the commendable aim of Miss Lurie's first work for a young audience – i.e., to combat the stereotype of fairy-tale females as weak and helpless – the royal fathers in these carefully crafted tales still arrange matches for their daughters according to whim; swains persist in choosing mates only if they are pretty as well as clever; and marriage remains the Shangri–La of every nubile maiden save one, Mizilca, gutsy heroine of the tale of the same name.

In the best of the stories the reader quickly forgets the protagonist's sex, so compelling are the narratives. This is as it should be, for any memorable tale chronicles a victory of the human spirit – surely androgynous – over one form of bondage or another. Whether the victor be male or female is incidental.

A Case for **The Five Chinese Brothers**

ONE OF MY FAVORITE neighborhood characters during childhood was a Chinese laundryman who worked and lived in a small, single-windowed store at the corner of our street. For a couple of years after I had first learned to read, I thought the sign painted on his window in large red capital letters said WASHING, with "Hand Laundry" lettered in black underneath, much smaller, to provide a fuller explanation of the service he rendered. It was only when experience turned me into a more discriminating reader that I realized it was his name, WAH SING, emblazoned bright and clear on the glass, his occupation taking a distinctly secondary place.

Wah Sing had a wife who ironed shirts at a remarkable clip and two or three small, cheerful children who played on the floor behind the laundry's wooden counter. To his steady customers, he dispensed a lichee nut each time a package of clean laundry was picked up and paid for (though never when even the largest batch of dirty shirts was delivered to him). As exotic as the flavor of the fruit he dispensed, Wah Sing was no stereotype to me, though I suspect he would never pass muster with the Council on Interracial Books for Children, Inc., should ever I decide to introduce him into a contemporary children's book.

Certainly, if Claire Hutchet Bishop's fictional *The Five Chinese Brothers* (Coward, 1938) is being relegated to the literary scrap heap as offensively stereotypical, what chance has a Chinese laundryman, real or imagined? According to Albert V. Schwartz, associate professor of education at the College of Staten Island (in *"The Five Chinese Brothers*: Time to Retire," *Interracial Books for Children Bulletin*, vol. 8, no. 3, 1977), this old-time favorite – now in its thirty-sixth printing – is rampant with negative stereotypes of the Chinese, including a reinforcement of the notion that all Orientals look alike, that they have "bilious yellow skin and slit and slanted eyes," that they dress in coolie clothes and often display that "humiliating symbol" of Chinese peasant subjugation, the queue. And, if this weren't bad enough, Professor Schwartz also finds the

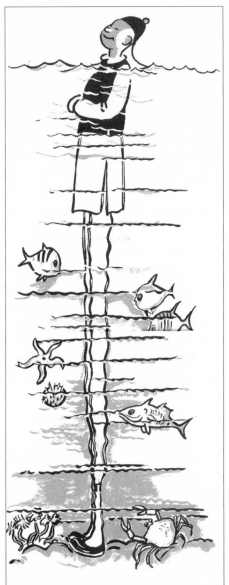

But he began to stretch and stretch and stretch his legs, way down to the bottom of the sea, and all the time

Clare Hutchet Bishop
and Kurt Wiese,
The Five Chinese Brothers

townspeople, as portrayed by the author, mean spirited and vindictive, the judge an injudicious dolt and the anonymous status of the five brothers "a relic of historical racism."

All this saddens me, because, as it happens, I was fond of *The Five Chinese Brothers* as a child, and I would be willing to swear on a stack of fortune cookies that the book – like my nodding acquaintance with Wah Sing – did nothing but encourage positive thoughts in me about the Chinese and the culture from which they spring.

Far from finding the five brothers' yellow skin "bilious," I always thought of artist Kurt Wiese's faces as being the color of sunshine or butter, cheerful and highly appealing. And if Mr. Wiese's heroes are rendered in a broad cartoon style, well, why not? This approach has been used by many a successful children's book artist from Peter Newell to Jack Kent without the intention of demeaning the subjects thus rendered. It is, in fact, a style particularly well–suited to the folk tale, a genre which deals in broad truths. We are not concerned with the names, ages or specific physical features of the characters in a Grimm fairy tale any more than we are in Bishop's confection.

The fact of the brothers' being exact look–alikes is the great joke of the book – not a racial joke on the Chinese, but a specific joke on the judge and townspeople in the tale. The great charm of the story, of course, is that the joke is never on us, its child–readers. We know from the very start that "once upon a time there were Five Chinese Brothers and they all looked exactly alike."

In a way, the Chinese setting is incidental to the tale. The brothers could just as well have been Kurdish, Peruvian or Bulgarian at the time the book was written. What the tale did require was a setting unfamiliar to readers, a place remote enough in time or space or our knowledge of it, so that readers could well believe in its inhabitants possessing magical powers (e.g., one brother could swallow the sea, a second had an iron neck, a third had infinitely stretchable legs, etc.). This said, I can well see that the tale might not cast the same spell on young Chinese readers. Chinese children might not so readily accept these impossible powers in their own people.

Professor Schwartz goes on at some length about the Chinese judge's reprehensible behavior in sentencing the first Chinese brother to death by beheading "without even hearing both sides of the story." But there was really no other side to be heard. The victim of the supposed crime, the little boy, is its only witness, and he has drowned as a result of his own disobedience. Again, child–readers alone are privy to the whole truth, one of the secrets of the book's longevity. I, myself, always found the judge to be a model of civilized behavior. Four times, on the morning of a scheduled execution, he grants the prisoner's last request to go and say goodbye to his mother. "'It is only fair,' said the judge."

I was also touched and impressed by the sense of honor and family solidarity among the brothers. Whenever one returns home safe, another goes to jail in the condemned man's place. After the fifth attempt to execute one of the brothers fails, the judge is willing to call it quits. "It must be that you are innocent," he concludes, a fact that happens to be true. And the townspeople all readily concur. Even the ending is one of pleasing measure: "The Five Chinese Brothers and their mother all lived together happily for many years."

I cannot remember a tale during my childhood that gave me a cozier sense of all being right with the world.

Thus, there seems to me to be a danger to the free growth of the human spirit, as well as an element of the ludicrous, in bringing contemporary social sensitivities (many of them entirely justified and commendable) so heavily to bear on books like *The Five Chinese Brothers*. Relegating this work to the literary junkyard is about as sensible as would be the banning of another book with a Chinese setting, *The Story of Ping* (also illustrated by Kurt Wiese) because the small duck hero has yellow feathers.

Professor Schwartz would commend to us, in place of *The Five Chinese Brothers*, a 1960 version of the Chinese folk legend from Peking, *The Five Little Liu Brothers*, in which the setting is specific and accurate, the characters all have names, their skin is accurately "beige" and all eyes are unslanted. But, judging from the few passages quoted from the more authentic tale, I would hazard the guess that few of its child–readers will remember the tale for a week. Readers of *The Five Chinese Brothers* usually have total recall of the book twenty or thirty years later. I feel that there are many small children today who would enjoy the book exactly as I did when it was first published.

I strongly suspect that my own good feelings toward the Chinese have stemmed in part from Wah Sing and *The Five Chinese Brothers*, with some latter–day help from Charlie Chan and Number One Son.

By all means, let's avoid using any picture book that might give offense, but let's also avoid blanket condemnations. It's just possible that one man's stereotype may be another's broadening experience.

School Library Journal
October 1977

BICENTENNIAL BOWDLERIZING:
THE SANITIZING OF YANKEE DOODLE

AT SOME POINT during his sophomore year at Harvard, Edward Bangs, Class of '77 – 1777, that is – tossed off the brash and jaunty chorus to the perennially popular patriotic air, *Yankee Doodle*:

> Yankee Doodle, keep it up,
> Yankee Doodle dandy,
> Mind the music and the step
> And with the girls be handy.

Beyond this lighthearted contribution, which may well be responsible for the song's subsequent longevity, Bangs did some felicitous weeding and rearranging of various verses that had proliferated like barnacles on a ditty sung on this side of the Atlantic at least since the French and Indian War in the 1740s.

Yankee Doodle's earliest lyrics were a satire on those New Englanders able to buy their way out of serving in the front lines of a British-backed, Massachusetts-launched expedition against the French in Canada. The present-day opening verse – about Yankee Doodle's pony ride and his feather called macaroni – is a nineteenth-century append-age. In deleting several meandering barroom stanzas and adding a few new ones to form a loose-jointed narrative, Bangs created a slight story about a father and young son visiting the American camp in Cambridge at the start of the Revolutionary War. So much for past history.

Some two years before the U.S. Bicentennial, the publishing firm for which I worked approached the versatile children's book illustrator Steven Kellogg with the proposal that he undertake a 200th anniversary edition of the seemingly immortal *Yankee Doodle* – a picture-book version appropriate to an audience of four- to eight- year-olds.

Kellogg, a serious student of the picture book, took to the idea enthusiastically, in part because he knew what good company he'd be keeping. Several of this nation's most gifted illustrators had tackled the job before him, among them Felix Darley in 1865, the young Howard Pyle in 1881, Thomas Nast in the 1890s and Norman Rockwell in the 1940s. After a year of ruminating and doing research into period cos-tumes and architecture, Kellogg delivered what we all felt was a remarkably fresh interpretation of the song, entirely accessible to youngest viewers and readers. (Kellogg's *Yankee Doodle* was himself a small boy no more than six or seven, a pint-sized patriot who high-tails it home to the safety of his "mother's chamber" after accidentally wandering off behind British lines.)

Here a juvenile publishing story might have ended happily if not for coincidental circumstances. From the beginning, there had been friendly banter between the artist and the publishing house's art direc-tor (a woman) about the politically incorrect Bangs line "And with the girls be handy." Was it appropriate to the enlightened spirit of 1976? Both Kellogg and I agreed that the line was an integral (and historical) part of a period song and should not be tampered with. Besides, the

Yankee Doodle
illustration by Steven Kellogg

words could certainly be interpreted as meaning "And with the girls be gallant" – or even solicitous. This was how Kellogg had illustrated the line; his small hero is shown helping a still smaller girl into a horse-drawn wagon.

By chance, at the time the final text for Kellogg's book was being copyedited, *Shoulder to Shoulder*, a BBC documentary on the women's suffrage movement in Britain, was running weekly on Channel 13 in New York. So moved were my sons and I by the unswerving principles and willingness to be imprisoned for their beliefs exhibited by these early twentieth-century crusaders that the *Yankee Doodle* chorus began to reverberate in my ears as flippant and dismissive – the sophomoric work of a callow undergraduate.

At the office, we reopened the "And with the girls be handy" discussion: The staff consulted *Webster's Third* (Unabridged) and found three shades of meaning for "handy." The second was "ready to the hand, conveniently near, convenient for reference or use." We felt that this definition allowed us to alter a single word – girls – to folks. The chorus still made perfect sense in relation to Kellogg's illustration. Not only was his young hero shown in the act of being gallant to a maiden, but it looked as though his parents were about to offer two elderly neighbors a ride. And "folks" had the virtue of not perpetuating a sentiment at best condescending, and at worst ambiguous and suggestive. Further, this use of folks was sanctioned by the song itself; an early verse refers to the beating of a drum "to call the folks together."

We were also heartened to discover that Louis Armstrong, in his singing of *My Old Kentucky Home*, has deftly changed the line "'Tis summer, the darkies are gay," to "'Tis summer, the folks they are gay."

Thus feeling we were on solid ground, we persuaded a less than enthusiastic artist to agree to the change in the chorus of *Yankee Doodle*. We then added what we felt was an obligatory note of explanation to the book's brief preface: "And just as Bangs took liberties with the lyrics to suit the realities of his time, this Bicentennial edition alters his chorus to suit the realities of our own." Finally, alas, we gilded the lily by sending out a mildly self–righteous press release documenting Parents' Magazine Press's discovery of the newfound American author of *Yankee Doodle*, and explaining the decision to alter his chorus.

In February '76, the earliest reviews lulled us into a false sense of security. Most notably, *Booklist* gave the Kellogg rendition a starred review, praising the artist's virtuosity and humor, with no notice taken of the minor text adjustment. (Other major review media – including *Horn Book, Children's Book Review Service*, the *Book-of-the-Month-Club News*, and *School Library Journal* – either made no mention of the word change or accepted the new version good–naturedly.) In March, however, *Publishers Weekly*'s Jean Mercier wound up an otherwise enthusiastic review with an overly generous condemnation: "But Kellogg's rewording of some of the well-known verses [Ed. note: it was just one word] are downright silly. In an attempt to please feminists, for instance, he has changed, 'Mind the music and the step, and with the girls be handy' (which meant something) to 'with the folks be handy' (which means nothing)."

This was followed in mid–April (almost on the anniversary of the Battles of Concord and Lexington) by an Olympian note of distress in the *New York Times Book Review*'s "Book Ends": "We are disturbed to learn of a bowdlerized version of the lyrics to *Yankee Doodle* in a children's book published by Parents' Magazine Press. The altered lyric goes 'with the folks be handy,' instead of 'with the girls be handy.' Since 'handy' means either 'skillful' or 'conveniently near,' we fail to see what is sexist about our *Yankee Doodle* boy being one or the other or both with the girls, and the substitution of 'folks' makes the whole line pointless."

If this weren't enough, two weeks later the Children's Book Issue of the *Times* underscored the disapproval. Reviewer Stephen Krensky wrote: "Of further interest is Kellogg's tinkering with *Yankee Doodle*'s famous chorus. According to a press release, Kellogg was convinced by the editors of Parents' that the familiar chorus was 'sexist.' So instead of the traditional 'Mind the music and the step/ And with the girls be handy,' the last line now reads, 'And with the folks be handy.'... Not only is the change of dubious historical propriety, but such misguided sensitivity is solely a triumph for the sort of people who want to integrate 'penpersonship' and 'personkind' into the English language."

Harper's Bookletter, less exercised, merely commented in passing: "For some ridiculous reason, our era is evoked by the substitution of the amorphous 'folks' for 'girls'...."

The politest cut of all came from Mrs. Hope Middleton Wood, Secretary-General of the Descendants of the Signers of the Declaration of Independence, who wrote at the end of a long letter of praise for Kellogg's interpretation: "This cheerful, robust and lighthearted little story is inexplicably marred by tampering with the final line for so-called 'sexist' reasons. Apparently someone felt a 'principle' was involved, though it would appear that the principle here is a denial that two sexes do in fact exist. I find this capitulation to a completely arbitrary authority contrary to any of the principles and ideals of the Revolution itself."

Not ordinarily being un-American, ridiculous, the sort of person who'd want to integrate one-up-personship into the English language, or, for that matter, even an ardent feminist, I continue to feel that a legitimate change was made – yes, on editorial principle – for a good and sufficient reason. Had Kellogg's *Yankee Doodle* been published in an historical context, such a change would, of course, have been unthinkable. But the editors felt that, in the age group the book was aimed at, few children were likely to know the original words of the chorus, and none would be damaged or deprived by the word change. Certainly no latter-day denial of the existence of two sexes was thereby intended; we simply felt there was no justification for perpetuating in 1976 a line richer in innuendo than meaning – particularly for an age group that would suffer no loss in the alteration.

Also, given *Yankee Doodle's* catch-as-catch-can development, the song hardly rated as sacrosanct. Just as the counting rhyme "Eenie, meenie, minie, mo/ Catch a ——— by the toe" underwent a salubrious alteration of the original word "*nigger*" to "*tiger*" some twenty years ago, Kellogg's editors felt that this Bicentennial edition provided a suitable occasion for putting *Yankee Doodle* in tune with the times. We even suspected that Bangs, a word tinkerer himself, might have approved this contemporary alteration to suit the realities of yet another American revolution. (It was this last point that won the assent of a still somewhat reluctant artist to making the change.) Certainly *Yankee Doodle* will survive the change, either incorporating it or discarding it. Only time will tell.*

As Steven Kellogg's editor on the book and a confessed bowdlerizer, I do own up to one genuine regret: that so many articulate critics have given more space and passion to the word switch than to the artistic achievement as a whole.

Library Journal
September 1976

MALE CHAUVINIST RABBITS

WHAT WITH *Watership Down* firmly entrenched on the best-seller list, the time has come to put in a good word for lady rabbits.

So intimidating is author Richard Adams in his frequent invocations of the authority and scholarly reputation of one R. M. Lockley (who in 1966 wrote an unassuming little book of field naturalist's observations, *The Private Life of the Rabbit*) that the average reader is hardly likely to question any of the so-called givens of rabbitry – male and female – that Adams flatly presents as Lockley's Laws. We simply accept, early on, Adams's own contention, voiced on Robert Cromie's "Book Beat," that "The novel is perfectly true to rabbit life.... You

---

* *Time has, in fact, told. When Simon & Schuster reprinted Kellogg's* Yankee Doodle *in the late 1990s, the politically corrected word change was restored. "And with the girls be handy" is back. With the gift of hindsight, I can't say I am sorry. It was much ado about too little – as a great deal of political correctness continues to be.*

become a rabbit." Yes, a male rabbit. There's no payoff in being a doe.

The first 168 pages of Adams's 426-page chronicle are a celebration of developing male camaraderie, competence, bravery and loyalty as a scraggly bunch of yearling bucks outwits or dodges a variety of elil (enemies) to arrive triumphant at a prospectively ideal spot, *Watership Down*. The book might have ended there, except for a crucial oversight. As Hazel, the epic's chief rabbit, informs his assembled followers: "We're doing well here.... But all the same, there's something on my mind. I'm surprised, as a matter of fact, that I should be the first one of us to start thinking about it. Unless we can find the answer, then this warren's as good as finished, in spite of all we've done ... we have no does – not one – and no does means no kittens and in a few years no warren."

This curious oversight is explained, somewhat opaquely, by Adams as follows: "It may seem incredible that the rabbits had given no thought to so vital a matter. But men have made the same mistake more than once – left the whole business out of account or been content to trust to luck and the fortune of war." Clearly "the whole business" is a bother to Adams. Does are desperately needed, but only as instruments of reproduction, to save his male rabbits' triumph from becoming a hollow victory.

Fully the last two-thirds of Adams's saga is devoted to what one male reviewer blithely labeled "The Rape of the Sabine Rabbits," a ruthless, single-minded and rather mean-spirited search for females – not because *Watership Down*'s males miss their companionship or yearn for love, but rather to perpetuate the existing band.

Before the thorny female question arises, Adams has no qualms about anthropomorphizing his male rabbits – depicting them as capable of the most extraordinary displays of loyalty, courage and affection. Yet their human camaraderie does not extend to females. When *Watership Down*'s band makes a successful raid on nearby Nuthanger Farm and two does are spirited from a hutch there, Hazel, an otherwise thoughtful and compassionate buck, inquires concerning the female booty: "Are they any good?" To which his lieutenant Holly replies in similar tender–hearted vein: "I'll tell you. I think they're precious little to be the only thing between us and the end of everything we've managed to do thus far."

To justify a pervasively callous attitude toward females and mating, Adams falls back on the Olympian, nature–observer's tone of his mentor Lockley: "The kind of ideas that have become natural to many male human beings in thinking of females – ideas of protection, fidelity, romantic love and so on – are, of course, unknown to rabbits ... they are not romantic and it came naturally to Hazel and Holly to consider the two Nuthanger does simply as breeding stock for the warren."

This explanation must suffice when, later in the novel, the head-strong Bigwig infiltrates an unfriendly warren called Efrafa and asks his male guide: "By the way, what are the rules about mating?"

"Mating," his companion replies. "Well, if you want a doe, you have one – any doe.... We're not officers for nothing are we? The does are under orders."

When one of the two Nuthanger does is reported to be in heat, Hazel asks offhandedly, "Is anyone doing anything about it?" Throughout, the reader never has a sense of who pairs off with whom. On the bucks' triumphal return from Efrafa, does now secured, we learn only that "as Hazel had foreseen, there was some mating." No female is clearly enough delineated for the reader really to care about who belongs to whom.

And when a fox makes off with one precious Efrafan female, it's no matter for concern. As a practical buck philosophically points out: "Anyway, what's a doe more or less?" By contrast, whenever a buck is endangered, the entire band will put itself in jeopardy to effect his rescue.

As to love, romantic or otherwise, there is only one curiously Victorian reference, which comes in the lament of a young doe:

> The windy grass was waving. A buck and doe
> Ran through the meadow. They scratched a
> hole in the bank.

They did what they pleased all under the
hazel leaves.

The nearest male equivalent turns up in a bawdy refrain: "Sitting with
his rump in a chicory clump/ and longing for a nice plump doe."

What, finally, of Lockley as Adams's not-so-silent partner, cited
whenever the author seems to require corroboration of his own view
of rabbitry? Even a cursory reading of *The Private Life of the Rabbit* reveals
several dramatic, if not supportive, facts. The first is that does are at the
very center of any rabbit community, a decided matriarchy. Not only
do does provide the key to a warren's organization, but it is always
young, dissatisfied females who initiate the founding of new colonies.
Lockley also emphasizes the ferocity of mother rabbits in defense of
their young against ferrets, stoats, weasels, etc. "The nursing doe," Lockley reports, "can drive large cats from a nesting site." Yet Adams, during the novel's climactic battle against the avenging bucks of Efrafa,
injects a superfluous scene in which Bluebell, a rather effeminate buck,
sits reading a story to the does (one a nursing mother) to keep them
calm. "Good idea," Bigwig thinks, "Keep 'em happy. More than I could
do if I had to sit there."

Overall, Adams's work is a glorious paean to man's (or rabbit's)
resilience, to the instinct for survival against all odds. Though the
novel spans little more than eight weeks in time and a mere six miles
of English countryside in space, Adams has created within these modest confines a rich new world full of beauty and truth. Yet, one must
note with passing regret that so remarkable a maiden flight of the literary imagination is marred by an attitude toward females that finds
more confirmation in Hugh Hefner's *Playboy* than R. M. Lockley's *The Private Life of the Rabbit.*

New York Times Book Review
June 19, 1974

On Feminism and Children's Books

Such considerations as feminism or male chauvinism (or any other deliberate effort to raise a reader's social or political consciousness) have little or nothing to do with literature. They may be minor or major aspects of a literary work for an adult or child, but once they become its reason for being, we leave the realm of literature, or near literature, and enter the province of propaganda.

Now propaganda is an entirely legitimate and worthwhile endeavor when undertaken in a life–enhancing cause. But those of us who choose books for children should be both willing and able to recognize the difference between propaganda and literature.

Employing an inspired bit of propaganda, a major boys' sportswear company broke with American advertising tradition in the early 1960s and began using buck-toothed, nearsighted, freckled and even Chinese, Spanish and, at last, black boys as models for its shirt advertisements. It was a heady change from the standard blond, blue–eyed, regular-featured WASPs we had all grown accustomed to seeing in advertisements. In making this brave and unexpected gesture, the Donmoor Shirt Company was not telling any of us something we did not already know – that children of all colors, sizes, shapes and degrees of handsomeness wear clothes. However, by giving graphic emphasis to this fact in a realm where the fat, the freckled and the funny–looking (not to mention the nonwhite population in its entirety) had traditionally been barred, this company liberated advertising itself by permitting reality to invade its cloistered realm. And we who saw the ads were also liberated. We no longer had, even in this minor way, to measure our children or ourselves against an idealized and therefore false stereotype. Common physical imperfections and differences were finally being acknowledged publicly and thereby made acceptable. The cause of truth had been served by an inspired bit of healthy propaganda.

Feminist preoccupations in children's books can be regarded in much the same light. Long before Betty Friedan wrote *The Feminine Mys-*

tique or Gloria Steinem and company began putting out the magazine *Ms.*, girls and boys, and men and women, had been receiving equal time in literature. What then do various spokesmen for children's reading matter mean when they call for "better books showing girls as authentic human beings" or "a new literature liberated from sexist innuendo and insult"?

Ever since children began listening to tales, they have loved those that revealed some truth – positive or negative – about human character. Consider the fisherman's wife for a moment, that antiheroine of the well-known Grimms' fairy tale. After having received as gifts a cottage, a stone house and a castle from an enchanted flounder, she says, "Husband, get up and look out the window. Look, can't we be King over all that land? Go to the flounder and tell him we want to be King." And when the timid fisherman protests, she replies, "Well, if you won't be King, then I'll be King. Go to the flounder. I want to be King." Was there ever a more authentic being than this greedy, overbearing, endlessly ambitious female whose aspirations stopped nowhere short of being God Himself on His throne in Heaven? Her characteristics are neither feminine nor masculine, only all too human.

What our social critics often seem to be asking for are children's books that portray not–yet–existing women characters doing what few women in real life have done thus far: being telephone linemen, big league baseball players and Presidents of the United States. Not that anything is intrinsically wrong with this. Part of the function of books, for children or adults, is to open the reader's eyes to the wider possibilities of life. Artist Richard Scarry, who had early in his career depicted the female animal characters in his encyclopedic books for small children as always wearing aprons, cooking, baking or cleaning, eventually had his consciousness level raised to the point where, in one book, he gave us a mother pig who pays no attention whatever to a whiny offspring because she is busy writing a children's book. This is all to the good. In these small ways, young children's minds are opened to the possibility that mothers, as well as fathers, are not always available or at their eternal beck and call. If the heroine of even a mediocre children's book can be the captain of a ship, or the leader of a gang of boys, or a pathologist in a hospital, surely she will inspire at least some girls who read her adventures to do as much in the world. As for the boys who read about her, they will perhaps begin to look on girls as their equals in aspiration and possible accomplishment.

Certainly a book like Charlotte Zolotow's *William's Doll*, with illustrations by William Pène du Bois, has a commendable message: it is perfectly normal, even admirable, for a young boy to want to have a doll of his own to hug and cradle in his arms. "Sissy, sissy, sissy!" chants a friend next door when he finds out that William wants a doll whose eyes make a little click when they close. "Don't be a creep!" cries his brother. "Wonderful," says his grandmother. And "wonderful" we educators of the young must also agree. This does not, however, alter the fact that in real life most boys will still think William is both a sissy and a creep for having such a wish. Nor does it alter the fact that the book itself fudges in a major way in order to put its lesson across to the widest possible audience. The author makes it quite clear that William is a regular little boy in all the other respects that fathers, and even mothers, would be likely to approve. He enjoys playing with model trains and is a first-rate basketball player. Still, he would like a doll, too. But what of those little boys who would like dolls and are perfect duds at all or most so-called masculine activities? A book about such a hero that could still win over a large audience might possibly attain the status of literature because it would have to come to grips with a complex human being, rather than a well-meaning, idea. Books like *William's Doll* are useful but not of much enduring human content.

The Feminist Press in Old Westbury, Long Island, whose entire output is devoted to works that will improve the self-image of girls, published *Firegirl* by Gibson Rich, a picture book about a girl named Brenda who is six or seven years old and loves fire engines. The story's most dramatic moment comes when the child's father breaks the terrible news: "I've been meaning to tell you, Brenda, girls can't be fire-men. Only boys can. That's just the way things are, honey." Well, Brenda, a girl of our times, instead of taking her father's words as gospel, says, "I am too going to be a fireman." She even manages to come closer to her goal than would be possible for any real-life six or seven year old of either sex. Three small cheers.

Also representative of the genre is Eve Merriam's picture book, *Boys and Girls, Girls and Boys*, with pictures by Harriet Sherman. It is a pleas-ant, horizon-expanding catalog reminding us that it is okay for boys to be chefs, read books, and take piano lessons, and for girls to be airline pilots, collect worms, and play the snare drum. Ms. Merriam also points out that either boys or girls can be lion tamers and ballet dancers. Her message is a salubrious one, and, insofar as all such books serve to make young children more accepting of the differences – and the sim-ilarities – in human beings of both sexes, they are commendable.

Such books are seldom, however, regarded as literature. One of the salient differences between books of propaganda and those of lasting merit is that in a literary work it does not matter whether the leading characters are male or female, black or white. Whatever our sex or color, we care about Charles Dickens' David Copperfield because we are caught up in his human plight. The same is true of Princess Irene in George MacDonald's *The Princess and the Goblin*. And surely the pro-tagonist of Maurice Sendak's *Where the Wild Things Are* might just as well have been a Maxine as a Max. The best books are always about human beings first – male or female, black or white, Muslim, Christian or Jew secondarily.

This is not to deprecate feminism. A good many hours of my child-hood were spent aching to be free to do the things that boys were allowed to do: climb trees, jump off the garage roof next door, play in the middle of the street and do a lot of yelling. And there was no piece of news that pleased me more this past fall than hearing that my thirteen-year-old niece was voted the first girl goalie on a rather serious-minded local ice hockey team on her block in Philadelphia. Also, I appreciate the value of a strong female figure to identify with and emulate. Though it's hard now for me to remember exactly why, this figure in my life was Madame Chiang Kai-shek. Reading her biography in a run-of-the-mill work called *Famous Women*, when I was about thirteen, made me determined to go to college (she was a Wellesley graduate) as a first step in my own liberation.

Undoubtedly children's books can do a fine propaganda job in breaking down unfortunate and limiting stereotypes. Surely healthy aggression and the desire for worldly success are not masculine traits alone, and every children's book that today depicts a heroine leading an orchestra, building a building, or landing a jet is on the side of the angels. Such stories and picture books may not immediately alter everyday reality, but they certainly help us to see what we long avoided seeing: that women as well as men can have meaningful careers. They may have nothing to do with literature, just as putting one black or Puerto Rican face into every group of five characters in nearly every children's book today does not necessarily make that work worthwhile. But they do achieve something. This healthy propaganda in children's books serves the real purpose of making us take note of what hundreds of years of social conditioning and history have made us impervious to. The deeper reaches of the human soul, however, are neither touched nor illuminated by the great majority of such works. The memorable books we read as children or as adults usually deal with the triumphs of human beings over one sort of spiritual bondage or another. And while it is certainly true that members of minority groups and women in contemporary society do face special problems, it is also true that long after women have attained equal rights and today's minorities have achieved acceptance, the great human problems – failure to communicate with one another, love unrequited or lost, an individual's grasp forever exceeding his reach – will still confront us all, both young and old. And we will continue to look to works of quality and depth to shed light on them. Thus, let's welcome books of healthy propaganda, but let's recognize them as just that and not make them the mainstay – or chief preoccupation – of our children's reading diets.

School Library Journal
January 1974

TWENTY

Songs of Praise

THOUGH FEW THINGS are more ephemeral than book reviews (particularly those of children's books), I have willingly spent a good part of thirty-plus years reviewing mostly children's books, or books about children's books. The pieces that follow are, for a variety of reasons, ones I remember fondly, and their content seems still to be of more than fleeting interest.

SNOW-WHITE WITHOUT WALT

IT IS SOMEHOW FITTING, in an era of renewed feminist ardor, that Snow-White should at last be liberated from thirty-five years of thralldom to Walt Disney. Appropriate too that her deliverer be a woman, Nancy Ekholm Burkert, whose notable children's book illustrations include those for Roald Dahl's *James and the Giant Peach* (1961), Edward Lear's *The Scroobious Pip* (1968), and now the late Randall Jarrell's pellucid translation of the Grimms' *Snow-White and the Seven Dwarfs*.

Mrs. Burkert eyes with suspicion an entire group of contemporary children's book illustrators whom she has dubbed "the nillies." Their work, she feels, pleases with surface brightness and precious, vaguely conceived people and places, but totally lacks educative value for the inquisitive eye.

Mrs. Burkert is preeminently a fine draftsman. Her *Snow-White* is a paean to particularity, as well as testimony to her conviction that a tale

Snow White and the Seven Dwarfs
illustration by Nancy Ekholm Burkert

very like it probably happened in medieval times. Seven real dwarfs might well have banded together then for mutual safety and support. In Mrs. Burkert's imagination, Snow-White became a French princess who fled into the Black Forest, eventually to be rescued by a traveling Italian prince.

To support these assumptions, the artist has fabricated a Gothic world of stunning beauty and authenticity. Snow-White, whose model was Mrs. Burkert's fourteen-year-old daughter Claire, wears a head-dress borrowed from a Dürer portrait. Admirers of medieval art may even recognize the table's floral centerpiece as plucked from a Hugo van der Goes *Nativity*. No detail is irrelevant; the heroine's apron is bordered with meadow rue, an herb to ward off witches; the white dog, basket of cherries and lilies all signify virginity. The dwarfs themselves are not imagined grotesques but real people, the product of weeks of medical-library research into characteristic dwarfish proportions and deformations. Every architectural detail, fabric and piece of crockery in the artist's six grand double-page visions of the tale have their existing medieval prototypes at the Cluny and the Museum of Decorative Arts in Paris, the Unterlinden Museum in Alsace and elsewhere. There's more than enough to sate the most inquisitive eye.

Life Magazine
December 8, 1972

Higglety Pigglety Pop! A Nonsense Rhyme Transmogrified

> *Higglety Pigglety Pop!*
> *The Dog has eaten the mop!*
> *The Pig's in a hurry,*
> *The Cat's in a flurry,*
> *Higglety Pigglety Pop!*
> Samuel Griswold Goodrich

POOR OLD Samuel Griswold Goodrich! Setting out, in 1846, to save the children of America from *Mother Goose*, he improvised a rhyme so patently absurd as to laugh the frivolous old girl off the literary stage. Alas, his *Higglety Pigglety Pop!* became an immediate hit in her repertoire. If that weren't bad enough, a Sealyham terrier named Jennie has now accomplished for Goodrich's folly what only a Helen Hayes could do for Victoria Regina: immortalized it by sheer force of theatrical personality.

"There must be more to life than having everything!" Jennie observes on running away from an indulgent master, thus providing Maurice Sendak with the subtitle of his latest and most personal work. Never has this meticulous craftsman drawn so lovingly, with flora so lush or fauna so tenderly observed. In some respects, *Higglety Pigglety Pop!* is reminiscent of Beatrix Potter, with a totally convincing animal heroine, a palpably real milieu. True, there are not the cozy furnishings of Miss Potter's old English farmhouses, but rather Sendak's magical remembrances of things past: a horsedrawn milk–wagon, a marvelous old iron stove and gas heater, a robust baby who seems transposed from a yellowed photograph, and – for elegance and fantasy – a parlormaid named Rhoda and a ferocious "downstairs lion." Like the elements in a Giotto fresco, all seem drawn together not for the moment, but forever.

Jennie proves her mettle by putting her head in the lion's mouth, much as Sendak does in attempting a children's work that plumbs depths accessible only to the fully grown. Prose and pictures, the book is like a dream. "The winter is nearly here and I am discontented," wails an ash tree. "I'll soon have nothing but the empty, frozen night." Jennie herself, in a reversal of fortune, laments: "There must be more to life than having nothing." One senses that this work is wrought from the winter of Sendak's own discontent.

Yet such musings seem extraneous once Jennie assumes her role within a role as heroine of a bona fide theatrical production of *Higglety Pigglety Pop!* She and Mr. Sendak pull out all stops in a slam–bang, slapstick Caldecottian finale. Like Charlie Chaplin's *tour-de-force* appearance as himself in the closing frames of *Limelight*, Sendak, with Jennie's complicity, brings off one of his best and most poignant performances to date. Children will guffaw and even shudder, but the resonance of this essentially melancholy work remains adult in register.

Book World
1967

LAURA INGALLS WILDER: AN AFFECTIONATE PORTRAIT

What impulses – creative, scholarly or Sherlockian – propel biographers to their task? In the case of a subject as long-lived as Laura Ingalls Wilder (1867–1957), author of *Little House on the Prairie* and seven other much-loved works of autobiographical fiction for children, it must, in good part, be the desire to compare the unvarnished biographical facts with the highly-polished fiction, the better to take the measure of Mrs. Wilder's artistry.

In *Laura: The Life of Laura Ingalls Wilder*, by Donald Zochert, this staff writer for the *Chicago Daily News* scrupulously records facts and, with courtly forbearance, resists any impulse to point out the widely disparate glimpses of Laura's life in the Big Woods and the Prairies that emerge from his investigations.

Where the "Ma" (Caroline Quiner Ingalls) of Laura's books is all docile assent to her spouse's incurable wanderlust ("Well, Charles, you must do as you think best."), Zochert shares with the reader an early school composition by Caroline, herself the daughter of Wisconsin pioneers. She writes wistfully, around 1850, "Who could wish to leave home and wander forth in the world to meet its tempests and storms?... Give me a place at home, a seat at my father's fireside, where all is so happy and free." How much her quiet acquiescence in her husband's pioneering forays must have cost her!

It was Caroline Quiner's fate to marry a rolling stone. Charles Ingalls was charming and self-reliant; he was also a fair fiddler, an indifferent farmer and a hapless businessman. He grew wheat in Minnesota where grasshoppers devoured his crop; he bought half a share in an Iowa crossroads hotel when the crossroads was about to become a backwater.

What a reverse side of the coin to the all-competent, cheerful father Laura's novels present: hunter, meat-curer, cabin-builder, killer of bears and panthers, etc. Laura's real-life father was not a complainer. When dreams failed, he took odd jobs to support his growing family. But like Laura, he was happiest jouncing along in a covered wagon "to the very end of the road, wherever it was." His feckless ways enabled the Ingalls family to take part in the great westward migration of the nineteenth century; to witness the forced withdrawal of the Osage Indians from their prairies; to be among the legions who tamed the American frontier.

Laura was born in Pepin County, Wisconsin – the Big Woods of her first children's book. Her seemingly total recall of a peripatetic childhood doubtless was sharpened by her elder sister Mary's sudden blindness (an after-effect of measles) when Laura was twelve.

Laura's father, by whom her sun rose and set, told her: "Your two eyes are quick enough – and your tongue – if you will use them for Mary." Thus Laura "saw out loud" not only for Mary, but for the generations born since the great Depression of 1929 who have devoured her books. She highlighted the details of life in frontier settlements – the joys of making snow-and-syrup candy, of churning butter, the poetry of winter blizzards and solitude.

To read Zochert's well-researched account is to learn also of settlers who went berserk and shot themselves and their families in despair, of girls who married at thirteen for lack of any alternative, of drunken lawlessness, of children who froze to death in flash snowstorms.

Where Mrs. Wilder remembers that "Laura was 6 and Mary 8" and they had never seen a town, the facts are that, at four, Laura was already enrolled in a small Wisconsin township school, that both she and Mary had been to Missouri and back, travelling through several towns, and that most of their frontier life was lived on the fringes of civilization.

Zochert makes us appreciate how much artistry went into Mrs. Wilder's shaping of the happenings of her long and adventurous life. She began to write her fiction only in 1931, when she was already sixty-four. Looking backward with the eye of love, she often telescoped events and softened rough edges. The remembered self-sufficiency of the old days took on exaggerated glamour and charm. The father of her girlhood dreams dwarfed the bumbling duffer who was also Charles Ingalls.

Unlike those soaring literary biographies that acquire an existence all their own, Don Zochert's book is an affectionate account, written to fill in the chinks of time, space and logic left by Laura Ingalls Wilder's own fiction. Certainly he lays to rest the notion that the *Little House* books are "unadorned autobiographical remembrance."

On its modest merits, his biography is a solid, honest labor of love. It brings to Mrs. Wilder's remarkably ingratiating tales a therapeutic dash of hard-headed reality.

Chicago Daily News
April 24, 1975

Ghost of the Hardy Boys: An Autobiography

Just as there are compulsive eaters and talkers, so, too, there are compulsive writers. And surely Leslie McFarlane, self-styled "ghost of the Hardy Boys," must rank among the most charming and least pretentious of this often recondite literary lot.

From 1926 to 1946 the genial dispenser of fictional V.S.O.P. (very superior old pulp), McFarlane "hammered out" – in his own apt phraseology – some twenty volumes of adventures for those red-blooded, all-American heroes, the Hardy Boys. These included the three inaugural works that launched the series on the low-road to seeming immortality. For this, his most lasting literary accomplishment, the author modestly eschews full credit. Not without reason. Each Hardy saga was, in fact, written under the pseudonym of Franklin W. Dixon and composed from an explicit outline prepared by the near-legendary "Stratemeyer Syndicate" of Orange, New Jersey. This bizarre fiction factory was a breeding farm for such other U.S. series thoroughbreds as the Bobbsey Twins, Nancy Drew, Tom Swift and a stableful of less durable juvenile stars from the turn of the century on.

A curiously American phenomenon, the Syndicate was the inspiration of one Edward Stratemeyer, author of the jingoistic "Old Glory" series that flourished in the wake of the Spanish–American War. In 1899, he also created the Rover Boys. Something of a merchandising wunderkind, Stratemeyer realized early in his career that while books in series sold well, they never picked up momentum until several were on the market. Why not, then, launch a series by threes – *The Rover Boys at School*, *The Rover Boys at Sea* and *The Rover Boys in the Jungle*? In this way, not only could the author provide each individual book with a judicious plug for the other two, but he could also drop enticing hints about glorious adventures yet to come. In fact, were Stratemeyer to cease entirely writing such books, merely devoting his talents to providing polished outlines for indigent, anonymous literary aspirants to flesh out for laughably low flat fees, why, he might really go places! As revolutionary in its way as Henry Ford's assembly-line approach to automobile production, Stratemeyer's plot dispensary in Orange (now defunct) made him a millionaire several times over by the time he died in 1930.

Via the Stratemeyer route, Leslie McFarlane, a lean and hungry twenty-three-year-old Canadian reporter desperate "to become an author," stormed the ramparts of literature. Answering a 1926 ad in *Editor & Publisher* –"Experienced Fiction Writer Wanted to Work from Publisher's Outlines" – he was soon transformed into Roy Rockwood, author of several terminal volumes in the waning Dave Fearless series.

McFarlane had no illusions about these maiden efforts: "They had less content than a football bladder and no more style than a drunken camel. Garbage." On completing his first book, McFarlane noted wryly, "A poor thing, but not entirely my own."

For his dogged hacking, McFarlane received the princely sum of $100 per book, unfreighted by any promise of future royalty sharing. But, wildly optimistic, our autobiographer dreamt of churning out four such Stratemeyer potboilers monthly, thereby staking himself to a solid income while he tried to write "better stuff." Though he never scaled any literary Everests, McFarlane did manage to quit his job as a reporter and eventually turn himself into a respected short-story, TV and film-script writer. An artist by temperament if not innate talent, the author even began perfecting his craft within the Stratemeyer straightjacket. Given the honor of breaking in a fresh pseudonym for the first three "feeder" novels in a new series – plus a raise to $125 a book – McFarlane decided that "the Hardy Boys deserved something better than the slapdash treatment Dave Fearless had been getting." It was still hackwork, but McFarlane "opted for Quality." His unsolicited plot embellishments and character embroidering may well account for the series' longevity, some thirty volumes after he had given up the ghosting.

It's hard to decide which provides the most surprises and delights in this offbeat literary memoir: McFarlane's disarming account of his apprenticeship on two unlikely sounding Canadian dailies, the *Cobalt Nugget* and the *Sudbury Star*; his affectionate recollections of eccentric (and often remarkably generous) editors he has known and learned from; his distilled wisdom about small-town reporting (never pan an amateur show – the worst performer is generally the best advertiser's wife); or his irreverent, almost parenthetical history of hackdom, from the priggish Martha Finley of *Elsie Dinsmore* fame to the great Horatio Alger and the prolific Gilbert Patten. Not only is McFarlane a born raconteur, he is a kindhearted and thoroughly civilized man. No rancor stains his chronicle of a life successfully lived in the remote suburbs of literature. Though he has netted about five thousand dollars over the years for his twenty Hardy Boys books – while the syndicate and various publishers have, by this time, raked in well over $15 million – McFarlane bears no ill will. "No one forces anyone to become a writer," he says. "I was not swindled ... the importance of the money was related to my needs."

His book implicitly raises, but never answers, the provocative question of what makes a man of limited intellectual curiosity and coarse sensibility decide to pursue the literary life. McFarlane is so genial and good-natured an autobiographical host that the reader is willing to enjoy him on his own terms. He can flash backward and forward in time like a literary athlete, bringing to life the great Haileybury Bush Fire, or an ancient hockey match between the Sudbury Wolves and the Sault Sainte Marie Greyhounds. His style, hearty and permanently Hardy–Boys tinged, skates effortlessly over the surface of events witnessed and people encountered. Entirely without regrets at seventy-four, the author looks back on two happy marriages, three grown children, and ample fulfillment as a writer able to make his way in a part of Canada he loves.

About his own literary achievement, McFarlane is refreshingly clear-eyed: "I knew I was not a genius and moreover, that genius cannot be achieved by effort. I also knew that I was not a writer of great talent, although even a small talent can be improved and developed by diligence." His book should be required reading for any teenager who thinks he wants to be a writer. No work gives a better sense of the drudgery and joys of writing – not as high art, but as an honorable craft capable of being mastered. There is unlikely to be any sunnier reading than this unique bit of Americana, this chronicle of a modest literary life well lived.

Bookletter
July 5, 1976

A GRAPHIC FEAST

There are certain works so grand in intent that simply for their authors to have nurtured them into being merits a respectful doffing of the cap. Barbara Bader's hefty, broad-spectrum survey of children's picture books from the turn of the twentieth century to the mid 1970s is such an effort.

Mrs. Bader's opus, *American Picturebooks: From Noah's Ark to the Beast Within*, is not, as her publisher claims, "the first comprehensive review of American picture books." (For all their genteel fustiness, the two volumes by Bertha Mahoney Miller, Ruth Hill Viguers, et al., *Illustrators of Children's Books 1744–1956*, cover much the same territory with a less strident aesthetic bias.) Nor is it an incisive historical analysis of "the evolution of the picture book from a medium of moral instruction to a medium of psychological revelation." It is, nonetheless, a landmark in children's books.

Bader, a former librarian and editor of *Kirkus Reviews*, succeeds unqualifiedly in making us look at children's picture books as works of art and, by extension, at their authors, artists, editors and printer-engravers as copractitioners of a constantly evolving, exacting art form. The welded term "picturebooks" is Bader's own shortcut to describe that happy harmony of art and text which is the hallmark of the best children's books. Alas, it is almost her only success at telescoping thought.

Fortunately, Bader provides nearly 700 well-chosen illustrations (130 in full and reasonably faithful color), a virtual parade of the changing fashions in children's picture books through the decades. There are selections from the self-consciously beautiful books of the '20s; the outgoing, unpretentious limited-color tales of the '30s; and the vibrant harvest of color and graphic innovation following World War II. Nearly every illustration is reproduced within the framework of the full book page on which it appeared, and, in each instance, overall page dimensions are indicated.

By this seemingly elementary device, Bader forces her readers to acknowledge and examine not pictures alone, but pictures in relation to words and surrounding white space. Often, she provides two and even three consecutive spreads from a given work, thus affording an unprecedented opportunity to savor the graphic rhythm and flow that are too often taken for granted as one turns the pages of the actual book.

In her zeal to make us aware of every nuance of a given book's charms, Bader unfortunately refuses to let illustrations speak for themselves. Seeing a double-page spread from Leo Lionni's *Inch by Inch*, or three sequences from Roger Duvoisin's *A for Ark* side by side, tells us more about color and line than several thousand words.

Curiously enough, though Bader writes about an art form that values verbal economy, she squanders language and often uses three words where one would do: "Visually – graphically, pictorially – it doesn't hold a candle to *Millions of Cats*," she says at one point. More distressing is her proclivity to reach for the awkward, jarring locution: words like attractant, confoundment, concision, and divorcement turn up regularly to clog an already viscous prose. Also, while much of what she tells us is randomly interesting, it is disconcerting in a critical survey to sense an overall lack of focus or directing intelligence. Too frequently she seems carried along by her welter of material, her words serving merely as a kind of calligraphic cotton batting to hold the art in place on the felicitously designed 8-by-10½-inch pages.

But, if she is often turgid, she is sometimes acute, as when she notes of one Joseph Low book that "it has every virtue except an appeal to its intended audience." And, if she exasperates, she can hit home, too. Commenting on that well-known phenomenon in juvenile publishing, the Harper book, she says: "There is, or was, such a thing as certainly as there once existed Venetian painting or Irish theater: a fusion of form and spirit." And the fusion is one she traces clearly from the days of Margaret Wise Brown in the '40s through those of recently retired editor Ursula Nordstrom.

Never parochial, Bader relates, where possible, picture-book developments to happenings in the larger world of fine arts: to Matisse's innovative cutouts for his book, *Jazz*, in the late '40s, to the advent of action painting in the '50s. And though she may have a decidedly tin ear, there is nothing wrong with Barbara Bader's eye. What a treasure chest of superior pictures: E. Boyd Smith, Boris Artzybasheff, Nicolas Mordvinoff, Paul Rand – one-time luminaries, now all but forgotten. True, there are puzzling contemporary omissions – notably M. B. Goffstein and Arnold Lobel – but it is certainly gratifying to see Harriet Pincus get her due, alongside Sendak, Steig, Charlip, Ungerer and other present-day stars. And if it seems a pity that Bader passed up the opportunity to compare different major illustrators' handling of the same tale, she has nevertheless provided a handsome and invaluable tool for editors, reviewers, librarians, students and lay enthusiasts – complete with footnotes and full bibliography. No one has ever before served up quite so rich a graphic feast of what publisher William Scott once characterized as "the simplest, subtlest, most communicative, most elusive, most challenging book form of them all."

Bookletter
May 24, 1976

A CRITICAL DELIGHT

In *Fairy Tales and After: From Snow White to E. B. White*, Roger Sale has written a most unusual work of criticism on the subject of children's literature: one that refuses to pigeonhole its subject matter as a distinct – and, therefore, implicitly minor – literary genre. What's more, he doesn't once apologize for taking seriously books generally remembered with pleasure by large numbers of adults, yet seldom discussed, "except," as the author notes, "very chattily." It is this very elusiveness of the subject matter, the fact that the magic and power of so many children's books are difficult to pin down, that seems most to have engaged the author's considerable critical acumen.

Sale is a professor of English at the University of Washington, and he writes as an adult for other adults. Wisely, he makes no effort to cover all bases, concentrating instead on just those "books for which I feel some marked imaginative sympathy." No lukewarm enthusiast, he asserts from the start that "children's literature is one of the glories of our more recent literary heritage."

Yet he eschews any definition of his chosen subject, contenting himself with the Olympian assertion that "we all have a pretty good idea of what children's literature includes." Without a trace of pedantry, Sale addresses himself more to literature's broad function, "that it gives profit and delight, and by this definition children's literature has given as much profit and delight as other kinds of literature." Because he finds the category "children's literature" too uncomfortably vague and loose to permit much generalizing (and the great children's books themselves "too different from one another to suggest more than occasional comparisons between two or three"), Sale focuses on particular works and their creators.

And what a joy it is to join so interesting a mind and so responsive a literary sensibility in reexamining books by Dr. Seuss, Lewis Carroll, Frank Baum and others. Refreshingly, there is not a hint of condescension in Sale's sharp scrutiny. Of *Peter Rabbit*, he says simply, "It is one of the world's best known and best loved books because without it humanity would be the poorer."

Not of the school of criticism that would isolate the work from its author, Sale soundly observes that Beatrix Potter's power to charm her readers "has to do with smallness ... with the way Potter uses smallness to force concentration from her reader." And, offered several telling glimpses into Potter's genteel and suffocatingly claustrophobic youth, we can only nod assent to the judgment, "Given the confined nature of her life, given her tendency to write in tiny letters, given her desire to copy little things other people usually ignored, it is not surprising that enclosed spaces gave her the crucial assurance that within them she could be brash and full of pronouncements." And what Potter aficionado will not raise a small cheer for his ultimate appraisal: "How loose and baggy, how easy on themselves she makes most other writers and artists seem."

Seldom do Sale's insights fail to deepen our appreciation of even the most familiar nursery favorites. Commenting on Jean de Brunhoff's "somber equilibrium," Sale notes, "He shows us misfortunes of a kind seldom found in children's books: betrayal, desertion and cruelty ... de Brunhoff's tone in the presence of these events is impassive and accepting.... The impassivity that seems for a moment like indifference also assures us that this moment will pass." It is only mildly disconcerting that Sale makes no distinction between the early Babar stories written by Jean de Brunhoff (those under discussion) and the later, lesser tales by his son Laurent, with which today's children are probably more familiar.

If Sale is generous and incisive with his praise, he can also be firm and withering in his judgments. He does not hesitate to point out A. A. Milne's "shallow snobbery" (that author's tendency "to calculate one's superiority to someone else"), nor to condemn the distasteful underlying premises of a traditional fairy tale like *Rumpelstiltskin*, with its "alien insistence that the king must always be accepted, and even married, no matter how dreadful, and that the little man in the woods must always be thwarted, no matter how sympathetic." Of so sacrosanct a figure as Hans Christian Andersen, Sale writes, "What is wrong with his work is, almost without exception, what is wrong with all inferior children's literature and what mars even some of the masterpieces." The fault Sale pinpoints is the tendency "to make the central relation be between the teller and the audience rather than the teller and the tale." Thus he finds, not only in Andersen but in much of Kipling as well (notably the *Just So Stories*), "an essentially patronizing attitude toward the audience."

Nowhere is Sale more compelling than when he is examining fairy tales (and the oral tradition) as they relate to later works specifically intended for children. He reminds us that children's literature is a product of "the latter days," dating only from the beginning of the seventeenth century, by which time magic had been generally discredited and childhood was invented. In fairy-tale literature, "What was was, and was equally for everyone." Thus, Sale cautions, when we return to the old Grimm tales today, "We need to adjust or even temporarily to abolish our sense of older and younger, parent and child, and let the tales give us their sense of these people and these relations." But, admiring as he is of the purity of fairy tales in their portrayal of good and evil, the ugly and the beautiful, he cannot subscribe to the near mysticism of writers like Tolkien who look on these primitive works as an open sesame into some realm of the Other, a place beyond human experience. "I hear testimony in a story or a collection of tales, and a voice is speaking across a large abyss," Sale confesses to us. "But it is only a voice, or some voices, not something beyond human personality, not something beyond human relationships."

What makes *Fairy Tales and After* so much a work to be reckoned with is the wholeheartedness of its author's own responses. It is exhilarating to find the world of children's books so openly welcomed – at long last! – into the larger cosmos of general literature. How refreshing to witness Kenneth Grahame's Toad of Toad Hall, for example, compared unselfconsciously to another antihero, Hemingway's Robert Cohn of *The Sun Also Rises*. And what a pleasure to read that "de Brunhoff shares with Flaubert and Proust those qualities for which the more famous adult authors are admired, and if their display of these qualities is more copious than de Brunhoff's, it is no more pure."

What doubtless gives most resonance to Sale's observations and pronouncements is that they are informed by a sober awareness of mortality, by that tragic sense so often purposely excluded from children's books by those who would protect their readers from what they already know in their growing bones. In admiring the stark closing line of a Grimm tale ("And so they were all dead together."), Sale writes, "One minds mortality less when remembering that we will all be dead together, along with the hen and the cock and the teller of that tale."

Perhaps never has so urbane, so civilized – in sum, so adult – a voice been raised on behalf of children's books.

Inquiry
November 13, 1978

PICTURE-BOOK PERFECT: **CLEVER BILL**

In an era when new picture books numbering in the thousands are published annually and, in all too many instances, are far from being inspired, this work by the distinguished English artist and illustrator William Nicholson (1872–1949) remains as fresh and pertinent to the lives of small children today as it was in 1926 when it first appeared in England. Happily, it has been returned to print in a faithful new 50th anniversary edition.

The charm of *Clever Bill* lies in its artful simplicity, a tribute not only to Mr. Nicholson's particular gifts as draftsman and designer but also to the rich English picture-book tradition from which his work sprang. Perhaps best known now as the illustrator of Margery Williams's *The Velveteen Rabbit* (1922), he did both words and pictures for only one other children's story – *The Pirate Twins* (1929).

There is not a wasted word nor an extraneous graphic detail in *Clever Bill*, but rather a mesmerizing synchronization between spare text and uncluttered drawings. In fact, we scarcely perceive a division between words and pictures. The text is rendered in a hand-penned script that is inseparable from the artwork and contributes immeasurably to the book's natural, deceptively casual pace. Once begun, the story cannot be put down.

"One day the Postman brought Mary a letter from her –," we read on the first page. Page two reveals the sender to be "Aunt." We need not know her name to see that she is a prototype of the doting female relative. Mr. Nicholson is a master at letting his pictures speak volumes: There are Aunt's lorgnette and brooch, her elaborate Victorian inkwell, and the quaint wall bell-ringer used to summon a servant. There is even a Nicholson print hanging above Aunt's desk – his well-known lithograph, done in the 1890s, of Queen Victoria strolling with her dog. We needn't take in all of these details, yet they add richness and verity to the atmosphere.

On the third page the reader is at liberty to peruse Aunt's invitation to visit her at Dover, but only by turning the book upside down. This is an inspired psychological ploy. Not only does the artist thereby invest the words with as much drama as he does the pictures, but the reader is drawn into a minor – though delicious – infringement of Mary's privacy. Somehow, the border between art and life has been crossed. By being made privy to authentic documents – Aunt's letter and Mary's typewritten formal acceptance – we become active participants in the story itself.

The pages run on at breakneck speed, each connected to the next by a breathless, childlike "and." No writers' workshop would endorse the formula, but how beautifully it works for Nicholson playing at being Mary. The child catalogs the absolute necessities to be packed: her small wooden horse, gloves with thumbs, dear Susan (a doll), sundry other items every young child will delight in examining closely, from the cracks in a well-worn pair of red patent-leather party shoes to the seam running down a rag doll's face, and of course, "clever Bill Davis," a stuffed guardsman doll.

These belongings must now be made to fit into a small green suitcase, and we watch, entranced, as Mary packs "this way and then that way" and "that way and then this." At last the heroine departs, "and!! and!!!" she forgets poor Bill Davis, who weeps inconsolably. But not for long. Bill runs down the stairs and, lickety-split, across the English countryside "so fast that he was just in time to meet her train at Dover." Mary is no more delighted than the reader at the miraculous sight of Clever Bill, standing at military attention, awaiting her arrival.

Like life, the book abounds in unexplained minutiae that we may notice or miss, depending upon how much we bring to it. *Clever Bill* is chock full of those elements George Eliot once proclaimed vital to all beautiful fiction: genuine observation, humor and passion.

From the curlicues of train smoke that decorate the endpaper borders to the topsy-turvy placement of the book's dedication on the inside back cover, the work is a tour de force. There are only twenty-two pictures, yet we have lived through a complete and satisfying drama. Clever Bill Nicholson!

The Horn Book
December 1977

JOAN OF ARC: BOUTET DE MONVEL'S MASTERWORK

Two of the rarer commodities in the world and in literature today are heroism and piety. So it is a particular pleasure to welcome back *Joan of Arc* – in a handsome Viking reprint made from a first edition in New York City's Pierpont Morgan Library – the masterwork of the French illustrator Louis Maurice Boutet de Monvel.

Published in Paris in 1896, the picture-history of France's national saint was, in part, a labor of love: the artist had been born in Orléans, the city liberated by Joan from the English in 1429. Boutet de Monvel also had a more timely motive – to create for the children of his day a stirring picture book about a past moment of French glory. The nation was still smarting from its defeat in the Franco-Prussian War of 1870–1871; and in his introduction (not included in the new edition), the artist exhorted his audience, "Open this book with reverence, my dear children, in honor of the humble peasant girl who is the

Patroness of France ... the Saint of her country as she was its Martyr. Her history will teach you that in order to conquer you must believe that you will conquer."

An academic painter who eventually won international fame as a portraitist of children, Boutet de Monvel had already illustrated several notable juvenile works, among them two collections of songs, a popular book on etiquette and a brilliantly designed selection of La Fontaine's fables. But nothing ever matched his *Joan of Arc*, a story with unbeatable ingredients – religious fervor, court pomp, massed armies, pitched battles and a unique heroine. Joan's life bore many parallels to Christ's and to the lives of other Christian martyrs. Chosen by God, she struggled and briefly triumphed; she was cruelly denied by those she aided, betrayed to her enemies and executed in 1431. She died in Rouen – burned at the stake – when she was only nineteen.

Unquestionably first among *Joan of Arc*'s enduring qualities are its forty-three majestic paintings done in watercolor and ink with black line, covering the major events in her brief existence. Handsomely composed, deeply felt, and executed with a consummate sense of color as well as a healthy respect for historically accurate settings and costumes, the pictures remain fresh and moving today. Boutet de Monvel's full-page illustrations have a nobility and grandeur akin to the great church frescoes of the Renaissance. Their pleasingly flat rendering combined with a sophisticated use of design elements – the patterns on wall coverings, floor tiles and court dress – owe a debt to the Japanese prints so popular in the artist's day.

The intimate opening picture, dominated by tender tones of pastoral green, introduces us to the peasant child of Lorraine. Dressed in drab homespun, she winds flax while tending the family cow. What a contrast to the next illustration, a mesmerizing rendition of Joan's initial vision at the age of thirteen. The Archangel Michael appears, golden-haired and gold–armored; he is enclosed in a silvery aura, which is itself ringed by luminous tongues of golden flame. This brilliantly lit version announces Joan's mission to help the Dauphin be crowned

King of France. The book closes with a decidedly sepulchral apparition of two female martyrs, Ste. Margaret and Ste. Catherine, comforting a spent Joan before her burning at the stake.

Uncannily, with only the subtlest alterations in his pale backgrounds, Boutet de Monvel manages to convey the quality of light in each picture – indoor or outdoor, morning or late afternoon, dawn or dusk. Employing a palette at once muted and daring, the artist constantly surprises and delights the viewer with his unexpected color combinations: The Dauphin's palace contains a peach rug strewn with pink roses, and court costumes are aglow with sumptuous yellows, rich reds and burnt

The next day, May 6th, she captured the bastion of the Augustinians. Then, very early on the morning of the 7th, the attack on the Tourelles bastion began. Joan was in the moat, raising a ladder against the parapet, when an arrow from a crossbow pierced her between her neck and shoulder. She pulled the iron shaft out of the wound. When someone offered to help her with a magic charm, she refused, saying that she would rather die than do anything contrary to the will of God. She made her confession, and she prayed a long time while her troops rested. Then, giving the order to begin the assault again, she threw herself into the thickest of the fight.

The bastion was captured, and all its defenders perished.

Louis Boutet de Monvel, *Joan of Arc*

oranges. Throughout, the artist makes brilliant use of browns, black and white. Joan's formal battle dress is inspired: a splendid sleeveless tunic worn over her silver armor. Long and white with a delicate fleur-de-lis pattern in gold, her graceful robe has wondrously scalloped edges. It manages at once to suggest the wings of an angel, the fragility of a bird and the vulnerable femininity of this reluctant soldier of God.

As in a passion play or tableau, each gesture is exaggerated for maximum narrative clarity. But, despite the simplicity of his figures, Boutet de Monvel manages to suggest the heroine's single-minded devotion, the nobles' arrogance, the Dauphin's vacillation. Like the old Cecil B. De Mille biblical extravaganzas with their casts of thousands, the artist's pictures are teeming with soldiers, nobles and clerics. Yet every visual detail is deftly exploited for dramatic impact. When Joan first marches into battle, we can clearly read her banner – the names of Jesus and Mary embroidered on one side next to a winged angel kneeling before Christ. The graphic high point of the work is a double-page illustration depicting the English defeat at Patay. Worthy of Paolo Uccello, it is a panorama of armored soldiers, thrusting lances, and mounted horsemen at full gallop. Each of the picture's two parts is a separate framed unit. But a French steed on the right-hand page bursts through its frame, racing headlong toward the left-hand page. And the rows of poised lances and spears, although interrupted by the white space between the pages, carry across from the right side to the left. Gaps in the margins add to the cinematic sense of frenzied action.

Boutet de Monvel's own text, reverent if somewhat wooden, quotes liberally from Joan, as her words were reported in accounts of her own time. Her statements are touching in their unflagging faith. Examined by a council of clerics, the untutored girl says, "I may not know my A B Cs, but I come on behalf of the King of Heaven." Captured at Compiègne she cries, "I have sworn and given my faith to Another ... and I will keep my vow to Him." And on being tried as a heretic, she offers no defense but "I am sent by God.... Send me back to God, from whom I came."

Almost as remarkable as his stately pictures is the fact that the artist managed with incredible felicity to accommodate one of the longest picture-book texts ever – some 5000 words – in ink-bordered rectangular blocks incorporated into his picture space. So deftly are the words locked into each illustration that the reader or listener never suffers any loss of visual detail. No matter how long the text block is, we somehow manage to see the picture whole – right from the start. Curiously, despite the book's elegance, this juxtaposition of boxed words with pictures is reminiscent of a comic strip – a regal one, to be sure.

The English text has been skillfully pared down by Gerald Gottlieb, Curator of Early Children's Books at the Morgan Library, from a translation done in 1897. Mr. Gottlieb has also provided an illuminating new introduction. The shortened text gains in clarity and grace for a contemporary American audience, and only a few gems are lost. Unfortunately, the book's overall size has been slightly reduced – just enough to diminish the luxuriousness of the original edition. Although the color reproduction overall is felicitous, the present book is printed on shinier, whiter stock than was its predecessor, resulting in some muddling of the original limpid colors: Greens are occasionally altered to blues, oranges deepened to red or bleached out to yellow, blues rendered brighter and harsher. The design modifications on the book's cloth cover and title page, however, are effective and respectful of the original.

Never before in the brief history of children's picture books in color had so handsome and exalted a work appeared. On grounds of both aesthetic purity and narrative content, Boutet de Monvel's masterwork merits a place of honor on the contemporary child's bookshelf.

The Horn Book
February 1982

Beautiful Dreamers: Winsor McCay and James Marshall

It is difficult to imagine two illustrators as unlike in style and temperament as Winsor McCay and James Marshall. Though each was a consummate master at bringing a page of illustration to vibrant fictive life, their subject matter and results were worlds apart.

McCay, a cartoonist of awesome graphic virtuosity, was best known for the flamboyant full-page color comic strip *Little Nemo in Slumberland*, which he turned out for the Sunday *New York Herald* from 1905 to 1911 and, again, from 1924 to 1927. At the height of its popularity, in 1908, *Little Nemo* was appropriated by Broadway, becoming a hit musical with a score by Victor Herbert.

In contrast, James Marshall, who died in 1992 at the age of 50, was a contemporary master of the children's picture book. His was a quietly successful and decidedly unflashy career. Its crowning achievement was a septet of disarmingly simple picture books about two irresistible buck-toothed hippopotamuses, George and Martha, whose near-unshakable friendship rivals that of Damon and Pythias.

Now, seventy years after the final *Little Nemo* strip graced the funny papers and twenty-five years after the first of James Marshall's small-canvas tales, *George and Martha*, reached the eyes and ears of children, two generous anthologies – *The Best of Little Nemo in Slumberland* and *George and Martha: The Complete Stories of Two Best Friends* – appear almost simultaneously to offer us not so much a sampling as a full-course meal of the best work of two unique artists.

The medium of the color comic strip was scarcely a decade old when McCay's *Little Nemo* burst onto the American scene. The artist had done an earlier strip, *Little Sammy Sneeze*, but it was no match, in either innovative techniques or surreal imaginative scope. In *Little Nemo*, McCay introduced panels that expanded or contracted – horizontally or vertically – as his artwork demanded. His pages gave an uncanny illusion of motion, of animation. The strip's weekly installments never deviated from a single unchanging formula: A small boy, about six, dreams a fantastic dream (more often than not crossing the border into nightmare) set in a rococo slumberland of mammoth architectural splendor and bizarre, unpredictable happenings. Just as the action in each episode builds to a crescendo of suspense, Little Nemo dependably (and reassuringly) awakens in his own little bed at home. Often an episode was completed in one strip; occasionally the dream extended over several weeks, even months. But there was always the same weekly ending: Nemo awakening, at home in bed, in the strip's final panel.

The possessor of a wild and seemingly limitless visual imagination, McCay luckily had the graphic virtuosity to bring his slumberland fantasies to life before the viewer's bedazzled eyes. In McCay's imagined world, a volcano may erupt inexplicably from the page; floors can open and characters disappear before our eyes; the columns of a large hall may be transformed into giant tree trunks with monsters lurking behind each one. Without warning, Nemo and his two sidekicks, Flip and the Imp, will suddenly grow to giant size or shrink helplessly. In one magical strip, Nemo and Flip are ice skating on a shiny surface that gradually reveals itself to be Nemo's grandfather's bald pate! There's never a dull moment.

With such unremitting graphic high jinks to beguile us, plot, dialogue and characterization are almost beside the point. McCay's protagonists are little more than cardboard foils for the artist's incredible flights of fancy.

In sharp contrast to McCay's busy and ingeniously complex dream world, Marshall creates a familiar, but entirely uncluttered, real world: a minimalist's paradise for two undeniably real hippopotamuses, George and Martha. Each of the seven picture books, united here for the first time, contains five vignettes about George and Martha's enviable relationship.

These mini-stories vary in length between four and ten pages. Their brief texts are unfailingly on a left-hand page, smack in the center of a comforting sea of white. The droll illustrations, black-ink line with watercolor washes, are always on the right, each measuring 7 inches square and enclosed in a black–outline frame surrounded by a generous border of white page. Every vignette is separated from the one that follows by a blank white page, a kind of curtain between acts, a respite to digest what we've seen and heard.

If, at first glance, this all seems too simple–minded, something a talented child might toss off on a good day, forget it. Marshall has purposefully constructed this wondrously welcoming, entirely reliable world of words and pictures in perfect synchronization. His childlike drawings effectively erase any barrier between grown–up artist and young audience.

A serious student of the picture–book genre, Marshall greatly admired the simplicity and *sotto voce* wit of both Jean de Brunhoff and Tomi Ungerer. He did his mentors proud: George and Martha are captivating. From the very first vignette (1972), in which George pours his bowl of split pea soup into his loafer (to keep from hurting the feelings of Martha who "was very fond of making split pea soup") to the thirty–fifth and final episode (1988), in which Martha doesn't let undying friendship stand in the way of an antic act of revenge on George, the reader/viewer painlessly absorbs nourishing kernels of truth about friendship. In George and Martha's world, friends don't lie to one another; they try to make each other feel good in moments of crisis or pain; they forgive and forget; and they never say "I told you so." The words and pictures are so happily wedded that the two are, in fact, inseparable.

We grow so accustomed to George's and Martha's peccadilloes that we forgive George his macho boasting ("I used to be a wicked pirate.") and Martha her occasional know-it-all bossiness. They become our friends, and so our laughter is affectionate when Martha does her "Dance of the Happy Butterfly" or comes bouncing down the lane on a pogo stick. And we do not sneer when poor George is too afraid to jump from the high–diving board and must beat a cumbersome retreat. Like us, they have their failings: George has the bad habit of spying on

James Marshall
illustrations from the
George and Martha books

Martha, and Martha can be vain and a trifle heedless ("How I love to look at myself in the mirror.")

Because the artist's pictures are so unencumbered and plain, every graphic detail counts. At the end of the first book, George loses one of his two front teeth in a skating accident. The dentist replaces it with a gold one that is, ever after, George's identifying feature. From the second book on, Martha always wears a jaunty red tulip bud behind her left ear. If she is feeling ill, it droops in sympathy. Each rereading of the tales is guaranteed to reveal more treasures.

Marshall's attention to both pictorial and narrative details is punctilious. When the hippos ride the "bump" cars at an amusement park, George's fedora pops straight off his head, the only indication of a collision with Martha's vehicle. Under George's sink is a detergent called Ker Pow, and the title of a scary movie the friends attend is "The Mummy's Toe." George's dentist is named Buck McTooth. Children are particularly appreciative of such unexpected bonuses, and adults take pleasure in pointing them out.

Certainly no two illustrators could offer a more dramatic contrast. To McCay, a blank page afforded the challenge to dream an impossible dream and capture it in gloriously theatrical images and detail. To Marshall, the same page cautioned disciplined restraint; his motto as an artist may well have been "less is more." The work in neither of these anthologies has been tarnished by the passage of time, and both are of interest to children and adults. In the case of the Marshall anthology, the amalgamation of all seven *George and Martha* books between sunny yellow covers somehow strengthens the hippos' charms. *Little Nemo*, on the other hand, like any rich confection, is best taken in measured helpings. Each of their collected works deserves a wide audience.

Los Angeles Times
December 8, 1997

TWENTY-ONE

Hogwarts: Harry Potter's Brave New World

What is style for one art is style for another, so blessed is the fraternity
that binds them together, and the worker in words
may take a lesson from the picture maker.
Henry James, *Pictures and Text*

J. K. ROWLING was a struggling single mother living in Edinburgh, Scotland, in 1997. There she began writing her first Harry Potter novel (*Harry Potter and the Sorcerer's Stone*) on random scraps of paper in a neighborhood café. A generous, unexpected award from the Scottish Arts Council helped her finish that volume and proceed directly to the second (*Harry Potter and the Chamber of Secrets*).

Thus was launched as awesomely successful a career in children's books as the world has ever seen, with equally successful editions in sixty-one foreign languages soon following suit. It is rumored that Rowling's annual income now surpasses that of the Queen of England. Some fans worried that the author of seven novels about a spunky, bespectacled orphan at an exclusive English public school for the education of fledgling witches and wizards might run out of steam before her promised series ever reached completion. But the timely appearance of each consecutive volume gave ample reason for optimism and cheer. Every work to date is longer than its predecessor: *The Sorceror's Stone* (1998) has 309 pages, *The Chamber of Secrets* (1999) 341 pages, *The Prisoner of Azkaban* (1999) 435 pages, *The Goblet of Fire* (2000) 734 pages, and *The Order of the Phoenix* (2003) a garrulous 875! If the remaining books follow this near geometric pattern, two hefty weightlifter editions should come our way by 2006.

What feeds the loyal reader's near–insatiable appetite for Harry's escapades and misdemeanors with his schoolmates and teachers at Hogwarts (the adolescent wizard's Harvard) is what one of Rowling's admirers characterizes as "her light–hearted fertility of invention" played out by "a cast of characters from two worlds."

Two worlds? No question about it. There are the everyday inhabitants of the reader's familiar world, comprised of human beings of no imagination and no ability to appreciate the magic all about them. They are called Muggles. And there are the descendants of old, respected wizard families eager to learn the spells and incantations that will empower them to ply their inherited trade. They will earn their witch and wizard titles by the time seven Hogwarts school years have passed.

Aficionados of Rowling's series know that Harry attends Hogwarts from his eleventh to his seventeenth year, and that he and his two best school friends – Ron Weasley and Hermione Granger – must constantly be alert to unexpected dangers from the evil wizard Voldemort, who has already murdered Harry's parents. Rowling's prose is sophisticated, as is her turn of mind; she's more than likely to hold onto her audience through Harry's last academic year.

Each book begins with the students of Hogwarts School of Witchcraft and Wizardry departing from King's Cross Station, London, for the new academic year. An initial letter from Hogwarts' headmaster informs Harry that his train will leave at 11 A.M. from "platform nine and three-quarters." Harry's Muggly Uncle Vernon ridicules this directive: "Don't talk rubbish." But another departing student's mother reassures Harry:

> All you have to do is walk straight at the barrier between platforms nine and ten. Don't stop and don't be scared you'll crash into it, that's very important. Best to do it at a bit of a run if you're nervous. Go on, go now...."

Suspension of predictable reality works, and Harry finds himself near a scarlet engine next to a platform packed with people. Somehow, witnessing this suspenseful, magical scene makes the reader grant greater credibility to the author.

It is curious how a series that has received so much notice for both a first-time author and a likable young hero should have almost no attention paid to its accomplished illustrator, Mary GrandPré. The artist not only gives the school its castle-like setting on the cover and title page of the first book, but she provides the color jacket pictures of Harry in action and growing visibly older with each new work. In addition, GrandPré provides a single, chalk-pastel drawing in black and white – either of a figure or an object relevant to the chapter that follows – for each of the 130 chapters in the five published books. None of these drawings ever exceeds three inches horizontally or vertically, and none violates or upstages the author's words. Afloat in a metaphorical sea of Rowling's text, GrandPré's pictures contribute significantly to the reader's belief in and understanding of Harry Potter's Hogwarts world.

The depictions of Harry are based on a limited number of hints from the author: He has "a tuft of jet-black hair over his forehead," under which can be seen "a curiously shaped cut, like a bolt of lightning." He also wears his fat cousin Dudley's baggy old hand-me-downs and a pair of broken glasses held together by scotch tape. The artist refers to her dark drawings as "soft geometry," and we can understand this when we look at her first drawing for the first chapter of the book. It might well be construed as an abstract, oval design until a closer look reveals it to be Harry as a baby being left on his uncle's doorstep. Yet GrandPré does not shy away from Rowling's more difficult challenges. Hear the author's description of a horrific watchdog:

> They were looking straight into the eyes of a monstrous dog, a dog that filled the whole space between ceiling and floor. It had three heads. Three pairs of rolling, mad eyes; three noses, twitching and quivering in their direction; three drooling mouths, saliva hanging in slippery ropes from yellowish fangs.

GrandPré both does the author's words justice and avoids arousing terror in a young viewer. The artist also attends carefully to Rowling's description of Hagrid, the outsized gamekeeper of Hogwarts:

> He was almost twice as tall as a normal man and at least five times as wide. He looked simply too big to be allowed, and so wild – long tangles of bushy black hair and beard hid most of his face. He had hands the size of trash can lids, and his feet in their leather boots were like baby dolphins.

Even when she is illustrating an exaggerated character like Harry's spoiled and selfish cousin, Dudley, GrandPré softens Rowling's verbal judgment. As for Dudley:

> He had a large pink face, not much neck, small watery blue eyes, and thick, blond hair that lay smoothly on his thick, fat head. Aunt Petunia often said that Dudley looked like a baby angel – Harry often said that Dudley looked like a pig in a wig.

The artist, who lives with her family in St. Paul, Minnesota, is clearly no beginner; she has illustrated more than fifteen other books.

The fifth Potter volume leaves Harry infatuated with his classmate Cho Chang. He is also being warned by Hogwarts' headmaster, Albus Dumbledore, that he is more dangerously threatened by the evil Lord Voldemort than ever before, because that black wizard has managed to return to his own body after thirteen years of marginal survival living off frightened former followers.

Readers around the globe, meanwhile, are as at home in Harry's Hogwarts wizard world as they are in their own everyday Muggle one. The portraits on the walls of the castle can visit from one frame to another. Mail is delivered by owl; everyone except first-year students can travel by flying broomstick; and elves, gnomes, trolls, poltergeists, vampires, pixies and ghosts are common sights. Ms. Rowling's lucid and lengthy prose skillfully encourages the reader's suspension of disbelief, allowing us willingly to join Harry at "platform nine and three-quarters" for the annual return to Hogwarts.

What is surely Rowling's most remarkable achievement with her Harry Potter series is its permanent annihilation of the widely disseminated canard that children really want short, easy books and won't expend the effort required by a work more than 300 pages long – particularly one that makes no attempt to simplify the author's language or tone down the occasional truly scary moments. Listen to Harry's first encounter with his would-be killer, Voldemort:

> Harry felt as if Devil's Snare [a magic potion] was rooting him to the spot. He couldn't move a muscle. Petrified, he watched as Quirrell [a turncoat Hogwarts professor] reached up and began to unwrap his turban. What was going on? The turban fell away. Quirrell's head looked strangely small without it. Then he turned slowly on the spot.
>
> Harry would have screamed, but he couldn't make a sound. Where there should have been a back to Quirrell's head, there was a face, the most terrible face Harry had ever seen. It was chalk white with glaring red eyes and slits for nostrils, like a snake.
>
> "Harry Potter..." it whispered.

Rowling is equally compelling in describing lighter moments, as at exam time:

> Professor Flitwick called them one by one into his class to see if they could make a pineapple tap-dance across a desk. Professor McGonagall watched them turn a mouse into a snuffbox – points were given for how pretty the snuffbox was, but taken away if it had whiskers.

In addition to a seemingly endless capacity for inventing new words and droll names for her characters (as befits the creator of a fantastic new world) Rowling has also created a compelling new game called

Quidditch. This soccer-like encounter between two seven-player teams, who must keep four balls in motion, is played while mounted on broomsticks. The winning team is the one that manages to catch the smallest ball (about the size of a walnut), the Golden Snitch. Harry turns out to be a natural at the sport.

Another noteworthy feature of Rowling's books is their frank dealing with prejudice and a class system that is no doubt more deeply entrenched in England than in the United States, but which is endemic on both sides of the Atlantic. We see it in the prejudice of most students against "mudbloods" – wizards of mixed blood (or of no wizardly blood whatsoever) and, in the case of Harry's adoptive parents, against Hogwarts, wizardry in general, and Harry and his parents. Rowling presents the case from both points of view, but she never preaches. Listen to an exchange between Harry and his most arrogant classmate, Draco Malefoy:

> "Where are your parents?"
>
> "They're dead," said Harry shortly. He didn't feel much like going into the matter with this boy.
>
> "Oh, sorry," said the other, not sounding sorry at all. "But they were our kind, weren't they?"
>
> "They were a witch and a wizard, if that's what you mean."
>
> "I really don't think they should let the other sort in, do you? They're just not the same, they've never been brought up to know our ways. Some of them have never even heard of Hogwarts ... I think they should keep it all in the old wizarding families."

Rowling pulls out all the stops when Harry's hateful cousin Dudley tries on his newly acquired private school uniform:

> That evening, Dudley paraded around the living room for the family in his brand-new uniform. Smeltings' boys wore hats called boaters. They also carried knobbly sticks used for hitting each other while the teachers weren't looking. This was supposed to be good training for later life.

As for our knowledge of the vicious renegade Voldemort – why he ever wanted to kill Harry in the first place; what his intentions are should he manage to achieve immortality; how, bodiless, he managed to survive for thirteen years – we know precious little. Information is tendered slowly and guardedly. His power is substantial, increasing from volume to volume, but it is ambiguous and shrouded in Gothic mystery. All we really know about the villain's beliefs is a quote reported by one of his followers: "There is no good and evil. There is only power and those too weak to seek it." How did Hogwarts turn out such a wayward alumnus?

J. K. Rowling is an exceptionally visual writer. If she occasionally errs on the side of providing the reader with extraneous information, her devoted fans consume it greedily. And illustrator Mary GrandPré subtly embellishes Rowling's texts. As a team, they do Harry and his wizard world proud.

In recognition of the magic J. K. Rowling has brought into so many children's lives all over the world, she has deservedly been named an Officer of the Order of the British Empire, an honor richly deserved.

Mary GrandPré
illustration from
Harry Potter and the Sorcerer's Stone

Permissions Acknowledgments

Cartoon on p. ii © The new Yorker Collection 1993 Danny Shanahan from cartoonbank.com. All rights reserved.

Illustration from *Richard Scarry's Best Word Book Ever* by Richard Scarry, Copyright © 1963 by Random House, Inc. Renewed 1991 by Random House, Inc. used by permission of Golden Books, an imprint of Random House Children's Books, a division of Random House, Inc.

Illustration from *Grandpa's Too-Good Garden* by James Stevenson. Reprinted courtesy of Darhansoff Verrill Feldman Literary Agents.

Cover of *An Actor's Life for Me!* by Lillian Gish. Illustration copyright © 1987 by Patricia Henderson Lincoln.

Illustration from *A Prairie Boy's Winter* by William Kurelek, Copyright © 1973 by William Kurelek. Reprinted by permission of Houghton Mifflin Company. All rights reserved.

Illustration from *The Tale of Peter Rabbit* by Beatrix Potter, Copyright © Frederick Warne & Co., 1902, 2002

Illustration from *The Griffin and the Minor Canon* by Frank Stockton (illustrations by Maurice Sendak). Copyright Maurice Sendak.

Illustration from *The Tale of Mrs Tiggy-Winnkle* by Beatrix Potter, Copyright © Frederick Warne & Co., 1905, 2002

Illustration from *The Juniper Tree and Other Tales From Grimm* translated by Lore Segal and Randall Jarrell with pictures by Maurice Sendak. Translation copyright © 1973 by Lore Segal. Pictures copyright © 1973 by Maurice Sendak. Reprinted by permission of Farrar, Straus and Giroux, LLC.

Illustration from *Dominic* by William Steig. Copyright © 1972 by William Steig.

Illustration from *No Kiss for Mother* by Tomi Ungerer. Copyright © 1974 Diogenes Verlag AG Zürich

Illustration from *The Snowy Day* by Ezra Jack Keats, Copyright © 1962 by Ezra Jack Keats, renewed © 1990 by Martin Pope, Executor. Used by permission of the Ezra Jack Keats Foundation and Viking Penguin, a Division of Penguin

240

Index

*Numbers in **bold** refer to illustrations.*

Index

DESIGN AND COMPOSITION BY CARL W. SCARBROUGH